CARTOONING
for Suffrage

CARTOONING
for Suffrage

Alice Sheppard

Introduction by
Elisabeth Israels Perry

University of New Mexico Press

Albuquerque

Library of Congress Cataloging-in-Publication Data

Sheppard, Alice, 1945–
    Cartooning for suffrage / Alice Sheppard.
       p.   cm.
    Includes bibliographical references and index.
    ISBN 0–8263–1458–9
    1. Women—Suffrage—Caricatures and cartoons.   2. Women cartoonists—United
States—Psychology.   3. Cartooning—United States—History—19th century.
    4. Cartooning—United States—History—20th century.   I. Title.
NC1425.S54 1993
741.5′082—dc20
93–10570
    CIP

Designed by Linda M. Tratechaud

For Doris E. Mount
and in loving memory of
Robert J. Klak

Contents

Illustrations

2.9.   William Charles, "Bruin becomes Mediator or Negotiator for Peace." Hand-colored engraving, 1813. Courtesy the Lilly Library, Indiana University, Bloomington, Indiana.

2.10. Amos Doolittle, "Brother Jonathan Administering a Salutary Cordial to John Bull." Etching, $9^{7/8} \times 14^{7/8}$ inches, 1813. Courtesy Winterthur Museum.

2.11. E. W. Clay, "Uncle Sam's Taylorifics." 1846. Courtesy New-York Historical Society, N.Y.C.

2.12. "Over the Way." *Punch*, 16 November 1861.

2.13. "Columbia's Fix." *Punch*, 28 December 1861. Courtesy Collection of Nicholas Marshall

2.14. John Tenniel, "Columbia's Sewing-Machine." *Punch*, 1 October 1864. Courtesy Collection of Nicholas Marshall.

2.15. Thomas Worth, "Uncle Sam and Miss Columbia Open the Vacation Season." *Judge*, 23 June 1883. Courtesy Alice Marshall Collection, Camp Hill, Pa.

2.16. Joseph Keppler, Jr. [Udo J.], "A Trifle Embarrassed." *Puck*, 3 August 1898.

2.17. [Louis Maurer], "The Great Republican Reform Party Calling on Their Candidate." 1856. Currier lithograph. Courtesy New-York Historical Society, N.Y.C.

2.18. William Henry Hyde, "A Matter of Duty." *Life Magazine*, 8 October 1885.

2.19. Thomas Nast, "'Who Stole the People's Money?' Do Tell. 'Twas Him." *Harper's Weekly*, 19 August 1871. Courtesy American Antiquarian Society.

2.20. Thomas Nast, "The Tammany Tiger Loose." *Harper's Weekly*, 11 November 1871. Courtesy Collection of Nicholas Marshall.

2.21. Thomas Nast, "Uncle Sam's Thanksgiving Dinner." *Harper's Weekly*, 20 November 1869.

2.22. Thomas Nast, "The Lightning Speed of Honesty." *Harper's Weekly*, 24 November 1877. Courtesy Collection of Nicholas Marshall.

2.23. Thomas Nast, "Beware." *Harper's Weekly*, 3 July 1875.

3.37. Sara Moore, "The New Masculinism." 1915. Courtesy the Schlesinger Library, Radcliffe College.

3.38. Promoting the March, 1912. Courtesy Prints and Photographs Division, Library of Congress.

3.39. Suffrage Parade, New York City, 6 May 1912. Courtesy Prints and Photographs Division, Library of Congress.

3.40. Lore Rogers, Suffrage Parade, Washington D.C. Courtesy Susanne MacLean Boone.

3.41. Suffrage Parade, Washington D.C. 3 March 1913. Courtesy Bain News Service, Prints and Photographs Division, Library of Congress.

3.42. "Suffrage as a War Measure." New York State Woman Suffrage Association flier. 1917.

3.43. Suffrage pickets outside the White House. Courtesy Prints and Photographs Division, Library of Congress.

3.44. Charles Dana Gibson, "Congratulations." *Life,* 28 October 1920. © 1920 J.B.R.

3.45. Nina E. Allender, "Every Good Suffragist the Morning after Ratification." *Suffragist,* September 1920. Courtesy the National Woman's Party and Social Welfare History Archives, University of Minnesota.

4.1. Annie "Lou" Rogers. Courtesy Elliott Hersey.

4.2. Ida Sedgwick Proper. Courtesy the Schlesinger Library, Radcliffe College.

4.3. Nina Evans Allender. Courtesy Kay Boyle.

4.4. Blanche Ames Ames. Courtesy the Schlesinger Library, Radcliffe College.

4.5. Rose O'Neill. Courtesy Prints and Photographs Division, Library of Congress.

4.6. Cornelia Barns. Courtesy Charles Garbett.

4.7. May Wilson Preston. Courtesy Archives of the Society of Illustrators/Museum of American Illustration.

4.8. Mary Ellen Sigsbee. Courtesy Katrina Sigsbee Fischer.

6.26. Edwina Dumm, "Well, Well." *Columbus Daily Monitor,* 1 January 1917. Courtesy Edwina Dumm and the Ohio State University Libraries.

6.27. Katherine Milhous, "Votes for Women." Postcard, 5¹/₂ × 3¹/₂ inches. c. 1915. Courtesy Alice Marshall Collection, Camp Hill, Pa.

6.28. Lou Rogers, "A Nut She Doesn't Try to Crack." *Judge,* 13 March 1915.

7.1. Lou Rogers, "His Mistake." *Judge,* 16 March 1912.

7.2. Nina E. Allender, "Horatius at the Bridge." *Suffragist,* 13 May 1916.

7.3. Lou Rogers, "A Modern Woman's Task." *Judge,* 21 September 1912.

7.4. Lou Rogers, "The Woman Behind Columbus." *Woman's Journal,* 12 October 1912. Courtesy Alice Marshall Collection, Camp Hill, Pa.

7.5. Nina E. Allender, "A Modern Eliza." *Suffragist,* 4 May 1918. Courtesy the National Woman's Party.

7.6. Nina E. Allender, "Madame Defarge—1918 Model." *Suffragist,* 6 April 1918. Courtesy the National Woman's Party.

7.7. Nina E. Allender, "The Wise Women of the West Come Bearing Gifts." *Suffragist,* 18 December 1915. Courtesy the Schlesinger Library, Radcliffe College.

7.8. Rollin Kirby, "Pauline Revere." *Woman's Journal,* 11 November 1916. Courtesy the Ohio State University Libraries.

7.9. Lou Rogers, "Alas, Poor Yorick." *Woman's Journal,* 25 April 1914.

7.10. Edwina Dumm, "A Modern Sir Walter?" *Columbus Daily Monitor,* 15 January 1917. Courtesy Edwina Dumm and the Ohio State Universities Libraries.

7.11. Lou Rogers, "If Lincoln Were Alive." *Judge,* 20 June 1914.

7.12. Nina E. Allender, "Great Statues of History." *Suffragist,* 23 January 1915. Courtesy Sophia Smith Collection, Smith College.

7.13. Nina E. Allender, "Fairy Godmother Wilson." *Suffragist,* 4 December 1915. Courtesy the Schlesinger Library, Radcliffe College.

7.30. Lou Rogers, "Progressing in Spite of Themselves." *Woman's Journal*, 11 January 1913.

7.31. Lou Rogers, "Ridding a State of a Moral Nuisance." *Judge*, 26 July 1913. Courtesy Periodicals Division, Library of Congress.

7.32. Lou Rogers, "Using the Back Way." *Judge*, 19 July 1913. Courtesy Periodicals Division, Library of Congress.

7.33. Lou Rogers, "En Route for Social Betterment." *Judge*, 15 November 1913.

8.1. Boardman Robinson, "The Type Has Changed." *New York Tribune*, 24 February 1911.

8.2. Nina E. Allender, "Our Hat in the Ring." *Suffragist*, 8 April 1916.

8.3. May Wilson Preston, "Votes for Women." *Woman Voter*, January 1915. Courtesy Periodicals Division, Library of Congress.

8.4. Fredrikke S. Palmer, "A May Basket for the Parties." *Woman's Journal*, 29 April 1916. Courtesy the Ohio State University Libraries.

8.5. Lou Rogers, "Ready to Serve." *Woman's Journal*, 23 November 1912.

8.6. Lou Rogers, "A Simple Case of Common Sense." *Judge*, 22 August 1914. Courtesy Periodicals Division, Library of Congress.

8.7. Lou Rogers, "Mrs. Sam: 'It's Terribly Humiliating to Me, Sam. . . .'" *Woman Citizen*, 7 July 1917.

8.8. Edwina Dumm, "Fashion Hints from Darkest Russia." *Columbus Daily Monitor*, 30 March 1917. Courtesy Edwina Dumm and the Ohio State University Libraries.

8.9. Laura Foster, "Uncle Sam and Aunt Susan." *Judge*, 1 July 1916. Courtesy Periodicals Division, Library of Congress.

8.10. John Bengough, "On the Road to Victory." *Woman's Journal*, 20 July 1912.

8.11. C. D. Batchelor, "An Important Choice." *Woman Voter*, August 1916. Courtesy Periodicals Division, Library of Congress.

8.12. Fredrikke S. Palmer, "Will Congress Heed?" *Woman's Journal*, 11 December 1915. Courtesy the Ohio State University Libraries.

9.3. John Sloan, "The Return from Toil." *The Masses*, July 1913. Courtesy Collection of American Literature, The Beinecke Rare Book and Manuscript Library, Yale University, New Haven, Conn.

9.4. Nina E. Allender, "Supporting the President." *Suffragist*, 3 August 1918. Courtesy the National Woman's Party and Social Welfare History Archives, University of Minnesota.

9.5. Maurice Becker, "Woman's Proper Sphere Is the Home." *The Masses*, January 1914.

9.6. Nina E. Allender, "Woman's Place Is the Home." *Suffragist*, 29 August 1914. Courtesy the Schlesinger Library, Radcliffe College.

9.7. Mary Ellen Sigsbee, "Woman's Place Is in the Home." *New York Evening Journal*, ca. 1916. Courtesy Katrina Sigsbee Fischer.

9.8. Fredrikke S. Palmer, "When Will Their Independence Day Be?" *Woman's Journal*, 1 July 1916.

9.9. Cornelia Barns, "One Man—One Vote." *Woman Voter*, April 1914. Courtesy Periodicals Division, Library of Congress.

9.10. Boardman Robinson, "Just Like the Men." *New York Tribune*, 1 March 1913. Courtesy the Ohio State University Libraries.

9.11. Alice Beach Winter, "Puzzle: Find the Race-Problem." *The Masses*, March 1914. Courtesy Tamiment Institute Library, New York University.

9.12. Nina E. Allender, "The President's Valentine." *Suffragist*, 19 February 1916.

9.13. Nina E. Allender, "December 16, 1915." *Suffragist*, 25 December 1915.

9.14. Lou Rogers, "Forcing Him Out of the Rut." *Judge*, 12 April 1913. Courtesy Periodicals Division, Library of Congress.

9.15. Nell Brinkley, "When Poverty Comes in the Door Love Flies Out The Window." *Philadelphia Evening Bulletin*, 29 January 1912.

9.16. Mary Ellen Sigsbee, "The Easiest Way." From What Breaks Up the Home, *Woman's Journal*, 3 August 1912. Courtesy Katrina Sigsbee Fischer.

9.17. Lou Rogers, "Mrs. Poor Patient." *Birth Control Review,* June 1918. Courtesy Sophia Smith Collection, Smith College.

9.18. Alice Beach Winter, "He Ain't Got No Stockin's." *The Masses,* January 1913. Courtesy Tamiment Institute Library, New York University.

9.19. Cornelia Barns, "Voters." *The Masses,* December 1915. Courtesy Tamiment Institute Library, New York University.

9.20. Mary Ellen Sigsbee, "The Question Why Are We Here." *The Masses,* April 1912. Courtesy Tamiment Institute Library, New York University.

9.21. "A Happy Home." *Imperial Highway,* 1883.

9.22. Charles J. Taylor, "An Unpardonable Mistake." *Puck,* 21 April 1897.

9.23. Lou Rogers, "Breaking into the Human Race." *Woman's Journal,* 2 December 1911. Courtesy Miriam Y. Holden Collection, Princeton University Libraries.

9.24. Mary Taylor, "Equal Rights." *Maryland Suffrage News,* 3 July 1915. Courtesy Sophia Smith Collection, Smith College.

9.25. Cornelia Barns, "Waiting." *Suffragist,* 17 May 1919. Courtesy the National Woman's Party.

9.26. Nina E. Allender, "The Thinker." *Equal Rights,* 7 April 1923. Courtesy the National Woman's Party and Alice Marshall Collection, Camp Hill, Pa.

Cartooning for Suffrage is an effort to explore, interpret, and preserve a particularly distinctive segment of women's history. Unfortunately, the artwork central to this study survives in crumbling newspapers, fliers, and posters of the American woman suffrage campaign—ephemera maintained in precious few research libraries and private collections today. Compelling and imaginative in appearance, this artwork was produced by a group of energetic, talented, and idealistic turn-of-the-century suffragist artists, whose personal stories link political history with the psychology of modern gender roles.

My decade-long research led me to pursue fascinating, though uncertain evidence, as I delved into family chronologies, regional histories, institutional archives, and repositories of popular culture. Locating productive leads and important materials became possible only through the cooperation and support of dozens of persons and agencies to whom I am deeply indebted.

My appreciation and admiration goes first of all to the relatives of the artists who with enthusiasm and generosity yielded little-known facts, family memorabilia, and personal recollections. Susanne M. Boone, Kay Boyle, Richard Elliott, Katrina Sigsbee Fischer, Charles Garbett, Elliott Hersey, Pauline Plimpton, Lewis G. Proper, and Col. Louis W. Proper proved to be most helpful. Those I met personally confirmed the ebullience, personal strength, and wisdom that I had come to associate with the ancestor or relative about whom I inquired. All were eager to help recognize the woman artist so significant in their family histories.

Among the historical societies and institutions that willingly searched their archives for relevant materials were the Art Students League of New York, Corcoran Museum, Farnsworth Library and

Preface

Museum, Historical Society of Denver, Iowa State Historical Society, Kansas Historical Society, Massachusetts College of Art, Maine State Library, Michigan State University Libraries, National Museum for Women in the Arts, Schlesinger Library, Sophia Smith Collection, and the Oneida County Historical Society. Those who assisted most in locating and preparing the visuals were Marie-Hélène Gold of Radcliffe College, Susan Boone of Smith College, Georgia Barnhill of the American Antiquarian Society, Erika Gottfried of New York University, and Marita Clance of the Library of Congress.

Scholars who shared their considerable expertise included Shelley Armitage, Lawrence Campbell, Lucy Shelton Caswell, Melissa Dabakis, Mary Davison, Edward Deci, Zita Dresner, Britta Dwyer, John Evans, Monika Franzen, M. Thomas Inge, Mary Lee Lunde, Alice Marshall, Judith Schwarz, Nancy Walker, and Rebecca Zurier. They helped fill missing gaps, offered new interpretations, and reduced potential sources of error. Irene A. Bradford supplied an important list of Rogers relations. Reference librarians at the State University of New York, College at Fredonia; Bloomsburg University; and Eastern Oregon State College were helpful in locating materials and verifying sources. I also appreciate the extensive inter-library loan services provided by these institutions.

I was fortunate to obtain the services of talented photographers dedicated to the importance of obtaining quality reproductions—even from damaged, deteriorating originals. Most especially I want to thank Jerry and Cathy Gildemeister of Union, Oregon, for their diligence, commitment, and impressive results. Their copy photographs did much to regain the intensity and artistic quality of the original artwork. It is a pleasure to acknowledge the exemplary prints produced by Ronald Pretzer, as well as the photography of Yoas Services, Schindler Studios, Hoyers Photo, Deborah Lanni, Charlotte Morse, Raymond Mayo, and Oscar Studios.

Private collectors and dealers located rare and significant materials needed for the book. Alice Marshall of the Alice Marshall Collection proved a boundless supply of knowledge and material on women and contributed expertise and friendship throughout the book's creation. Nicholas Marshall generously opened his private collections and shared his wealth of information on nineteenth-century periodicals and illustrators. Monika Franzen of Historical Pictures Service kindly provided resources from her extensive collection.

A fellowship from the National Endowment for the Humanities enabled me to devote a full year to my research and writing. Financial support for cartoon reproductions was generously contributed by the Swann Foundation for Caricature and Cartoon, Eastern Oregon State College, and by the State University of New York at Fredonia. Media centers at SUNY-Fredonia and SUNY-Geneseo also lent support.

The University of New Mexico Press has been consistently helpful in enhancing the quality of this work. I am grateful to reviewers, copyeditors, and staff, some of whom remained anonymous. I appreciate the skill of Linda Tratechaud in designing the book and, most especially, the patience, expertise, and commitment of my editor, Barbara Guth.

Jane Mont commented thoughtfully on an early draft of the manuscript and contributed an artist's eye. I am grateful to Doris Mount for careful reviews of several manuscript forms, as she attended to accuracy, clarity, and a consideration of the reader.

Randall Scott contributed scholarly insights, enthusiasm, and a librarian's perspective as he prepared the index. Joanne Foeller of SUNY-Fredonia cheerfully added her skills in word processing to final versions of the text. Finally, the love, support, and enthusiasm given me by my husband, Robert J. Klak, have long shaped my aspirations and scholarly accomplishments. His keen sense of humor and delight in memorable cartoons prompted his anticipation of the present book.

CARTOONING
for Suffrage

Almost as soon as the American woman's rights movement got underway in the mid-nineteenth century, negative visual images of women activists began to appear in the popular press. Sometimes the image was of a lecturer on "free thinking" portrayed as "evil temptress," sometimes of a reformer in bloomers smoking a cigar. As late as the 1910s, popular publications such as *Life Magazine* were still printing similarly negative images of women activists that showed them as aggressive, overbearing shrews who neglected their children and forced their menfolks into domestic drudgery. By conveying the message that women seeking to change traditional gender roles would harm society's moral and political structure, this pictorial rhetoric helped subject the campaign to costly and disheartening delays.

By the turn of the twentieth century, the campaign for woman suffrage had won a few victories, but only in the West. The majority of Americans were either indifferent to the idea of new terms for female citizenship or, worse, openly hostile to it. As women prepared to renew their campaign in the early 1900s, they began to harness the power of images to work for their side of the argument. *Cartooning for Suffrage* reconstructs this little known aspect of the campaign, an aspect that until recently has not received adequate scholarly attention.[1] Alice Sheppard presents here the first full-scale study showing how artists committed to suffrage ideals reshaped a visual rhetoric that helped create a climate more favorable to change in America's gender relations. By giving close and analytical attention to this neglected subject, she not only introduces the reader to a group of dedicated, creative women artists but also provides scholars with broadly useful resources for locating the

Introduction

IMAGE, RHETORIC, AND THE HISTORICAL MEMORY OF WOMEN

Elisabeth Israels Perry

woman suffrage story into a more central place in human political history.

We cannot always predict what will become fixed in a society's historical memory. Art Historian Lisa Tickner makes this point in the introduction to her study of the imagery used in the British suffrage campaign. Tickner recounts how, in 1908, British suffragist Emmeline Pethick-Lawrence anticipated that certain movement memorabilia, such as the large processional banners used in suffrage demonstrations, would become possessions of great historical importance to British women. "Alas, she was wrong," Tickner laments. "What becomes 'historic' is not just a question of accident—of letters and diaries lost and conversations unrecorded—but also a question of power, . . . the power invested in particular institutions and discourses, and the forms of knowledge that they produce."[2]

Cartoons for suffrage, American as well as British, fell into oblivion not because they weren't powerful in and of themselves but because the event they represented, the winning of the vote for women, has not been central to political history. Even those historians who have specialized in the struggle of subordinated groups for justice have only recently begun to include women's causes as integral to that struggle, or to ask whether changes traditionally seen as "progressive" actually benefitted women. And, as Tickner also observed, even scholars who specialize in women's topics have not necessarily valued women's pictorial rhetoric. Historians of women's art, for example, have tended to dismiss cartoons as "too political," calling them "agitation by symbol" and thus not worthy of serious study.[3]

Yet, as Tickner shows about British suffrage art, cartoons contain a wealth of material that helps us understand how women have been stereotyped and treated in society. ". . . [I]t was not a footnote or an illustration to the 'real' political history going on elsewhere," she writes, "but an integral part of the fabric of social conflict with its own contradictions and ironies and its own power to shape thought, focus debates and stimulate action." According to Tickner, the art of the British woman suffrage campaign presented in vivid relief not just the specific struggle for the vote but also "a broader debate about *definitions of femininity and women's place in public life.*"[4]

Because American suffrage cartoons played precisely this role, the images and messages they contain shed light on the discourse about women that took place in the latter years of the suffrage campaign. They show the depth and extent of American ambivalence, fears, and hopes about the roles women might play in new, more modern times. In addition, the cartoons portrayed images of active, public womanhood that have persisted long into the post-suffrage era. From a feminist standpoint, most of these images have tended toward improving women's position in society. They did not go far enough, however, in freeing women from narrow conceptualizations of their social roles in American public life.

Today's sophisticated visual technology makes us keenly aware of the power of images to mold public opinion. Showing that reliance on visual imagery predates modern practice, Sheppard demonstrates that turn-of-the-century suffragists were equally aware of that power. Political cartoons in general had taught them that visual rhetoric could be highly effective in getting a viewpoint across to a wide public. By crystallizing an idea or an argument into a simple image, visual rhetoric permits the argument to be grasped in a flash and thus to reach an audience wider than that reached by verbal means, either spoken or written. Humor, irony, or satire allow the release of laughter, and thus ease communication to those who might otherwise find an idea uncomfortable or unacceptable. Evocative images of oppression or cruelty arouse feelings of pity or outrage that can galvanize the passive into action. The visual rhetoric of the American woman suffrage movement played both of these communicative and inspirational roles.

American suffrage cartoons used two persuasive techniques. The first approach presented the franchise as a means to end woman's oppression. Oppression appeared across a range of female experience. In the cartoons that portrayed one end of the range, women struggle under handicaps as they attempt to join men on an equal footing in the public sphere. At the other end, they are deeply wronged by social evils such as sweatshops, prostitution, and vice.

By far the predominant approach, however, was to point out that civilization lost ground by excluding women from active citizenship. It sought to awaken the general public to woman's potential as social contributor. Such cartoons contended that women voters, given the chance, would improve, perhaps even be the salvation of, humanity.

Women's images in this second category of cartoons conform to traditional types. They are well-dressed, stereotypically feminine or matronly, with Anglo-Saxon faces. Applying their "natural" skills as housekeepers to municipal concerns, the women pursue idealistic, nonpartisan causes. They sweep away dirty politics, graft and corruption, and the interests behind commercialized vice. They promote controls over child labor and women's working hours.

They also oppose war. Mothers, made more politically aware through the franchise, are better equipped to educate their children; young women serve their country alongside men; and women in male garb (dangerous ground, this!) lead the forces of righteousness toward victory. In a contrasting but perhaps necessary corollary, the prevailing male image in the pro-suffrage cartoon is stupid, lazy, indifferent to the suffering of others, authoritarian, or down-right vicious.

Thus, the early twentieth-century suffragist vision of womanhood was twofold: in one view she was subject to oppression and therefore in need of the vote in order to protect herself; in the other her enfranchisement would bring into politics a superior moral conscience and thus improve conditions for all. In its own time, this dual vision was highly effective. After all, it confirmed what most members of the public already believed—that women needed special protection and were morally superior to most men. But it left an ambiguous legacy to the future. Woman as victim entrenched conceptions of female weakness that inevitably held her back as she tried to compete with men in the public sphere. Woman as virtuous voter raised ex-pectations that could not possibly be met.

After the suffrage victory, the persistence of the idea that women needed special protection led to a painful split among former suf-fragists. The split was grounded in a fundamental disagreement over the social consequences of biological difference. Some suffra-gists believed that, because women's maternal functions were unique, society needed to devise special protection for them in the work place. These reformers thus fought for, and continued after suffrage to justify, special legislation that protected women from exploit-ative conditions—including below minimum wages, excessive work hours, especially at night, or contact with hazardous materials—that might harm their child-nurturing capabilities. Others among the suffragists took issue with this approach to worker protection. They argued that, since special protective legislation excluded women from certain jobs, or kept them from working enough hours to earn their living, it had wrought economic hardships on women. For this group, discriminatory treatment of women in the workplace was the worst possible way to achieve protection for industrial workers. They argued for absolute legal equality between men and women and for industrial protection laws that protected all workers, regardless of sex. Until more modern times, however, courts continued to reject such laws as improper government interference in the free enterprise system.

The campaign for an Equal Rights Amendment divided the woman's movement into opposing camps. On the one side were the protectionists, led by groups such as the League of Women Voters; on the other were the egalitarians, led by the National Woman's Party. The split had serious political consequences for women in the post-suffrage era. Although the two sides were able to work together on some issues, such as maternity and infant care, the conditions of international citizenship for married women, or the winning of a woman's right to sit on juries, they were unable to cooperate on other important goals. Thus, organized political women were severely hampered in their ability to develop an effective political role for themselves in the post-suffrage era.

Women's experience at the polls after suffrage showed that the optimism of suffrage cartoonists about the impact of the woman's vote was based on shaky ground. After suffrage, women failed to vote in large numbers. Many were reluctant or felt ill-prepared to vote; others had become as indifferent toward politics as many male members of society. Furthermore, when they did vote, with the exception of some local contests in which former suffragists managed to organize a bloc woman's vote to win a specific political goal, women tended to vote similarly to men. Not surprisingly, corruption, vice, and war continued. Although women activists won a few legislative battles, the idea promoted in suffrage cartoons that women would be a mass force for social good proved unfounded.[5]

Perhaps of even greater significance, as a guard against the frequent charge that involvement in public life "unsexed" women, most of the cartoonists had used images that appealed to current aesthetic standards of femininity widely accepted in the suffrage movement as a whole. Whether ethereal, matronly, or allegorical, the cartoonists' images announced that women, once enfranchised, would still play the decorative, nurturing, and moral roles society expected of them.[6] In other words, gender relations would go on pretty much as before. Only a daring few of the cartoonists portrayed women as capable of strong or heroic behavior, challenging men of lesser worth than they, or competing with men in spheres previously closed to them. Such cartoons put into opponents' hands an easy weapon for counterattack: the charge that feminism inflames "sex warfare." In seeking their own visual devices, the "antis" exploited public suspicion along these lines. In their cartoons, men unlucky enough to be connected to suffragists appeared as henpecked or forced to baby-sit, cook, or wield a mop, usually making a mess of all of these tasks. Women activists took the form of ugly, cigar-smoking, pants-wearing, anti-family spinsters. In authoritarian poses, they looked down their noses at others, stuck out their tongues, pointed fingers, and threatened war between the sexes if their demands were not met. Similarly negative images of feminists have dogged them to this day.[7]

The images in suffrage cartoons hold clues to the difficulties politically active women faced in trying to succeed in public life after suffrage. Despite the effort of the cartoonists to legitimize women's potential for political agency, they hesitated to push this idea beyond acceptable contemporary limits. Their caution is understandable, for, had they pushed too far, the resulting conservative reaction could have been disastrous to the suffrage cause. Still, they missed an opportunity, which would not recur until the revival of feminism some forty years later, to advance the dialogue about woman's public place.

The only images of strong, authoritative females in suffrage cartoons were those of Amazonian Wonder Women or allegorical figures drawn from classical culture. Suffrage cartoonists rarely represented women in the roles of judge, legislator, or president. After over seventy years of suffrage, women still occupy less than 20 percent of the nation's elected political offices. Despite the advances won in the 1992 elections, their presence at top levels of other policy-making bodies—in business, finance, or education— also remains low. In short, giving women access to the vote did not make them equal to men. After suffrage, most Americans continued to think of women's holding of office, almost any office with the authority to make policy and execute it, as inappropriate to their sex. The winning of the vote increased women's chances of changing that stereotype, but suffrage cartoonists did little to help the change come sooner.

Instead, both suffrage rhetoric and the cartoons that encapsulated that rhetoric reinforced the very prejudices that kept some old attitudes in place. Their "strong women" were, for the most part, if not in allegorical form then shown working for nonpartisan, idealistic causes. After suffrage, women active in politics held on to this imagery. They shrank from direct contests with men in the political arena. They had good reasons for doing so. Since most of their opponents would have been incumbents, such contests seemed (and usually were) unwinnable. In addition, the women felt that political campaigns subjected families to many hardships, not the least of which were long absences from children and the loss of privacy. Of even greater influence on their hesitancy to run for office, however, was their continuing conviction that the wielding of public power would put into jeopardy woman's greatest strength: her idealism. They believed that the seeking of office (what at the time they called "political pie") led inevitably to the compromise of one's ideals. Since the preservation of ideals was woman's most important contribution to society, she could not take the risk of pursuing the concrete rewards of power. Instead, she should seek political "influence," a form of "private" power less likely to corrupt her and, in the long run, playing a more significant role in the advancement of civilization.

In the immediate post-suffrage era, there were many women—professional and non-professional—who had accumulated vast political expertise. They had led large national organizations and mounted national reform campaigns. They were highly experienced, strong, executive types who knew how to define agendas and who had the energy and managerial skills to fulfill them. But suffrage cartoonists never depicted women in powerful public roles once the vote was won. The best of the suffrage campaigners were neither career-oriented nor personally ambitious. After decades of working for political goals from within their own separate sphere of women's organizations, they still felt most comfortable and effective working for change from that sphere.[8] They wanted the vote. They wanted to be full American citizens, to be a part of the American democracy, and to have a significant influence on government policies. But winning policy-making power for themselves was, for most of them, beyond desire or imagination.

Suffrage campaigners are hardly to blame for this failure. Suffrage cartoons testify to the power of the gender socialization most women had experienced. Men had undergone that socialization, too. For their part, they were content to leave things the way they were, with men in power and women in the service of causes. And without male cooperation, no further changes in the gender division of public role, function, and power would take place.[9]

In short, suffrage cartoons, reflecting larger themes present in the suffrage movement as a whole, helped win the battle for the vote but never shook loose long-entrenched views of how men and women should interact once the vote was won. There was yet another, equally disturbing aspect of the cartoon legacy. By depicting the woman voter as almost exclusively white and well-educated, the cartoons played to contemporary racial and class prejudices. With notable exceptions such as Cornelia Barns's "One Man, One Vote" (figure 9.9), they therefore did little to advance what suffragists had always claimed was their larger goal, to bring greater democracy to American society. Many suffragists were ambivalent about the impact of newly arrived immigrants on politics, especially in large cities where party machines often bought newcomers' votes in return for jobs and other favors. Some suffragists were openly racist, arguing to southerners that the granting of the franchise to women would guarantee the preservation of white supremacy in the south. Suffragists were among the many strong supporters of literacy tests, used systematically at the polls to keep people of color and foreigners from exercising their voting rights.[10] Suffrage cartoons reflected the values of the suffrage organizations, values widely held by their contemporaries and enduring long into the twentieth century.

In their own time, suffrage cartoons helped convince the American public of the need for a reform now widely taken for granted in modernized countries. Their immediate purpose fulfilled, their influence lingered on in the imaginations of American women and men, who continued to function under the spell of their rhetorical power. Now, through the efforts of modern feminists and supported by Alice Sheppard's painstaking research, the cartoons have been made easily accessible to a wide audience and available for a new interpretation of their social meaning. Thus, they can continue to play roles of historical importance. First, they can serve as a positive learning tool, especially for today's generation of young people, whose historical memory of women is not only impoverished but for whom the ideals and goals of the feminist cause have little meaning. Second, they can provide tactical models for women activists still searching for means to attract a broader spectrum of adherents to the pursuit of feminist goals.

Ask any group of young people to name a famous American woman of the past and chances are they will come up with Betsy Ross, whom they remember seeing in a picture book from their childhood, sewing stars on the first American flag.[11] If pressed, older youth, especially African-American youth, may think of Harriet Tubman, the legendary rescuer of slaves from bondage, whose life they have seen eulogized in a televised drama. Others may cite Carrie Nation, the temperance crusader, whose ax-wielding exploits they have seen in photographs or cartoons in school textbooks, or Eleanor Roosevelt whom they remember from the film "Eleanor and Franklin" or widely disseminated pictures of her from the Depression era or the 1940s. They seldom know that Nation was a marginal figure in a widespread woman's movement for moral and social reform, or that Roosevelt played important political roles apart from her status as the wife of a president. That they tend to cite these particular women, however, attests to the power of images to communicate information in a lasting way.

In the last quarter of the twentieth century the field of women's history has made astoundingly rapid progress. Books in the field have won Pulitzer Prizes and other national awards, professors of women's history hold prestigious appointments in major universities and professional associations, and students receive advanced degrees in the field in over seventy graduate programs across the United States. Most departments of history in institutions of higher learning boast at least one, if not more, professors who specialize in the history of women. The body of confirmed knowledge that the field has established appears in new history textbooks published at all levels of the educational process. Major archival repositories of women's papers and other memorabilia now exist to help preserve a historical memory of women. Despite this progress, most of our youth still lack an awareness of women's historical experience. Without such an awareness, they will remain unprepared to meet the challenge of the rapidly changing gender relations of our contemporary society.

In my own teaching over the previous decade, I have found that students often resent the inclusion of material on women.[12] They want to know if it is "really important," or, phrasing the question another way, if it is "going to be on the exam." More hostile students—most of them male, but some female—let me know in no uncertain terms that, if they had wanted to know about women, they would have signed up for a Women's Studies course. To these students, history is wars and politics and economic change. Since they know little or nothing of women's roles in these areas, they do not see the relevance of "women's issues" to them. They have seldom, if ever, given thought to the exclusion from power of over half of the human race. If they have thought about it, they have accepted it. "That's the way it's always been," students often say to me, "and nothing's going to change it." Some women in the class may groan in protest, but they themselves do not have readily at hand the images and examples that might raise the consciousness of their peers.

Because suffrage cartoons offer such vivid, easy-to-grasp insights into women's historical experience, they can help raise young people's consciousness. The cartoons' graphic display of the injustice of disfranchisement rapidly reveals the larger significance of denying the vote to women. The sight of women in old-fashioned clothes making demands for other rights and opportunities still not won alerts viewers to the ongoing importance of feminist issues. It also brings home to them the injustice of the continuing difficulty women face in winning a sympathetic hearing for their concerns and grievances. Even the cartoons' limited vision of woman's public place is an important device for teaching, for this vision helps explain why more than the vote was needed to end women's subordinate status. Finally, by revealing suffragists' narrow notion of the connections between their own struggle and that of other races and classes, the cartoons teach another important lesson: that suffragists, like any other group in history, should not be idealized but must be seen as real human beings caught up in the conflicts and dilemmas of their time.

Cartooning for Suffrage can thus be a resource for scholars as well, for the cartoons offer new explanations both for why the climate of the early 1900s became favorable to the campaign's success and why suffrage alone was not enough to propel women into roles in the public arena equal to those of men. Finally, wider audiences, especially those who think of themselves as supporters of feminism but who know little of its roots in the past, will find the cartoons useful. There are few quicker ways to achieve legitimacy for one's actions than the discovery of a historical precedent for them. By showing the length of time women have been asking for opportunities and rights equal to men's, suffrage cartoons give those demands, when uttered by contemporary feminists, greater urgency. The cartoons can also open up fruitful discussion of strategies and tactics used by feminists in the past, including the viability of the cartoon medium to communicate reform goals.

Feminists today still have not conveyed the justice of their goals to the broad cross-section of the public they must convince in order to win them or to prevent the loss of those they have already won. They need support from women who do not identify themselves as feminists; they need support from men. Gender wars have no winners but instead give rise to a backlash that endangers not only the feminist cause but the causes of others who are asking for equitable treatment. Can feminists today take a cue from the suffrage era and develop a visual rhetoric aimed at winning wider support for the contemporary feminist agenda? A rhetoric that might not only amuse, stimulate, and inspire proponents of that agenda but also sway the indifferent, perhaps even convert the hostile? The suffrage cartoons have offered us many lessons. Their ability to win support for their cause with minimal antagonism is surely one lesson still worth heeding.

Notes

1. Among other examinations of cartooning and suffrage are Martha Bensley Bruère and Mary Ritter Beard, eds., *Laughing Their Way: Women's Humor in America* (New York: Macmillan, 1934) and Monika Franzen and Nancy Ethiel, *Make Way! 200 Years of American Women in Cartoons* (Chicago: Chicago Review Press, 1988).

2. Lisa Tickner, *The Spectacle of Women: Imagery of the Suffrage Campaign* 1907–14 (Chicago: University of Chicago Press, 1988), ix.

3. *Ibid.*, 16.

4. Emphasis mine. *Ibid.*, ix.

5. The best introduction to this topic remains J. Stanley Lemons, *The Woman Citizen. Social Feminism in the* 1920s (Champaign: University of Illinois Press, 1975).

6. Martha Banta, in *Imaging American Women: Idea and Ideals in Cultural History* (New York: Columbia University Press, 1987), discusses the preference of suffrage leaders for self-portraits surrounded by signs of traditional feminine identity, e.g. flowers, flowing gowns, and angelic-faced children.

7. As I write this, I have at hand a recent *New York Times* "Essay" by columnist William Safire (27 January 1992), entitled "Macho Feminism, R.I.P." In it, Safire derides "professional feminists" who would automatically presume a man wrong, a woman (no matter what her background) right. He also links feminism with "anti-male, anti-child, anti-family, anti-feminine" attitudes. Reading this piece, I felt as though I were back in the pre-suffrage era.

8. Studies that develop these themes include, in addition to J. Stanley Lemons's cited above: Felice D. Gordon, *After Winning: The Legacy of the New Jersey Suffragists, 1920–1947* (New Brunswick: Rutgers University Press, 1986), and Nancy F. Cott, *The Grounding of Modern Feminism* (New Haven: Yale University Press, 1987). My own work on women's political groups after suffrage explores these themes in the local context of New York City: "Training for Public Life: Eleanor Roosevelt and Women's Political Networks in New York in the 1920s," in Joan Hoff-Wilson & Marjorie Lightman, eds., *Without Precedent: The Life and Career of Eleanor Roosevelt* (Bloomington: Indiana University Press, 1984), 28–45 and "Women's Political Choices after Suffrage: The Women's City Club of New York, 1915–present," *New York History* 62/4 (October 1990), 417–34.

9. I develop these themes at greater length in *Belle Moskowitz: Feminine Politics and the Exercise of Power in the Age of Alfred E. Smith* (New York: Oxford University Press, 1987; New York: Routledge, 1992).

10. On the interplay of these themes in the suffrage movement, see Aileen Kraditor, *The Ideas of the Woman Suffrage Movement, 1890–1920* (New York: Norton, 1965, 1981). Sources on the themes

can be found in Mari Jo Buhle and Paul Buhle, eds., *The Concise History of Woman Suffrage. Selections from the Classic Work of Stanton, Anthony, Gage, and Harper* (Champaign: University of Illinois, 1978).

11. Historian Michael Frisch has also noted the predominance of Betsy Ross in student historical memory. Surveys taken at the State University of New York at Buffalo between 1975 and 1988 of students asked to write down names of people, excluding statesmen, whom they associated with pre-Civil War U.S. history, uniformly yielded her name first. Frisch attributes her prominence to the power inherent in the image of her "giving birth" to the American flag, our first "collective symbol." See "American History and the Structures of Collective Memory: A Modest Exercise in Empirical Iconography," *Journal of American History* 75/4 (March 1989), 1130–55.

12. I base these observations on almost ten years of teaching history in different kinds of institutional environments (a large midwest state university, a southern private university, and a northeastern urban public college) and on conversations since 1987 with over forty high-school teachers from all over the country whom I have directed in summer seminars on feminist studies sponsored by the National Endowment for the Humanities.

1

Cartoons, Politics, & Gender

Dr. Anna Howard Shaw's experience
with cartoons had been very
unhappy. I am sure this unladylike
picture filled her with horror. It was
certainly not welcome . . .

—*Lou Rogers,* "Lightning Speed
Through Life"

"The Ballot Box is Mine Because it's Mine!"

1.1.
Lou Rogers, "He Does the Family Voting."

1.2.
"Justice Demands the Vote."

In 1911 Miss Lou Rogers entered the New York offices of the National American Woman Suffrage Association to display a cartoon sketch that even these radical women would find too controversial to publish. It was a caricature of male pomposity, achieved through the figure of a proud-chested man with asses' ears and paper crown, asserting his monopoly over the ballot box by standing on it (figure 1.1). "The Ballot Box is Mine Because It's Mine," he expounded. The suffrage association consulted its president, Dr. Anna Howard Shaw, an ordained Methodist minister and trained physician, who was evidently shocked by the cartoon. The *New York Call*, a socialist daily, was more sympathetic and immediately published it. Years later, Rogers chronicled the episode in an autobiographical essay for the *Nation* and even then remained pleased with her drawing.[1]

Lou Rogers, a woman artist from rural northern Maine, was demonstrating properties then unknown to the cartoon in American popular culture. She defied established tradition in the target of her satire—male pretentiousness and power. She was innovative in making a visual appeal for American women's enfranchisement. That she was a woman drawing political cartoons itself constituted an anomaly. In these three aspects—as humor attacking male behaviors, as art promoting women's issues, and as political art by women—lies the historical significance of her early cartoons. From 1910 to 1920, at least three dozen American women seized their drawing pens, pencils, grease crayons, and brushes to contribute cartoons for suffrage. Examples of pro-suffrage art, numbering in the hundreds, assumed many forms: magazine cartoons, posters, illustrated fliers, calendars, decorative stamps, figurines, and postcards. There were paintings of suffrage parades and statues of

Cartooning for Suffrage

allegorical and emancipated women.[2] Suffrage art emerged within an international movement, where, for example, British suffrage art inspired and set a precedent for American practices, and designs from other nations were distributed and displayed widely (figures 1.2 and 1.3).[3] Impressive in purpose and composition, suffrage art is useful for reconstructing women's historical perceptions and providing insight into women's gender roles and social position in the early twentieth century.

Women's visible action for suffrage appeared unprecedented, incomprehensible, and, to some, appalling. Society pronounced early woman's rights advocates "unsexed" for daring to speak in meetings and "unwomanly" for transgressions into the public sphere.[4] When, after six decades of activism, suffragists adopted the political cartoon, some powerful and provocative examples aroused ambivalence even among supporters. The *Woman's Journal* (figure 1.4), a weekly periodical founded in 1870 by Lucy Stone and Henry Blackwell in Boston, declined to publish Lou Rogers's early cartoon. The *Woman's Journal* was progressive in its demand for enfranchisement, but remained moderate in its strategies and philosophy, assuming that rational persuasion would be adequate to gain the ballot. The *Suffragist*, a more radical paper, was established in Washington in 1913 and became the publication of the National Woman's Party in its demand for a federal constitutional amendment. When Nina Allender satirized President Wilson in cartoons for the *Suffragist* (figure 1.5), suffrage artist Marietta Andrews severed her ties with the paper.[5] Suffrage was a struggle embedded in uncertainty and risk—how to effectively demand the ballot for women in a manner consistent with late nineteenth- and early twentieth-century women's self images. For many suffragists, pro-

1.3.
Anna Soós Korányi, "Internationaler Frauenstimmrechts—Kongress."

1.4.
Woman's Journal, 3 June 1916.

1.6.
Elizabeth Schippen
Green,
"Playthings."

1.7.
Mary Sigsbee Ker,
"Springtime of
Life."

1.5. *Suffragist*, 30 September 1916.

priety could not be sacrificed; for others, the objective justified the means.

The reluctance to embrace women's radical political art stemmed from a turn-of-the-century art tradition that channeled and confined women to genteel, ladylike activities of drawing and painting. Watercolors, miniatures, portraits, decorative objects, and sentimental illustrations, particularly ones of romantic settings or children (figures 1.6 and 1.7) were conventional, nonthreatening, and meshed with prevailing definitions of woman's sphere. Political cartooning and caricature, in contrast, were judged unrefined, coarse, and vulgar. These forms had evolved to define women not as potential originators, but as the targets, for example, in derogatory cartoon images of mothers-in-law and "masculine" women (figures 1.8 and 1.9). At the turn of the century, women who produced cartoons unconsciously challenged gender definitions.[6]

The role of political cartoonist was judged masculine because it wielded power and served as a privileged vantage point from which to expose and ridicule social structures and political leaders. Popular cartoon magazines were produced by men and featured the actions of men (figures 1.10 and 1.11). With increased momentum and political sophistication, suffragists increasingly chose to overstep propriety. They adopted cartoon techniques of satire and caricature, acquiring symbolic power expressed in bold, aggressive tones.[7] Suffrage artists used these graphic images to focus attention on woman suffrage and to encapsulate justifications for giving women the vote. It provided their arguments with a tangible form that proved more difficult to refute.

THE MASCULINE WOMAN
She is mannish from shoes to her hat,
Coat, collars, stiff shirt and cravat.
She'd wear pants in the street
To make her complete,
But she knows the law won't stand for that.

1.8.
H. H., "The Masculine Woman."

THE MOTHER-IN-LAW
A husband of whom I have heard
Declared his wife's mother "a bird!"
She smiled, but just then
He murmured "a hen!"
The ambulance call then occurred!

1.9.
R. Hill, "The Mother-in-Law."

I.10.
Bernard Gillam,
"Grand Triumph
of Brains over
'Boodle.'"

*"We've had a —
— of a time since
we've been gone!"*

I.11.
Victor F. Gillam,
"Back to School."

Art and Politics

Early twentieth-century women's political cartoons have largely been ignored by art and cultural historians, due in part to a prejudice regarding women's activities as trivial and insignificant. Added to the bias against women's productions is the meager appreciation given the field of cartooning.[8] By the nineteenth century the fine arts or beaux arts were distinguished from industrial arts and crafts, and culture was segregated into highbrow versus lowbrow forms. Differences in their appearance and function came to legitimize implicit value judgments that favored the fine arts. Cartoons are acceptably frivolous, whimsical, and illogical, whereas painting, sculpture and other forms of high art are profound and serious. Political cartoons typically address particular persons, issues, and events, while more conventional art evokes universal themes or principles. Cartoons are mass produced, whereas the uniqueness of a painting enhances its value. Cartoons often seem "impulsive, spontaneous and 'dashed off,'" whereas paintings are esteemed for polished technique and detail.[9] Finally, cartoonists often acquire skills on their own through imitation and practice, while artists commonly attend art academies and institutions. As a result of these differences, when a highly trained artist produces cartoons, they may be considered mere diversions in an otherwise dignified career.

Paradoxically, on some occasions in history cartoons have been taken seriously enough to curtail individual freedom of expression and to influence government policy. In the seventeenth century one critic judged satirical representations of the English as sufficient grounds for war against the Netherlands.[10] An influential early Philadelphia engraver, William Charles, had been reputedly forced

26

to leave his native Scotland after unwisely caricaturing city officials. During the reign of King Louis-Philippe (1830–1848), the flourishing of French caricature brought about an era of repression. Charles Philipon, founder of the French periodicals *La Caricature* (1831–1835) and *Le Charivari* (1832–1893), was sentenced to prison in the 1830s for depicting King Louis-Philippe as a pear (la poire, slang for "fathead"), a likeness so fitting and appreciated that numerous imitations were spawned.[11] Honoré Daumier's portrayal of King Louis-Philippe as Gargantua similarly resulted in his imprisonment. Governor Pennypacker of Pennsylvania, insulted by derogatory images of himself in newspaper cartoons, succeeded in 1903 in outlawing visual representation of persons as animals (one inventive artist found they did very well as vegetables). Under the Espionage Act of World War I, cartoons by Art Young, Boardman Robinson, and Henry Glintenkamp were designated as treasonable, causing the August 1917 issue of the socialist periodical *The Masses*, in which they appeared, to be barred from the U.S. Mail. A Federal District Court judge concluded that the artists' freedom of speech had been abrogated, but victory was short-lived when a new government suit charged Young and Glintenkamp, along with five *Masses*' writers, with conspiring to obstruct the operation of military laws. The case was tried twice before a Federal Grand Jury, and ended in mistrial, the final vote being eight to four for acquittal.[12]

Taken seriously by politicians and governments, humor and cartoons have also attracted the interest of theorists. In 1858 Charles Baudelaire distinguished the "absolute comic" (a form based on fantasy and the grotesque) from the "significative comic" (containing allusions or references to specific events). Baudelaire recognized the association of representational humor to external reality,

1.12. Photo of Effie Romig and Friend.

making him one of the first to analyze humor as a symbolic form.[13] Cartoons, a form not addressed directly by Baudelaire, evoke specific questions on the relation between words and images. R. E. Williams pointed out that in some cartoons "picture and caption are inseparable," while others are purely visual.[14] William Murrell, in *A History of American Graphic Humor*, distinguished three types: the humorous drawing, the cartoon, and caricature. What Murrell identified as a cartoon focused on "a topical political or moral issue," consisted of "a forceful presentation by means of exaggeration," and was executed "with or without humor." It incorporated symbols and legends and conveyed the intent "to make something ridiculous."[15] Such considerations are not merely conceptual, but may affect behavior. As Charles Press asserted, the political cartoon contains "an implicit appeal to do something political."[16]

Women Cartoonists

Cartooning as a men's-only domain had begun to change by the late nineteenth century.[17] Among the factors permitting women to enter the field were the rise of training facilities, the rapid simplification of the process, and the acceptance of women into positions of skilled employment. By mid-century, women could obtain training as printmakers and engravers in women's schools of design including Pittsburgh's Design School for Women and the Philadelphia School of Design for Women.[18] They found employment in the lithography industry, where firms such as Currier and Ives hired women as colorists and artists.[19] When the invention of photoengraving methods eliminated the task of hand engraving, direct reproduction techniques meant that a sketch by any man, woman, or child could be reproduced quickly and easily for a newspaper or magazine. Artists could circumvent extensive technical training and still enter the field of cartooning. The proliferation of mass-produced illustrated magazines and an expanded public school curriculum in which art was emphasized encouraged new aspirations, and suddenly children of both sexes wanted to become cartoonists.

The public, nevertheless, continued to perceive the field of cartooning as masculine. Women were at a disadvantage because the established female cartoon prototypes—from Justice personified to the Gibson Girl—were created by men, and set the standards by which women's work would be judged. The cartoon form was created and consolidated around male sensibilities; it affirmed feminine glamour and denigrated independent women. To gain acceptance, women sometimes abandoned their own convictions and imitated men. When women first entered the cartooning field, they were welcomed as novelties; they captured attention simply by invading a male profession. One of the earliest women cartoonists, Rose O'Neill, contributed numerous cartoons and illustrations to *Puck* in the 1890s. An O'Neill cover titled "The Next Candidate for Statehood" (figure 1.13), depicts Columbia encouraging New Mexico to join the union. Columbia is a powerful, spiritual figure, a contrast to the charming young brown-skinned girl. O'Neill was later catapulted to fame when she invented the wide-eyed, pudgy-shaped Kewpie Doll. Another woman, Kate Carew [Mary Williams], came to New York around 1900 and was acclaimed, without regard to other women cartoonists, "The Only Woman Caricaturist."[20] A decade later Sara Moore of Detroit syndicated her "Cartoonettes," which the *Brooklyn Daily Eagle* placed on its women's page. While society would readily accept emotional

1.13. Rose O'Neill, "The Next Candidate for Statehood."

1.14.
Henrietta Briggs-Wall, "Woman and her Political Peers."

Mr. Openpurse Goodheart—More charity entertainments to subscribe to:—My dear girl, is n't it about time someone gave a charity entertainment to me?

1.15. Joseph Keppler, "Charity-Broke."

and flowery cartoons from women, O'Neill, Carew, and Moore overstepped this standard of sentimentality by probing social and political issues.

Turn-of-the-century women saw in the cartoons of Charles Daumier, Thomas Nast, Joseph Keppler, and others a symbolic form that could serve their cause. By 1893 when one of the earliest examples appeared some understood that women's oppression and social discrimination could be exposed, commented upon and debated in pictorial form (figure 1.14). Suffrage cartoons were blatant propaganda making a political appeal for the enfranchisement of American women. They were linked inseparably to the rhetoric of the movement, but themselves lacked an identifiable tradition, or even a clear precedent.

Suffrage Cartoons

The history of American women's suffrage cartoons raises many intriguing questions. How did women cartoonists develop the skills and the symbolic mastery needed to draw effective cartoons for suffrage? What were the chief influences on their imagery? What character types—suffragists, mothers, daughters, workers, politicians, or bosses—were prevalent in their art? Did women's portrayals differ from men's? How did women incorporate allegorical personifications of Liberty, Justice, or Democracy, and symbolize such concepts as progress, righteousness, patriotism, oppression, and enlightenment? Were most cartoons produced by women in isolation, or working through networks of mutual support within their organizations? Did suffrage art parallel the shifting rhetoric of the suffrage movement?

Cartooning for Suffrage

Although the varieties of propaganda art for suffrage shared a common purpose, examples differed in theme, imagery, and style, and showed the influence of distinct historical and contemporary styles. From late-Renaissance to nineteenth-century conventions came universal symbols modeled after allegorical figures such as Charity (figure 1.15), Fame, Justice, Liberty, and Victory. Thomas Casilear Cole's "The Spirit of May Second" (figure 1.16), contains a standard bearer reminiscent of the classical Victory, while an armored, mounted maiden sounds her trumpet, an established attribute of Fame. Symbols are the defining characteristic of the conventional political cartoon and in "Ring Around a Rosy," Edwina Dumm (figure 1.17) juxtaposed three men (Congress, the eight-hour day, and the high cost of living), a camel (Prohibition), and a woman (equal suffrage) labeled to symbolize representatives and the issues they faced.

Lou Rogers selected a classic image, that of a crowned goddess in drapery seated upon her throne (replacing the scepter as a symbol of authority and power), shackled by "disfranchisement" and "economic dependence" (figure 1.18). Her technique was hybrid, combining an allegorical meaning (oppression of women) with socially constructed shackles symbolizing specific conditions (Baudelaire's "significative" humor), and a third aspect: an emotional appeal made through the victim's despondent pose. Reminiscent of Thomas Nast's figure of Columbia weeping at the death of Lincoln, this illustrates what scholars term "physiognomic perception," a direct communication of feeling through posture and dynamic qualities.[21] The technique is also found in "Travail" (figure 1.19), in which universal woman is chained to man's side, her back bowed by the strain of her heavy burden. The details of the drawing, the figures'

1.16. Thomas Casilear Cole, "The Spirit of May Second."

1.17. Edwina Dumm, "Ring Around a Rosy."

1.18. Lou Rogers, "Enthroned."

1.19. "Travail."

primitive attire, and presence of the pyramids define a setting remote in time and place. This appeal is based on emotion, heightened by large figures looming out from within the cartoon frame.

Realistically drawn cartoons presented themes of poverty, worker exploitation, and child labor. Nina Allender depicted a sympathetic view of slum children and the difficult conditions in which they live in "The Inspiration of the Suffrage Workers" (figure 1.20), while Mary Ellen Sigsbee contrasted the comfort of the middle-class mother with the slum family's meager existence in "To the Woman in the Home" (figure 1.21). "How can a mother rest content with this—When such conditions exist as this?" demands the caption.

Women experimented by incorporating symbols from men's cartoons and appropriating them for their own use, but often discovered that concepts inherited from mythology and tradition reflected male perceptions. Greek goddesses and allegorical personifications, having served for centuries as ornate decorations on classic frescoes, pedestals, or coins, did not meet the image of liberated twentieth-century women (figure 1.22). There were several choices available. Women could reinterpret an existing symbol such as Justice, using additional or altered meanings to transmit the new political appeal made by women. Or, a cultural symbol, Liberty representing the complete absence of political bonds, could be shown to be defective or nonexistent. It must first be rejected in order to re-establish its true or latent meaning. New or unfamiliar symbols, such as Aspiration, Responsibility, Progress, and Suffrage (figure 1.23), lacked culturally prescribed forms or adequate codification and were thus limited as visual images. Likewise, if an image contained contradictory or poorly defined elements, even though familiar, its mean-

TO THE WOMAN IN THE HOME

How can a mother rest content with this—'   When such conditions exist as this?

There are thousands of children working in sweat-shops like the one in the picture. There are thousands of children working in mines and mills and factories. Thousands more are being wronged and cheated by Society in countless ways.

IS NOT THIS **YOUR** BUSINESS?

Intelligent citizens WHO CARED could change all this—providing always, of course, that they had the power of the ballot.

DO **YOU** CARE?

Mothers are responsible for the welfare of children— all children. Do your duty as a mother and demand

VOTES FOR WOMEN!

NATIONAL AMERICAN WOMAN SUFFRAGE ASSOCIATION
505 FIFTH AVENUE   NEW YORK CITY

1.21. Mary Ellen Sigsbee, "To the Woman in the Home."

1.20. Nina E. Allender, "The Inspiration of the Suffrage Workers."

1.22. William A. Rogers, "Can Not New York Protect Her Little Ones?"

33

1.23. *The Woman Citizen,* 21 August 1920.

Suffragette—
"Taxation without
representation is
tyranny."

Voter—"You
unwomanly
creature!"

1.24.
Lou Rogers, "It
Makes a Difference
Who Says It."

ing would be unclear. This was the case with Columbia, a customary American icon, who rarely offered a political statement for women (figure 1.24). Finally, strong, dominant female images could be fashioned by women artists, but these risked alienating men whose support was crucial to the campaign.

The chronology of events leading to passage of the Susan B. Anthony Amendment has been established and confirmed (see Appendix A).[22] However, the reasons behind the intense and prolonged struggle, its unsteady progress, the fierce opposition encountered, and the strange political alliances formed, leave room for considerable debate. The question of suffrage reached far beyond giving women the right to vote and became a catalyst for exploring social issues and ultimately bringing about extensive changes in occupational, civic, and personal arenas. The campaign spawned new organizations, networks, and patterns of collective action, and refocused the lives of hundreds of participants. Artists incorporated novel techniques and forms to produce suffrage propaganda and established fresh and vivid images for the movement. Their illustrations and political cartoons for suffrage provide a fascinating story that, like much of women's participation in history, has been little understood or appreciated.[23]

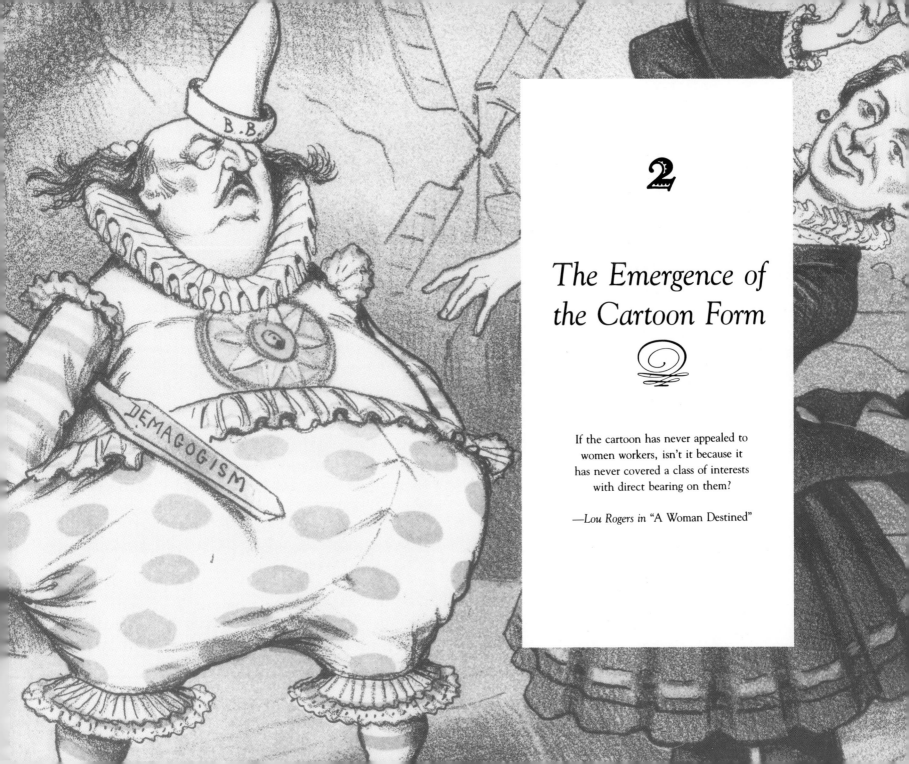

2

The Emergence of the Cartoon Form

If the cartoon has never appealed to women workers, isn't it because it has never covered a class of interests with direct bearing on them?

—*Lou Rogers in "A Woman Destined"*

2.1. "Bellum Symbolicum." 1620.

The cartoons produced by American women for the suffrage campaign are linked to long-established traditions of visual humor and propaganda art. They reflect the historical and cultural context in which this art was produced—a tradition in which artists' gender and gendered representations evoked distinctive meanings. From their inception, visual allegory and satire were created by men and focused on the world of men. Women historically failed to play significant public roles, and real women were rarely featured in cartoons, although the female figure was often used symbolically. Women artists of the early twentieth century, conscious of male political and social dominance, were determined to use their art to produce social change. They selected the political cartoon as their weapon, and adapted it to women's interests. To understand the significance of their work, it is necessary to consider the origins of the cartoon.

From Broadsheet to Cartoon

Renaissance broadsheets, topical and political images printed on loose sheets of paper and offered for sale to the public, were precursors to the modern editorial cartoon.[1] The form, which emerged in the fifteenth century, was often satirical or humorous, and rich in symbolism. A German broadsheet from 1620 uses allegory, elaborate detail, and intricate technique in its portrayal of war as a terrifying monster, brutally crushing the bodies of its victims beneath powerful paws (figure 2.1).

A demand for inexpensive art prompted the development of early woodcutting and engraving techniques that permitted images to be widely distributed. Once the design and carving were completed, images could be mass produced. Early craftsmen produced black and white prints with simple, outlined shapes, and later incorporated short, fine strokes to indicate shading, the genesis of cross-hatching.[2] Engravers in Germany and the Netherlands rendered detailed backgrounds and mastered the principles of perspective and figure drawing, pleasing customers who would scrutinize each acquisition carefully. The speech balloon, derived from medieval prototypes, was prominent in seventeenth-century prints and incorporated into later American graphics.[3] Remarkably, these essential features—symbolic codes, verbal labels, and line drawings—characterized the cartoon form into the twentieth century.

Medieval conventions of allegory and myth, in which persons or objects stood for complex ideas, helped establish a pictorial language. As Ralph Shikes explained, "In a period dominated by superstition, dogmatic faith, and uninvestigated natural laws, the artist treated his subject symbolically, rather than realistically."[4] This use of symbols was epitomized in the emblem book, a Renaissance form in which a picture allegorically presenting a moral truth was accompanied by a motto and a text, often in verse. One of the most famous emblem books was Sebastian Brant's *The Ship of Fools* (1494), a satirical commentary that portrays expressions of stupidity and self-defeating actions as those befitting a fool (figure 2.2).[5] Its symbol, the fool in cap and bells, is depicted in different situations, a device familiar to the modern cartoonist.

By the end of the sixteenth century, the use of symbolic personifications progressed to the point where artists relied on handbooks for selecting the characteristics associated with emblematic figures. The most important of these books was Cesare Ripa's *Iconologia*, a reference book published in Rome in 1593 describing personified virtues, vices, emotions, and other abstract concepts.

2.2. [Albrecht Dürer], Woodcut from Sebastian Brant's *Das Narrenschiff*.

2.3. Alexander Anderson, "Ograbme, or, The American Snapping-Turtle."

Ripa's extensively researched descriptions were based on classical mythology, Egyptian picture symbols, Biblical chronicles, medieval allegories and conventional wisdom. They were arranged alphabetically and, beginning with the 1603 edition, included several hundred woodcuts to supplement the detailed notes that explained each figure's appearance, attributes and properties. The need for the handbook was demonstrated by the appearance of many subsequent editions, including translations into French, German, Dutch, English, and Spanish.[6] A further tribute to these images is their strong influence on later works. Recognizable descendants of Ripa's figures—America, Britannia, Democracy, Justice, Liberty, and Victory—continued to populate political cartoons and public statuary through the nineteenth and twentieth centuries.

Retaining heavy use of a symbolic code, later broadsheets targeted specific persons and events. An 1813 American graphic, for example, represents an unpopular trade restriction with England as a snapping turtle, provoking a character to exclaim, "D—n it, how he nicks 'em" (figure 2.3). New England merchants viewed the embargo (spelled backwards "Ograbme," the turtle's name) as a severe assault on their livelihood.[7]

A cartoon's meaning, established through codes of graphic representation, signification, and allusion, must be readily decipherable, even as it distorts and transforms its subject. Characters may take on an inappropriate size, form, attire, or even gender. Recognizable features may be exaggerated, simplified, or juxtaposed against an incongruous setting. Objects are altered, reversed, joined, represented by their opposites, or represented by substitutes. As Freud explained, the mental processes bringing about symbolic transformations in dreams and jokes are condensation, unification, displacement, double meaning, representation by the opposite, and indirect representation.[8] The cartoon occupies a position in the realm of fantasy, a place set off by its black-lined frame, where talking animals and goddesses cavort among themselves or interact with humans.[9] Because the cartoon is visual, the mind accepts what art critic Ernst H. Gombrich terms its "specious" reality.[10] Cartoons appear real, irrefutable, vivid, and, ideally, unforgettable.

The nineteenth-century cartoon, which set the stage for the modern form, was marked by its symbolic code and the convention of labeling persons and elements, often in a laborious manner, to make the cartoon's message explicit. The cartoon could offer commentaries on abstract issues and principles, reflect on specific persons and situations and policies, and endorse candidates and action in political and social movements. As Maurice and Cooper observed in 1904, "The best and most telling cartoons are those which do not merely reflect current public opinion, but guide it."[11]

Although precursors to the cartoon had been around for centuries, the word *cartoon* did not assume its modern meaning until as recently as 1843, when the British magazine *Punch*, a prototype for the English-language humor magazine, parodied the inept proposals submitted for the new Houses of Parliament frescoes.[12] Soon the term, which previously designated a preliminary artist's sketch or layout, was applied to comical and satirical drawings of similar style and appearance.

America's Symbols

The cartoon symbols that dominate a particular historical period reflect a mixture of established tradition, such as those codified by Ripa, and new symbols imported to meet the artist's needs. Gom-

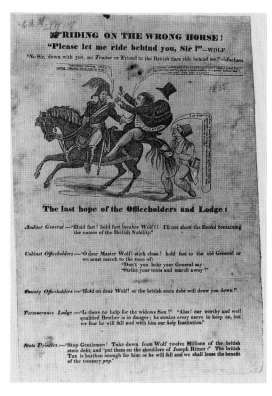

2.4. "Riding on the Wrong Horse."

brich recognized that cartoon symbols are derived from cultural conventions (mythology, folklore, religion, or history), natural metaphors (e.g., dark/light), and ad hoc symbols constructed for a specific use.[13] The nineteenth century witnessed an abundance of the latter, as cartoonists explored and consolidated a cartoon language. American emblems became standardized and immutable and included eagles, liberty bells, donkeys, and elephants. Older icons, including Uncle Sam and Columbia, took on updated appearances.

Presidential campaigns generated political cartoons by the 1830s. In an example from Andrew Jackson's term (1828–36), George Wolf tries to join Andrew Jackson on his horse. Jackson retorts, "No, Sir, down with you. No traitor or Friend to the British dare ride behind me" (figure 2.4). Integral to the development of the American political cartoon was the search for national symbols. In his sourcebook on imagery, Cesare Ripa used writings of Renaissance explorers and Jesuit missionaries to establish a native individual, adorned with body tatoos, animal skins, beads, and a feather headdress, to symbolize the American continent and serve as counterpart to the figures of Europe, Asia, and Africa. A male chieftain was alternated with an Indian Princess figure, a choice judged appropriate to become daughter or sister to Britannia, in various editions of Ripa. Art historian E. McClung Fleming discerned three primary themes governing the Indian princess' use: "her relationship to Britannia, her association with trade and commerce, and her passionate striving for liberty."[14] Other contenders as symbols of America included a goddess (the untamed continent), Columbia and Liberty, and Brother Jonathan as the counterpart to England's John Bull. Fleming pointed out that the enthusiasm for allegory and symbol in the late eighteenth century reflected a neoclassic style and that "Gentlemen on both sides of the Atlantic set to work borrowing old figures from Greek and Roman mythology or creating new ones to represent the United States."[15]

These gentlemen artists perpetuated male percepts and reflected the male subculture to which they belonged. They saw a parallel between the American continent and women, both viewed as unfettered, untamed, and unconquered. The conjunction is psychological, for as psychoanalyst Martin Grotjahn explained, "In the unconscious the land is the mother's body from which the child receives so much joy."[16] More than two centuries earlier, a vision of "America" was based on the goddess Artemis/Diana. Drawn by Maarten de Vos in 1594, she combined Amazonian power with earthy sensuousness (figure 2.5). Tamer of the animals, goddess of the hunt, her bare breasts reflected her primitive state, and she was the desirable body for man's conquest, although possessing powers unknown to men. Still, bare-breasted, armed native women would be ascribed less value than European men due to gender, race, and culture. In a 1782 British broadsheet, "The Reconciliation between Britania [sic] and her Daughter America," an elegantly dressed Britannia embraces her feather-skirted, red-skinned offspring, exchanging the latter's spear for the liberty pole and cap (figure 2.6). The uncivilized, indomitable, and recalcitrant daughter prepares to hug her progenitor, confirming an end to her rebellion. The presence of foreign diplomats accentuates the momentousness of the ceremonial reunion, for England still hoped to regain her colony. "Be a good Girl and give me a Buss [kiss]," urges Britannia.

The use of the woman Britannia to symbolize Britain has been

2.5.
Maarten de Vos,
"America."

2.6. Thomas Colley, "The Reconciliation between Britania and her Daughter America."

The Emergence of the Cartoon Form

41

2.7. *Boston Gazette,* 8 January 1770.

2.8. "Liberty and Washington."

traced to A.D. 119, when she was depicted as a captive on Roman coins. By the seventeenth century she was armed protector, gradually acquiring Athena's helmet, Neptune's scepter, and an emblematic shield, decorated with the crosses of St. George and St. Andrew.[17] Goddess of wisdom, skills, and warfare, Athena/Minerva and Liberty inspired a graphic symbol of America when in 1770 a new figure replaced Britannia on the masthead of the *Boston Gazette* (figure 2.7). The masthead was engraved by Paul Revere and extended the liberty motif through the symbolic use of the Phrygian cap of the freed slave, the liberty staff, the release of a caged bird, and the Tree of Liberty.[18] Revere repeated the imagery in engravings for the *Royal American Magazine,* using Liberty, a knight, and an angel to embellish a portrait of John Hancock. In a 1775 political cartoon by Revere, Liberty intervenes on behalf of the colonists' civil and religious freedom, opposing the unresponsive British cabinet.[19] Attired in classical drapery, Revere's icon is a goddess of imposing presence and dignity, who radiates a countenance of protective authority and latent sensuality (in one version her breast is exposed, a portrayal of invulnerability symbolized by the allegorical body).[20]

In 1789 the spirit of America was named "Columbia" by Timothy Dwight, the president of Yale University.[21] Although British cartoonists clung stubbornly to the Indian maiden as America's main symbol—it was found as late as the 1840s in *Punch*—Columbia's likeness flourished immediately at home.[22] Her countenance gradually softened and her clothing began to reflect cultural practices. One 1800s' painting depicts her in a close-fitting white dress (purity and virtue) rather than in classic drapery (figure 2.8). By the war

Cartooning for Suffrage

of 1812, she had acquired patriotic colors, arranged in a stars-and-stripes pattern. A hand-colored engraving by William Charles, a Scotsman who helped forge an American tradition of political caricature, depicts a regal Columbia, draped in red, white, and blue, holding the American flag (figure 2.9). Her crown, though anomalous in the new democracy, was integral to her goddess role, elevating her status and distancing her presence from ordinary women. But queenly and linked to the prototypic virgin goddess Athena, she would remain largely exempt from caricature and sexuality (*Miss Columbia*).[23]

Columbia's male counterpart, later known as Uncle Sam, was fashioned after Yankee Doodle and similar figures. His immediate predecessor was Brother Jonathan, an appellation used tauntingly by the British during the American Revolution and a character first appearing in a cartoon in 1813 (figure 2.10).[24] Brother Jonathan's costume, which at first seemed arbitrary, was standardized in the 1830s with striped pants borrowed from the stage Yankee, and later still the addition of a top hat and star-studded shirt. Brother Jonathan/Uncle Sam remained an unsophisticated country bumpkin and buffoon, a type of "wise fool," the antithesis of British culture and gentility.[25] British cartoonists retained the image of a belligerent and rebellious America, depicting both Uncle Sam and Columbia in *Punch* as carrying cat-o'-nine-tails or flogging whips.[26] England's male symbol, John Bull had evolved from "Farmer George," a dull-witted, heavyset farmer in eighteenth-century caricatures representing George III. Bearing a name certain to delight punsters enchanted with double meanings, one prototype acquired bovine horns, adding a graphic quality that replaced pliability with au-

2.9. William Charles, "Bruin becomes Mediator or Negotiator for Peace."

2.10. Amos Doolittle, "Brother Jonathan Administering a Salutary Cordial to John Bull."

The Emergence of the Cartoon Form

Mr. Bull, "Oh! If you two like fighting better than business, I shall deal at the other shop."

2.12. "Over the Way."

2.11. E. W. Clay, "Uncle Sam's Taylorifics."

Columbia: "Which Answer Shall I Send?"

2.13. "Columbia's Fix."

thority. John Bull overcame his coarseness and ignorance, was gradually transformed into a country gentleman, and paradoxically embraced as a noble national symbol.[27]

The juxtaposition of John Bull and Uncle Sam or Brother Jonathan created new possibilities of visual one-upmanship and diplomatic struggle (figure 2.11). In an American example pertaining to disputes with Mexico over the Southwest border and with England over the Northwest region ("Fifty-four forty or fight"), John Bull addresses Uncle Sam as Brother Jonathan, illustrating the blending of the two figures. Uncle Sam/Brother Jonathan assaults Mexico successfully, using oversized shears, while ignoring the northern region (destined to become British Columbia), which John Bull hooks with his fishing pole. In contrast, a British cartoon of the 1860s features a refined, gentlemanly John Bull, with top hat, jacket, boots, and walking stick, dismayed to discover the scruffy, belligerent Uncle Sam disrupting his cotton supply (figure 2.12). The unrefined Uncle Sam is engaged in a fist fight with the Confederacy and ignores John Bull.

For much of the nineteenth century and on both sides of the Atlantic, Columbia as a symbol of America operated as a solitary figure or together with Uncle Sam. She could appear classical or contemporary at the artist's discretion, and alternatively, seemed naive or sophisticated. Given realistic features and a heroic aura, she was often invoked in serious and catastrophic situations (figures 2.13 and 2.14). In a Civil War cartoon from *Punch*, Columbia is deliberating whether or not to allow the conflict to escalate. The burden is hers alone. A different representation of Columbia is the naive and girlish-figured (i.e., inexperienced) postwar character who seeks advice from matronly Britannia on mending the national

Mrs. Britannia, "Ah, my dear Columbia, it's all very well; but I'm afraid you'll find it difficult to join that neatly.".

2.14. John Tenniel, "Columbia's Sewing-Machine."

2.15. Thomas Worth, "Uncle Sam and Miss Columbia Open the Vacation Season."

rift. "Ah, my dear Columbia, it's all very well; but I'm afraid you'll find it difficult to join that neatly," cautions Mrs. Britannia. The artist was John Tenniel, known for his *Alice's Adventures in Wonderland* illustrations and a prominent cartoonist for *Punch*. In these renditions of Columbia, her downward gaze, long neck, and angular profile provide her with the ethereal features of a Pre-Raphaelite model, whose pure, allegorical appearance influenced late nineteenth-century British art. For one American cartoonist, however, Columbia, icon of national pride, was treated as a voluptuous and seductive caricature. On the cover of the humor magazine *Judge*, Columbia exhibits a mature, hourglass figure and well-endowed bosom (figure 2.15).

In late nineteenth-century efforts to symbolize America, the roles of Uncle Sam and Columbia became more disparate. One 1890s' *Puck* cartoon places Uncle Sam as director of the "U.S. Foundling Asylum," where he receives four infants (Hawaii, Cuba, Puerto Rico, and the Philippines) delivered by the arms of Manifest Destiny (figure 2.16). It does not seem incongruous that Columbia, in Greek gown and sandals, should stand at his side. In this representation she embodies a higher order—not an ordinary woman. Her mythic origins have resurfaced, unlike Uncle Sam, who though emblematic, was multi-faceted and essentially human. As the twentieth century accentuated the powers of masculinity and modernity, Uncle Sam would displace Columbia as the national symbol.[28] By this time her features, attributes, and insignia had become securely established as the Statue of Liberty, no longer to be transmuted and modernized by new generations of cartoonists.

Cartooning for Suffrage

Technology and the Cartoon

In the nineteenth century, technology, social values, and cultural patterns combined to elevate the cartoon's significance and to expand its functions. The steam-powered printing press, which made its way into the publishing houses of the 1850s, greatly increased production capacity for books and magazines. Lithography, a means of printing from a chemically prepared stone, was adopted for printing posters, advertisements, and magazine art. The heavy stones were cumbersome and the drawings had to be made in reverse, but the process eliminated the need for carving and allowed a fluid, more natural line to be drawn. Lithographic firms were established in large American cities by mid-century, when Nathaniel Currier and James Merritt Ives of New York, entering partnership in 1857, came to dominate the industry.[29] They offered a variety of news illustrations, decorative prints, social satire, and political cartoons, and for over four decades served as "printmakers to the American people."[30] Their approximately six hundred prints were produced commodity-style: furnished on demand and identified by the company trademark rather than the artists' names.[31] American experiments with color lithography, or chromolithography, were taking place in the 1840s, but early results disappointed Currier and Ives, who retained hand-coloring procedures.[32] The firm featured a number of artists—some specializing in drawing ships, sports, or landscapes; others, including Thomas Worth and Thomas Nast, producing cartoons. One typical political lithograph satirized the newly formed Republican party and its

Uncle Sam.—Gosh! I wish they wouldn't come quite so many in a bunch; but if I've got to take them, I guess I can do as well by them as I've done by the others.

2.16. Joseph Keppler, Jr. [Udo J.], "A Trifle Embarrassed."

2.17. [Louis Maurer], "The Great Republican Reform Party Calling on Their Candidate."

presidential candidate as a collection of radicals and malcontents (figure 2.17). The inclusion of two women in a reception line for candidate John C. Frémont at first seems progressive, until one realizes that the Republican party is being discredited because of its appeal to a masculinized Bloomer Girl and a skinny, aging, free love advocate.

Photography played a role in simplifying artistic reproduction, eventually displacing much of the art it initially aided. By the 1880s camera reproduction was used to capture the artist's drawing and transfer it to a plate (photoengraving). The rise of lithography and photoengraving created new possibilities for the cartoon. They allowed cheaper and more rapid reproduction of cartoons and encouraged freedom of expression. The initial pencil or ink drawing could be transferred directly, permitting smaller reproduction size without loss of detail, and allowing the final copy to resemble the original more closely. With the invention of the halftone screen, oil paintings and shaded drawings also could be mechanically reproduced. Accurate reproduction accentuated the artist's personal style, enhancing recognition and subsequent marketability. Distinctive cartoon figures, particularly those projecting images of female glamour, were rapidly associated with their originators: the Gibson Girl (Charles Dana Gibson), Christy Girl (Howard Chandler Christy), Fisher Girl (Harrison Fisher), and Phillips Girl (C. Coles Phillips).[33]

As the political cartoon evolved, it was transformed from an emblematic print importing personification of universal forces to a modern form combining caricature, symbol, and other expressive elements. Rosen and Zerner noted that Romanticism pushed art in divergent directions: on the one hand, toward an abstraction removed from specific contexts and objects and on the other, toward an appreciation of the aesthetic potential of naturally existing forms. This latter tendency culminated in realism and provided the foundation for a new, expressive caricature using the individual's recognizable features or physiognomy as inherently meaningful, and subject to shaping and manipulation by the artist.[34] The same elements underlie the process of physiognomic perception, conceived by psychologist Heinz Werner as holistic, immediate, and relying on primitive emotional qualities. The configuration of a line can make it appear angry or sad, a principle enabling the cartoonist to create a world where small signifies young and large indicates power. Indeed, Gombrich proposed that physiognomic qualities formed the basis of the cartoonist's power, an ability to "mythologize the world."[35] The political cartoon was taking on its modern appearance.

At the same time, a more affluent nineteenth-century public was eager to acquire cartoons, initially as broadsheets and later in magazine issues. Technological advance prompted use of cartoons as campaign art, social commentary, and commercial applications. The humor magazines of the nineteenth century fostered the cartoon as enlightening and entertaining. *Punch,* subtitled "the London Charivari" in acknowledging its inspiration from France's *Le Charivari* (the cacophony), published its premier issue in July 1841, offering commentary, reviews, poetry, a three-paragraph abridged novel, humorous drawings ("funny dogs with comic tales"), and a full-page cartoon. *Punch's* final issue appeared on April 8, 1992. In the United States, humor magazines would not become successful for several more decades and would be strongly influenced by their European predecessors. The most important and long-lived

American examples were *Puck* (published 1877–1918), *Judge* (1881–1939) and *Life* (1883–1936).[36] Like *Punch*, they were published weekly and offered a mixture of cartoons, illustrations, jokes, and commentary.

Joseph Keppler was the Austrian-born founder and chief cartoonist for *Puck*, an American humor magazine that was launched in German some months before the English edition and continued for more than a decade in both languages. *Puck* originated as a satirical cartoon weekly, attacking political corruption, social fads and affectations and religious fanaticism. Taking pointed shots at numerous politicians, it typically sided with the Democrats, supporting Grover Cleveland's and Woodrow Wilson's candidacies. The magazine was admired for its bold, multi-color cover cartoons, German in execution and appearance, its double-page centerfolds, and use of chromolithography by 1879. A former *Puck* artist, James A. Wales, who reportedly left after a disagreement with *Puck's* management, founded *Judge*. The new magazine was so similar to its predecessor that it offered little challenge initially. But the situation changed when the G.O.P. offered to back the paper financially in response to *Puck's* devastating cartoon critique of the 1884 Republican candidate, James Blaine.[37] Cartoonists Bernard Gillam and Grant Hamilton, both formerly of *Puck*, soon turned the tables against the Democrats in powerful attacks in *Judge*, and Hamilton's full dinner pail image was termed the "greatest single factor in [William] McKinley's election."[38] By this time artist John Ames Mitchell, together with fellow Harvard graduate Edward Martin, had launched *Life*, a satiric forum combining sophisticated black-and-white drawings with literary features—a magazine characterized by "a sense of humor, a playfulness, and a gentle exag-

VOLUME VI.   NEW YORK, OCTOBER 8, 1885.   NUMBER 145.

A MATTER OF DUTY.

2.18. William Henry Hyde, "A Matter of Duty."

2.19. Thomas Nast, "'Who Stole the People's Money?'
Do Tell. 'Twas Him."

geration" (figure 2.18).[39] Competition among the trio encouraged modernizing, change, and imitation. *Life* abandoned its black-and-white cover for full-color in 1899, while its appearance was already enhanced by the innovative and sophisticated pen drawings of Charles Dana Gibson. In the continuous race for commercial success, committees decided policies and assignments, adapted themes and styles to the magazine's orientation, and measured the adequacy of their product through circulation figures. In 1912 *Judge's* circulation of 100,000 finally surpassed *Puck's* (the latter ceasing publication in 1918), while *Life* soared on to reach 160,000 by 1916.[40]

Although illustrated magazines and newspapers expanded a forum for comic art, they clearly established a new hierarchy of influence and control. Editors, nearly always males, positioned themselves between the artist and the public, and imposed standards of worth and popular appeal. Collaboration was not unusual, as editors suggested topics and altered or added captions to the artist's work. Once published, however, these cartoons were admired and imitated, and became the prototypes for aspiring artists.

The major reform movements of the nineteenth and early twentieth centuries attracted skilled cartoonists to their ranks. Some reform-oriented cartoons appeared in commercial humor magazines, including *Judge*, which featured a page in support of woman suffrage, called "The Modern Woman," from 1912 through 1917. Interest in political reform, prohibition, and socialism, paralleled the rise of the American political cartoon, whose acknowledged master in the nineteenth century was Thomas Nast.

Thomas Nast (1840–1902), was proclaimed by biographer Morton Keller "the most powerful and influential cartoonist America has ever had," for using graphic imagery to elevate civic-mindedness to influence elections.[41] Even today his cartoons that appeared almost exclusively in *Harper's Weekly* from 1862 to 1886 are widely known, referred to, and reprinted. In 1871, after New York City's William Tweed and the Democratic Tammany machine swindled the city treasury out of millions of dollars, Nast drew a circle of men (the "Tweed Ring"), each pointing an accusing finger at the next in line (figure 2.19). Responding to this picture, Tweed reportedly stated, "I don't care so much what the papers write about me—my constituents can't read; but d—n it, they can see pictures!"[42] Nast was unrelenting in his visual attacks and soon invented a symbol for Tammany, a tiger. When the fierce-eyed, sharp-toothed beast assaulted the Republic/Columbia, it seemed an appropriate analogy for the effects Tammany's unscrupulous and dishonest political dealings had on national honor (figure 2.20).[43]

Nast conceived and refined a collection of well-known graphic symbols, including the rag baby of inflation, the worker's cap and pail, the G.O.P. elephant, and the Democratic donkey. He invented suitable images when none was found, and he modified familiar symbols, including Santa Claus, Columbia, and Uncle Sam, when they proved useful. As these skillfully executed figures became widely recognized, understood, and appreciated, they became the standard for American cartoonists into the next century.

Uncle Sam and Columbia appeared in many of Nast's cartoons, together on occasion (figure 2.21), but more often drawn separately. Uncle Sam acquired the tall, lanky build and rugged face of Abraham Lincoln, and despite his somewhat comic bearing, assumed power and leadership ability (figure 2.22). He was Nast's primary American symbol when dealing with economic, military,

2.20. Thomas Nast, "The Tammany Tiger Loose."

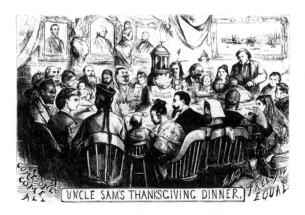

2.21. Thomas Nast, "Uncle Sam's Thanksgiving Dinner."

The Emergence of the Cartoon Form

2.22.
Thomas Nast,
"The Lightning
Speed of
Honesty."

2.23.
Thomas Nast,
"Beware."

or political issues. Columbia, in contrast, was heroic and righteous and was used for emotional, moral, or pedagogic settings (figure 2.23). The Columbia-type figure was less restricted in Nast's imagination, for he borrowed her image to represent the republic, civic government, or New York, as needed. In a New Year's engraving for 1869, Nast juxtaposed Columbia, Justice, and a winged "Spirit of '69" with two male figures (figure 2.24). Like his predecessors, Nast maintained different conventions for male and female icons. Men were politicians, leaders, and heroes; women were typically symbolic.

By the end of the nineteenth century, cartoons as propaganda were fairly common. The British artist Walter Crane produced socialist cartoons using an iconography adapted from the Pre-Raphaelites, which included angels, goddesses, knights, and peasants. Figure 2.25 relies on easily recognized symbols (shovel, pick, and trumpet) and sets forth the opposition of good (angel of socialism) against evil (vampire of capitalism) in a form readily adaptable to other situations of conflict. Crane's strong and original graphics influenced suffrage artists in England and are credited with shaping "the imagery of the British labour movement for more than thirty years."[44]

Americans relied on cartoons to express political, social, and religious concerns. For a weekly Christian paper, the *Ram's Horn*, "equal purity, equal suffrage" and "the saloon must go" were among its stated objectives. Its cartoonist, Frank Beard, offered a weekly "picture sermon," using a style indistinguishable from that found in either *Puck* or *Judge*.[45] In "The Artist and the Vandal" (figure 2.26), there is a curious fusion of nationalism (Columbia), Christian virtues (church and school as her tools), and social reform (against the destructive force of drinking). Woman, as symbolized by Columbia, is the keeper-of-the-morals and the architect of a better world, albeit one that is set on the pedestal of manhood and whose participants are inextricably male. Curiously, the only real person in the cartoon—the male vandal—attempts to undermine the idealized social order.

Although less inclined toward an iconography of goddesses and angels than their British counterparts, American socialists discovered advantages in using the cartoon form. Theirs was a more realistic style, influenced by the Ashcan school and favoring themes from the pragmatic worlds of men's politics and labor. Candidates' ideological positions were linked—sometimes awkwardly or forcibly—to recognizable graphic symbols. In a 1910s campaign poster (figure 2.27), Art Young countered the darkness, slums, and stagnant factories of capitalism with the prosperity, happiness, justice, and bright sunlight of socialism. The Statue of Liberty-like pose of candidate Charles Russell sends a subtle message that lends credence to the rising socialist movement.

John Sloan, an important American graphic artist, drew a series of cartoons for the *New York Call,* an early twentieth-century socialist daily (figures 2.28 and 2.29). In "The Socialist Giant Killer," young David (the *Call*) holds the torch of enlightenment in anticipated victory over Goliath, symbol of capitalism. In "Puzzle" a middle-class male voter deliberates whether to aid the workers through a socialist vote—or feed the gluttonous monster of capitalism (the "Dough Dough Class").[46] Both cartoons rely exclusively on male figures, for even seemingly radical socialists tended to

2.24.
Thomas Nast, "Peace on Earth and Good Will Towards Men."

2.25.
Walter Crane, "The Vampire."

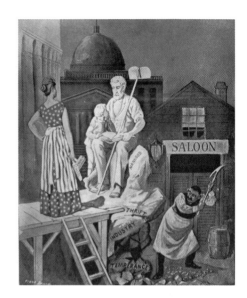

2.26. Frank Beard, "The Artist and the Vandal."

2.28. John Sloan, "The Socialist Giant Killer."

2.27. Art Young, "Charles Russell."

56

depict and perpetuate a man's world in cartoons where the setting was realistic. For symbolic cartoons, they employed women at best as angels or goddesses.

Female Representations

In the symbolic cartoon world created by men, allegories and satires embraced images of men as rulers, heroes, and suitors. In early broadsheets, women were excluded from the public realm and were depicted, if at all, as wives, servants, or other subordinates. Reinforcing a secondary status for women were medieval religious doctrines cautioning that women's influence invited temptation and heresy.[47] Viewed as obstacles to men's quest for religious salvation, women, in the extreme, were persecuted as witches. Aristotle's belief that women possessed a nature inferior to that of men was taken as further justification for setting women apart. It was a man's world even on the printed page; among the few recognizable women's images were Joan of Arc and Queen Elizabeth I.

From Greek origins, symbolic females continued to personify abstract concepts, such as the cardinal virtues (Prudence, Temperance, Justice, and Fortitude), theological virtues (Faith, Hope, and Charity), the liberal arts, and Philosophy.[48] An array of stock allegorical types—angels, goddesses, madonnas, virgins, temptresses and harlots—symbolized the forces and values in men's lives. As a result of historical and cultural processes, real women were represented as subordinate, while allegorical female figures were enshrined. This difference between the realistic and symbolic-allegorical models culminates in what Lisa Tickner termed a "symbolic ambiguity": "They [women] can come to symbolise in the

Puzzle—find a way to vote without helping the Dough Dough Class. (It's an easy one, but the Workers seem to find it difficult).

2.29. John Sloan.

abstract that from which they are excluded in the concrete."[49]

Consistent with this principle, nineteenth-century patriots exploited the imagery of Britannia, Marianne (France), and Columbia as symbols of their respective nations. Each appeared in paintings, posters, and coins as embodiments of nationalism, righteousness, and transcendent power. Female representations were used in the visual propaganda of World War I, and, according to Martha Banta, reveal one of two American motifs: the Protecting Angel (not necessarily displaying wings) and Militant Victory.[50] The Protecting Angel stood for the conventional feminine values of nurturance and the home (i.e., preserving cherished traditions), whereas Militant Victory reflected the unrelenting and compelling masculine forces of progress, expansionism, and domination (winged conqueror and Amazon warrior). Depicting Militant Victory as female conveyed the message that she transcends the mortal, thereby unleashing her superhuman power.[51]

According to Carl Jung, images of powerful females are projected from the human unconscious. For Jung, these *archetypes,* as he termed them, are universal and innate, not the products of social experience or culture. Female archetypes, moreover, influence males and females differently. The young male relies on exposure to his own mother to confirm the mother archetype, and as an outsider, he responds to his mother and to other women as symbols, a process that enhances his tendency to idealize them. He must later reconcile a contradiction between the pre-Oedipal mother (powerful, omniscient, complete) and a future female love object. For the female, the mother archetype is connected to her own being and experience and remains free of sexual connotations.[52] Jung viewed the dominant female archetype as the Great Mother or mother goddess (Sophia, Demeter, Isis), attributing to her a dual nature with "a positive, favourable meaning or a negative, evil meaning."[53] This duality is crucial to the young boy, as Jungian analyst Erich Neumann elaborated: "The youth's fears of the devouring Great Mother and the infant's beatific surrender to the Good Mother are both elementary forms of the male's experience of the female. . ."[54] Because men's representations of women retain this strong polarization, the powerful, virtuous, and transcendent (goddesses, queens, virgins) is contrasted with the impure, unworthy, and malicious (bitches, mothers-in-law, whores). The good/bad dichotomy is similarly reflected by images of pure, honorable, virtuous women ("angel at the hearth") versus debased, fallen women (prostitutes).

If women are both glorified and feared by men, albeit unconsciously, why does some graphic humor ridicule women and promote misogyny?[55] From mothers-in-law and women drivers to "suffragettes" (the latter still a classification in the Library of Congress, although almost always a pejorative term in the United States),[56] women have been belittled, laughed at, and reduced to ridiculous objects. The tradition of lampooning women can be traced to a primitive psychological process that transforms the feared object into a benign, often laughable entity. Through reiteration and codification of women as ludicrous, humorists acquire a means of social control.

Stereotypes demeaning women were prevalent in the satire and comedy of the sixteenth and seventeenth centuries and were transferred to graphic form with the rise of caricature, developed by the Italian artists Agostino and Annibale Carracci.[57] From the pompadour hairdos of Napoleonic times to the pug-dog infatuation of the eighteenth century, and the hoop skirts and bustles of the

"*Adieu, mon cher, je vais chez mes éditeurs, . . . je ne rentrerai probablement que fort tard . . . ne manquez pas de donner encore deux fois la bouille à Dodore. . . . s'il a besoin. . . . d'autre chose. . . . vous trouverez ça sous le lit. . . .*" [Goodbye, my dear, I am going to my publishers, and I probably won't be back until quite late . . . don't forget to give him two more feedings . . . if he needs anything else . . . you'll find it under the bed.]

2.30. Honoré Daumier, "Les Bas Bleus" [The Blue Stockings].

Victorian age, women's fashions and fads have often been lampooned. Women agitators who threatened male institutions became targets of disparagement. When women called for social equality and political opportunity before the French Revolution, artists responded with anti-feminist prints. In *Le Charivari*, Daumier portrayed intellectual women ("bluestockings") as self-centered, misguided individuals who abandon husband, home, and baby in pursuit of ephemeral literary rewards (figure 2.30). Traits that men judged undesirable in women were redefined as "unwomanly," leading to the proliferation of mocking images of women.[58] An American prototype of the female buffoon was Mrs. Partington, the shortsighted old lady from Shillaber's 1850 stories.[59] When artists began to create illustrations of the women's rights advocate, their characters differed little from Partington: old, unattractive, bespectacled, and unfashionably dressed. Unlike Mrs. Partington, however, advocates of women's rights were alleged man-haters and were depicted as spinsters.

Social institutions and customs hindered women's ability to create alternatives to men's images of women. The artist's role was considered male, and the tools of the pictorial image—wood blocks, copper plates, printing presses—were built and operated by men. Printed graphics required skills that talented young girls were unlikely to acquire on their own—nor did society offer to train them. Men were the producers and controllers of art, and their graphic representations perpetuated a male-centered view. Their portrayals of women were confused with social reality; alternatives would not be visible until women became interested in and acquired the necessary technical skills.

Men's images of women in nineteenth-century cartoons, although not mutually exclusive, fall into five categories: famous women who actually existed, ordinary women, grotesque women, ideal women, and symbolic women. By invoking female symbols, stereotypes, and abstractions, male cartoonists constructed a system from which women's perceptions were excluded.

Famous women appeared less often than most other categories of women in cartoons and were nearly always portrayed as radical, outrageous, or anticipatory of twentieth-century roles. Women identifiable in nineteenth-century cartoons included Amelia Bloomer, advocate of dress reform; Susan B. Anthony, woman's rights leader; and Victoria Woodhull, who endorsed free love and women's political advancement. Another was Belva Lockwood, lawyer and presidential candidate in 1884, who was portrayed as a farcical political Columbine alongside Benjamin Butler's political Harlequin/Clown (figure 2.31). The device was classic. As philosopher Henri Bergson explained in his principle of comedy as a social corrective: those who differ from society are ridiculed into conformity.[60]

Images of women in popular culture appeared gullible, simpleminded, and petty—preoccupied with fashion, social status, and overt signs of gentility. In the absence of caricature or distortion, these stereotypical qualities could be mistaken for female traits. These now-familiar characters appeared in both humorous and serious drawings; the caption determined which reading was intended. In a drawing from *Ballou's Dollar Monthly Magazine*, little Ella exclaims, "If the war will only last long enough, my sons shall fight for the Union" (figure 2.32). The humor arises from the childish perception of war as a desired state and the knowledge that anticipated sons—not daughters—constitute the real actors

Arrival of the Political Columbine to Join the Political Clown.

2.31. Frederick Opper, "Now Let the Show Go On!"

"O Ella, they want lots of soldiers!"

Ella—"If the war will only last long enough, my sons shall fight for the Union."

2.32. "Encouraging."

Miss Browning-Backbay.—Did n't I hear you say that you loved Keats?

Miss Lakeside Porkingham.—Keats! Keats! I don't remember him.

2.33. J. Ehrhart, "Escaped Her, For the Minute."

2.34. Gray-Parker, "A Society Belle's Toilet, with a Novelty in Bows (Beaus)."

on the public stage. There is an uncanny resemblance between the china doll and the two young girls, as if they, too, are decorative playthings. Young women were typically pictured in the home, their natural domain, where romance, fashion, and the arts dominated their lives and conversations. In an 1890s' cartoon, Miss Browning-Backbay inquires of her chum, "Did n't I hear you say that you loved Keats?" (figure 2.33). Miss Lakeside Porkingham responds, "Keats! Keats! I don't remember him." She fails to recognize Keats as a literary figure, only as an object of her romantic desires. In this vignette (in which women are further reduced in status through absurd names), Miss Browning-Backbay's familiarity with Keats is overshadowed by the ignorance of her frivolous companion. Later, suffrage artists imposed the stereotype of frivolous women on women who opposed suffrage.

Images of domineering, aggressive woman, according to Freud, reflect men's unconscious fears of their own drives and weaknesses. Jung suggested that the female archetype, a pattern from the unconscious mind, inherently possesses both positive and negative aspects—the good mother/terrible mother. Images of women as dangerous and evil are projections of the terrible mother. Her portraits are found in literature and art (the femme fatale, the dark lady, and the modern-day Eve) and were not uncommon in late nineteenth-century cartoons.[61] In figure 2.34, fashionably attired women use their beauty as a lure, constructing bouquets of hapless men and stitching strings of them to adorn their gowns. How could a culture that placed women on a pedestal of dignity, virtue, and service simultaneously degrade them as vicious and unfeeling? As psychoanalysts suggest, such distortions and transformations serve to remold women's characteristics to interpretable forms, albeit in opposite directions. They perpetuate views of women not as constituents of, but as outsiders to, the psychologically and politically based citizenry. Women are seen as possessing power which, if released, would collide with and weaken society. When British suffragettes armed themselves with bombs and bricks, cartoonists, as if lying in wait, responded with glee: their grotesque and fantastical images of women were finally legitimized by reality.

Charles Gibson's Gibson Girl of the 1890s epitomized, for men, the ideal female form. Gibson Girls, the epitome of American womanhood, were described by one turn-of-the-century British observer as:

> "Statuesque . . . with brows like Juno; and lovely heads perfectly
> poised on throats Aphrodite might envy; with mouths exquisitely
> cut, and noses such as were among the loveliest features of the Italian
> Renaissance; and beautiful eyes, with half-wistful lids. . . ."[62]

2.35.
Charles Dana
Gibson.

The Gibson Girl was rightly compared with goddesses, for she bore scant resemblance to everyday, mortal women. The only complaint from the British critic, moreover, was that she seemed deficient in "the crowning virtues of pity and charity." Her activities, limited to posing, promenading, and polite social conversation, combined with her aloof posture and studied facial expression invite the Gibson Girl to be seen as an object. Her mind was inscrutable, as revealed in the famous drawing of the question mark formed with her hair (figure 2.35). Sharing two key features with the New Woman of the 1890s—independence and sophistication—the Gibson Girl was no thinker or activist, nor even sexually provocative. She was a male fantasy, being eternally young, beautiful, and unobtainable—the perfect image to adorn the pedestal.

American cartoonists continued to represent abstract ideas as

The Democracy must stagger along until November as best it can under the burden which the crazy folly and treacherous selfishness of sixscore of its representatives have fastened to its back. N.Y. Sun, May 11.

2.36. Grant Hamilton, "Staggering Along."

Puck to Father Knickerbocker.—My friend, you'll never be happy till you get a divorce!

2.37. Charles J. Taylor, "Their Marriage Is a Failure."

female, incorporating Columbia, Liberty, Justice, Victory, and other women as agencies and institutions. Some icons preserved a neo-classic appearance, for example, Grant Hamilton's satirical representation of the Democratic party as an overburdened, sandal-clad figure in drapery (figure 2.36). Charles Taylor, in contrast, used modern attire to lampoon partisan politics as a heavy, domineering woman. She scowls at a harassed Father Knickerbocker, the emblem of New York, who is advised, "My friend, you'll never be happy till you get a divorce" (figure 2.37). That both cartoons draw on stereotypes associated with gender becomes clear if one reverses male and female characters. The nagging husband strikes us as less ridiculous than the nagging wife, and overworked men arouse less sympathy or pity, because they are stronger and expected to carry cumbersome, heavy loads.

Cartoonists persistently lampooned famous women and disparaged ordinary ones. They exaggerated women's negative qualities as prevalent or engulfing, and, alternatively, elevated their worthiness and virtue to an ideal impossible to attain in reality. Paradoxically, such idealization could but diminish women's humanness and in symbolic images structured to achieve emblematic or goddess status, they were not women at all. The women artists who created illustrations and political cartoons for suffrage refused to accept such models. They instead sought an imagery consistent with the nineteenth-century crusade for women's rights.

3

The Woman Suffrage Movement

Friends, we present ourselves here
before you, as an oppressed class, with
trembling frames and faltering
tongues, and we do not expect to be
able to speak so as to be heard by
all at first, but we trust we shall
have the sympathy of the audience,
and that you will bear with our
weakness now in the infancy of our
movement. Our trust in the
omnipotency of right is our only faith
that we shall succeed.

—*Abigail Bush*, in Proceedings of the
Woman's Rights Convention

3.1. Elizabeth Cady Stanton (1815–1902).

The nineteenth century marked a time of extensive change for American women. In 1800 women were insignificant, unobtrusive, subordinate beings whose names were not entered into population censuses or immigration records. They could not vote or go to college, and they did not dare to speak in public. After marriage, women were unable to own property, keep their wages, determine the fate of their children, or be punished for any crime committed in their husbands' presence.[1] Middle-class women's employment typically ended with marriage, but the responsibilities of running a household could be prodigious. Childbirth was frequent when children were economic assets, and information on birth control was scant. A new baby appeared every two to three years on the average, although half of all children succumbed to disease or accidents. The mother's life expectancy was less than forty years. Socially constrained for much of the century by the doctrines of true womanhood (purity, piety, and womanliness), women's increasing dissatisfaction with their situation helped forge a new model, what in the 1890s became known as the New Woman. The New Woman was self-sufficient, outspoken, and active—but she still was not a full citizen.

The woman suffrage movement in America was launched in 1848 at a convention at Seneca Falls, New York. Aimed at considering "the social, civil, and religious condition and rights of woman," it differed in purpose and style from the later suffrage campaign.[2] Organizers Elizabeth Cady Stanton and Lucretia Mott called for a meeting of women at a town chapel, but in keeping with tradition, they had selected a man—Mott's husband, James—to act as Chairman.[3] A number of men attended the meeting, and just as women were ambivalent about whether or not the men should be present, they lacked agreement on the movement's objectives. It was Elizabeth Cady Stanton's proposal that established the movement's course for the next seven decades (figure 3.1). She

> submitted a resolution on "the duty of the women of this country to secure to themselves the sacred right to the elective franchise." Lucretia Mott thought the resolution a mistake, and tried to dissuade her from presenting it. . . . Although the convention passed all other motions unanimously, it was seriously divided over the suffrage.[4]

Two weeks later a Rochester, New York, woman's rights convention ignored social propriety when it appointed Abigail Norton Bush, a stove-manufacturer's wife, to be its president. Not all participants accepted this arrangement; one woman withdrew her name from the officers' slate, and several others were reluctant to take their seats on the platform when they learned that a woman would preside.[5] Bush's rhetoric signaled a new emphasis: women were an oppressed class whom justice would inevitably aid. The claim would be reasserted for the next seventy years.

The voice of the white woman was heard with the earliest colonial settlers, although little significance was attached to it until the contemporary rediscovery of women's history. In the 1630s Anne Hutchinson of Boston urged women to express themselves publicly within the church (figure 3.3). Community leaders declared her a heretic and banished her from town.[6] Another early activist was Margaret Brent of Maryland, a competent lawyer and executor of Governor Calvert's estate. She addressed the Maryland Assembly of 1646–47, demanding a voice and a vote. Posterity took her more seriously than her own legislature, celebrating her

3.2. "Ye May Session of Ye Woman's Rights Convention."

3.3.
Anne Hutchinson
(1591–1643).

The Woman Suffrage Movement

67

role as "the earliest American woman to demand the right of suffrage."[7]

In the eighteenth century, questions concerning woman's mind and political place were raised sporadically. A writer to London's *Guardian* in 1713 urged consideration of education as uniquely suited to "woman's world," to her sedentary activity, and to her verbal proficiency.[8] Abigail Adams, as is often recalled, wrote to her husband in 1776, urging, "I desire you would remember the ladies and be more generous and favorable to them than your ancestors."[9] Her words produced no discernable effect, and statesmen assumed the word "citizen" to be so naturally male that they failed to include any reference to gender in the Constitution of the United States. In 1790 Judith Sargent Murray published an essay titled, "On the Equality of the Sexes." Murray challenged the assumption of woman's mental inferiority and provided a surprisingly contemporary analysis of social conditioning ("an education which limits and confines"):

> As their years increase, the sister must be wholly domesticated, while the brother is led by the hand through all the flowery paths of science. Grant that their minds are by nature equal, yet who shall wonder at the *apparent* superiority, if indeed custom becomes *second nature;* nay if it taketh place of nature. . . .[10]

British author Mary Wollstonecraft's 1792 treatise, *A Vindication of the Rights of Woman,* was based on John Locke's empiricist philosophy and called for an altered view of woman's nature and the removal of social obstacles to women's development. Wollstonecraft countered popular opinion with her insistence that women were indeed capable of rationality and supreme virtue.[11] Gender equality would be achieved, she asserted, through the education of women and by political representation.

Progress toward women's equality was slow and sporadic following the American and French revolutions. In 1838 Angelina Grimké, abolitionist and advocate of women's rights, addressed the Massachusetts Legislature—an act unusual for a woman of her day—stating: "*This* domination of women *must be* resigned—the sooner the better; in the age which is approaching, she should be something *more*—she should be a *citizen*.[12] Another leading advocate of woman's rights was Boston's Margaret Fuller, a brilliant, outspoken woman and the darling of the intellectual elite (figure 3.4). Her 1844 monograph, *Woman in the Nineteenth Century*, examined a variety of economic, religious, intellectual, and political issues. Fuller championed woman's emancipation as an extension of the principle of liberty. She believed that giving women their rights would elevate society: "We would have every arbitrary barrier thrown down. We would have every path laid open to Woman as freely as to Man. Were this done, and a slight temporary fermentation allowed to subside, we should see crystallizations more pure and of more various beauty."[13]

Enlarging Woman's Sphere

The American campaign for woman's rights emerged at a historical period in which the function, duties, and privileges of women were rigidly prescribed. The concept of woman's sphere, then in vogue for just over a century, had come to dominate thinking about women.[14] It advocated a code of conduct and manners, which historian Barbara Welter described as the "Cult of True Womanhood":

3.4. Margaret Fuller (1810–1850).

The attributes of True Womanhood, by which a woman judged herself and was judged by her husband, her neighbors and society could be divided into four cardinal virtues—piety, purity, submissiveness and domesticity. . . . Without them, no matter whether there was fame, achievement or wealth, all was ashes. With them she was promised happiness and power.[15]

Subdued and constrained by efforts to be womanly, early nineteenth-century woman had few legal rights. After a decade of petitioning, New York women in 1848 gained the right to hold property in their own names while married, an important step in social reform. Women, of course, could not have gained this right without the assistance of male voters concerned over the fate of their wives, mothers, and daughters.

Women's higher education, promoted by Abigail Adams, Judith Sargent Murray, Mary Wollstonecraft, and others, gradually became a reality.[16] There was a movement to establish female academies and seminaries, culminating in the founding of women's colleges such as Vassar (1865), Wellesley and Smith (1875), and Bryn Mawr (1884). By the 1890s not only were more girls than boys graduating from high school but 20 percent of all colleges were open only to women.[17] As historian Barbara Solomon observed, however, women's colleges perpetuated the idea of a woman's sphere. They developed curricula that emphasized literature, art and music, domestic science, and home economics. Women could be educated—but only for circumscribed roles.

As nineteenth-century American women actively sought change in the circumstances of their lives, they, in turn, were affected by historic transitions: geographic migration, foreign immigration, urbanization, war, technology, industrialization, and the social cli-

Cartooning for Suffrage

mate. In the home, women were occupied chiefly with food preparation and preservation, spinning and sewing, childbearing, farming, and factory piecework. When they first worked outside the home, it was seen as women's patriotic and community duty. Early in the nineteenth century, the economic base shifted from an exchange-based mercantilism to laissez-faire or open-ended production and commerce.[18] With the shift, women were relegated to the home, and paid labor was defined as outside woman's proper sphere. In 1840 only 10 percent of American women worked outside the home. As industry expanded, new jobs were created and a demand arose for an enlarged labor force. Young girls and women were recruited for the factories. Work, however, offered social mobility only for males, as Kessler-Harris has explained.[19] Soon women became concerned with the discrepancy between men's and women's wages and dissatisfied with labor conditions. The Civil War brought additional changes in work opportunities and attitudes. Women were needed to fill a wider variety of jobs, and the devastating loss of men left women outnumbering their potential mates. Society could hardly admonish these women for working outside the home. Nevertheless, psychological attitudes lingered, and women encountered ambivalence in the workplace.

Well-to-do midnineteenth-century women viewed leisure as a value and pursued gentility in habit and fashion. They dressed meticulously, in clothes that were impractical, restrictive, and promoted a sense of fragility and childishness (figure 3.5).[20] As woman's-rights leaders became less tolerant of society's constraints, they perceived women's fashions as another restriction. Elizabeth Smith Miller, a New York housewife, introduced an innovative outfit: pantaloons and a loose tunic. The costume was intended to provide

3.5. "Godey's Fashions For August 1869."

3.6. "Emancipation."

comfort and freedom of movement, and when pantaloons were adopted by Amelia Bloomer, they acquired the name by which they would later be known.[21] "Bloomers" were worn by advocates of woman's rights, including the Grimké sisters, Angelina and Sarah; Elizabeth Cady Stanton; Susan B. Anthony; and Lucy Stone. They provided detractors with a new symbol of masculinized women. Images mocking ambitious or unfeminine women, garbed in bloomers, became widespread in prints and cartoons (figure 3.6). One midcentury lithographer paraded the "Fe'he Males" (figure 3.7).[22] Out of personal anguish and the suspicion that bloomers detracted from issues of greater importance to women, adopters reluctantly abandoned them.[23]

Ideology, Organization, and Strategy

Early nineteenth-century women's societies helped prepare the way for suffrage organizations. In Rochester, New York, church-related societies of "benevolent women," appeared in the 1820s, and provided the community with "major social welfare institutions for half a century."[24] Protestant Evangelists, who proclaimed campaigns for "moral and social perfection—seeking to rid the world of vice, intemperance, and slavery," formed societies in the 1830s. By the 1840s, a third group became influential: women of the Society of Friends (Quakers) who "advocated, among other things, complete legal, social, and economic equality for blacks and women."[25] Local in scope, these groups established networks that brought women together, sustained their efforts, and trained them in organizational skills. As the societies grew, disagreements over goals and strategies, something that would plague the women's campaign, became more pronounced.

Cartooning for Suffrage

3.7. "Two of the Fe'he Males."

3.8. "Am I not a Woman and a Sister?"

3.9. Charles G. Bush, "Sorosis."

Abolition was the most prominent reform movement in the early nineteenth century. Both women and men participated in the crusade, and they attended meetings together. By the 1830s a newspaper column especially for women appeared in the Boston-based antislavery journal, the *Liberator* (figure 3.8), suggesting a special effort to include women in the campaign. The ready acceptance of women in American abolitionism was largely due to the influence of the Quakers. They provided the platform from which Angelina and Sarah Grimké took to the lecture circuit and spoke for the rights of blacks and women. Quaker Lucretia Mott and Elizabeth Cady Stanton traveled to London in 1840 as delegates to the World's Anti-Slavery Convention. Because they were women, they were refused seating at the conference. Shocked and humiliated, Stanton recalled their reaction: "We resolved to hold a convention as soon as we returned home, and form a society to advocate the rights of women."[26] This launched the American woman's rights movement.

Women's growing autonomy is evident in the post-Civil War growth of women's clubs, formed to promote literary interests, public service, and mutual support. One of the first of these clubs was Sorosis (figure 3.9), a New York City literary society, founded in 1869. It was organized in response to professional women being denied admission to a press club dinner honoring Charles Dickens.[27] Clubs for women were formed rapidly in cities throughout the nation and were eventually coordinated through the General Federation of Women's Clubs, organized in 1890. Other organizations for women were founded toward the close of the century: the Association of Collegiate Alumnae (later AAUW), the Daughters of the American Revolution (DAR), and the Women's Christian Temperance Union (WCTU). The latter, established in 1874 in Ohio, attracted a large following and became the most influential women's group in the country. More as an afterthought to its stated objective, the WCTU endorsed woman suffrage in 1881, perceiving it as a means to enhance the efficacy of its moral crusade. Other clubwomen, however, were reluctant to embrace politics, and the General Federation of Women's Clubs did not endorse woman suffrage until 1914.[28]

At the height of the suffrage campaign, another club, Heterodoxy, was established for professional women in New York's Greenwich Village.[29] Its founder was Marie Jenney Howe, an ordained Unitarian minister, who invited the most radical women of the city to become members: writers, artists, theorists, educators, and activists. Heterodoxy, which at its peak had a membership of more than one hundred women, met for lunch on alternate Saturdays. Each meeting featured a creative or provocative speaker, often a member of the group. As feminists, all members supported suffrage, typically by marching, canvassing, and addressing crowds. Some members served as editors, writers, theorists, and cartoonists for the increasingly important suffrage press.

The vote quickly became the preeminent issue of the woman's rights campaign, offering a tangible and symbolic goal. As the campaign aroused and mobilized women, it was promptly ridiculed. An 1864 *Harper's Bazar* illustration portrayed women as cadets and aldermen, and satirized their rhetoric with captions such as "We Can Ruin You" and "We are your Mothers in Law" (figure 3.11). The idea of women voting was viewed as preposterous. Actually, there was a precedent for American women's ballot: New Jersey's first constitution had specified state voting requirements of age,

3.10. "New York—Scene at the Women's Temperance Convention."

3.11. "Why Should We Not Vote?"

3.12. "Women Voting in New Jersey, Toward the Close of the Last Century."

property, and residency, with no mention of gender.[30] Although it is believed that few women voted (figure 3.12), by 1807 the right had been revoked. Its significance was recalled by suffragists, who issued a decorative stamp bearing the slogan "New Jersey Women voted 1776–1807, Why Not Now?"[31]

The success of the suffrage movement depended on an ideology, or belief system, and a network of organizations. Women acquired essential organizational skills through experiences with church, abolition, soldiers-aid, and temperance societies. These societies also served to extend the boundaries of woman's sphere while, at least initially, exemplifying traditional feminine values. The "opening wedge" in the women's campaign, however, came from certain principles of the Enlightenment encountered in the Constitution of the United States. Finding them coherent, forceful, and provocative, women applied these principles to the condition of women in society. According to a 1918 analysis by Kirk Porter: "Many of the liberals were shocked beyond expression and left speechless when women raided their armory, took their weapons, and went forth to use them as they had seen them used by men. Natural, inalienable, inherent right! No Taxation without representation! Government by consent of the governed."[32] Contemporary observers, such as Reverend Horace Bushnell, conceded that women's reliance on the "American doctrine of rights" as the cornerstone of their campaign was "to be expected."[33] Later, however, women superimposed principles befitting a pragmatic "expediency doctrine."[34] They argued that women needed the vote in order to accomplish their good works.

For many years woman suffrage was defeated repeatedly in state legislatures and referenda. The reasons were various: liquor inter-

Cartooning for Suffrage

ests, business interests, political machines, and people repulsed at "the thought of woman 'leaving her proper sphere.'"[35] The idea of separate men's and women's spheres had by now taken on an authority of its own and seemed the natural and moral order of the universe. Adversaries invoked the doctrine in response to any hint of change in women's status. In 1869 Reverend Bushnell was inspired to write *Women's Suffrage: The Reform Against Nature*, a work of nearly two hundred pages. Dedicated to his wife, it foresaw the destruction of the American way of life, should women be allowed to vote: "Women having once gotten the polls will have them to the end, and if we precipitate our American society down this abyss, and make a final wreck of our public virtue in it, that is the end of our new-born, most beneficent civilization."[36] Applying logic drawn from the natural order of the universe, as justified by the Bible and woman's distinct attributes (which he fully expected future scientific investigations to confirm), the core of Bushnell's argument was based on inherent differences between women and men. He asserted that "women are made to be subordinate, and men to be the forward operators and dominating authorities of the world."[37]

Other clergymen, not surprisingly, promoted woman's pious calling, believing the idea of women in politics to be an abomination.[38] As late as 1910, Reverend Lyman Abbott voiced his concerns in "Why the Vote Would Be Injurious to Women," written for the *Ladies' Home Journal*: "Should the woman go to the town meeting to determine the questions of boundaries and roads and police while the men meet to discuss the sanitation and adornment of the home and the care and education of the children? . . . Shall she force herself to assume the tasks which have hitherto been performed

3.13. Headquarters of the National Association Opposed to Woman Suffrage.

by men?"[39] For Abbott, suffrage would be an added burden, causing women to neglect their existing duties and increasing unduly their responsibilities in governing their communities and nation. It would be a calamity.

As the suffrage movement gained momentum, anti-suffrage associations were formed, attracting well-to-do women and wealthy businessmen. The Boston Committee of Remonstrants, a protest group founded in 1882, was reorganized in 1895 as the Massachusetts Association Opposed to the Further Extension of Suffrage to Women. It was composed entirely of women and would encourage formation of groups in other states.[40] In 1911 the National Association Opposed to Woman Suffrage was founded (figure 3.13).

Anti-suffrage sentiment and rhetoric clung to vestiges of true womanhood, but these traditional views of women were rapidly eroded by remarkable and unprecedented models of women: the coed, the career woman, and the Gibson Girl. By the 1890s, the New Woman was widely recognized. She was an individual who was self-sufficient, athletic, and better educated than her predecessors. As Rosalind Rosenberg summarized, "She rode a bicycle, played tennis or golf, showed six inches of stocking beneath her skirts, and loosened her corsets. She expected to marry and have children, but she wanted a life beyond her home—perhaps even a career."[41] Women who reached adulthood in the period of the New Woman widened suffrage support for and helped bestow social respectability on the movement. In the 1890s the press was sometimes willing to replace Bloomer Girls with society matrons in portrayals of suffragists (figure 3.14).

The initial woman's rights movement had been halted abruptly by the Civil War. After the war, male liberals advised women to be patient: this was the "Negro's hour."[42] For devotion to the Union and for aiding the cause of abolition, woman expected to be rewarded. Consequently, it particularly offended these women that for the first time, the language of the Fourteenth Amendment, inserted the word *male* into the Constitution. The irony was not lost on woman's-rights leaders, who increasingly perceived the nature of their struggle as political.[43] The war had provided a chance for women to assume greater, often previously male responsibilities and to participate in war efforts and volunteer service organizations, such as the Sanitary Commission.[44] These experiences shaped new perceptions, but also increased their impatience.

Although many women had worked for both abolition and woman suffrage, issues still closely connected, the emancipation of former slaves altered the balance between the two movements. The postwar woman's-rights convention of 1866 launched a new organization, the American Equal Rights Association, dedicated to human rights. It immediately took up the case of Kansas, where Negro suffrage and woman suffrage were to be decided by popular vote. Lucy Stone, Susan B. Anthony, and Elizabeth Cady Stanton, among others, volunteered to assist in canvassing. Although these woman's-rights leaders worked for both causes, tensions were felt between the promoters of Negro male suffrage and woman suffrage advocates.[45] When both Kansas referenda were defeated in 1867, the women felt the need to go their own way. Emergence of the autonomous women's movement, Ellen DuBois concluded, "was feminism's greatest achievement in the postwar period."[46]

In 1869 Elizabeth Cady Stanton and Susan B. Anthony decided to form a new organization, the National Woman Suffrage Association. An all-female organization, it welcomed working-class

Society Leaders Securing Signatures to Petitions to be Presented to the Constitutional Convention—Scene At Sherry's.

3.14. Benjamin West Clinedinst, "The Woman-Suffrage Movement in New York City."

3.15.
Susan B.
Anthony
(1820–1906).

3.16.
Carrie
Chapman Catt
(1859–1947).

women to the suffrage ranks and advocated a variety of reforms, including easier divorce, an end to discrimination in employment and pay, and improved health practices. They denounced established religion as a means of perpetuating women's subordination and condemned the Fourteenth and Fifteenth amendments as blatant injustices to women.[47] A separate pro-suffrage group, the American Woman Suffrage Association, was organized in Boston the same year under the leadership of Lucy Stone, Henry Blackwell, Thomas Higgenson, Julia Ward Howe, and others. It was more moderate than the National in its demands and adopted a single-issue strategy, solely seeking the woman's vote.[48] Reflecting the organization's eagerness for male support, it selected Henry Ward Beecher as its first president and formulated bylaws establishing an equal number of male and female officers.[49]

The National and the American suffrage organizations worked independently for two decades, but merged in 1890 to form the National American Woman Suffrage Association (the origin of that cumbersome name).[50] Elizabeth Cady Stanton was elected its president, succeeded by Susan B. Anthony, who served from 1892 until the turn of the century (figure 3.15). Leadership then fell to Carrie Chapman Catt, a former school teacher and one of the most competent and energetic suffrage leaders in America (figure 3.16). Her first term as president (1900–1904) marked the beginning of a new century and her second term the suffrage victory phase (1915–1920). The presidency was filled in the interim by Anna Howard Shaw, a physician and ordained Methodist minister (figure 3.17). Although Shaw was a dedicated and eloquent speaker, some later questioned her effectiveness as a national leader.[51]

Cartooning for Suffrage

The women's movement gained its supreme strategist in New Jersey Quaker Alice Paul (figures 3.18 and 3.19). The British suffrage movement had been her training ground and inspiration, for while a student overseas she had joined in demonstrations, been imprisoned, and participated in hunger strikes. Paul returned to Pennsylvania to pursue a doctorate in social work and soon chaired the Congressional Committee of the National American Woman Suffrage Association. The committee was conceived as the means to pressure Congress and transmit women's concerns to them. To shift emphasis from state campaigns to the federal government, Paul established a Washington office in 1913 and increased the Committee's budget from ten dollars to $25,000.[52] The small, dedicated Congressional Committee emerged as a political force, much to the consternation of the National American Woman Suffrage Association and its president, Anna Shaw. In a struggle over the group's autonomy, the Congressional Union separated from the National and became an independent lobby. It began to mobilize women whose states had already enfranchised them and in 1916 launched the National Woman's Party.[53]

In 1896 there were four states in which women were allowed to vote: Wyoming, Utah, Colorado, and Idaho. Their adjacent locations in the Rocky Mountain region encouraged use of a map to symbolize suffrage progress, a device used until the end of the campaign (figure 3.20). The extension of suffrage to women in the West was facilitated by the low female-to-male population ratio, the more egalitarian life-style of pioneer living, and the lack of corrupt urban centers with bosses and political controls. Territorial woman suffrage had been proposed by Congress some years earlier

3.17.
Anna Howard
Shaw (1847–
1919).

3.18.
Alice Paul
(1885–
1978).

3.19. National American Woman Suffrage Association members. *Front row center,* Alice Paul; *Back row, second from left,* cartoonist Nina E. Allender.

as a means to encourage settlement and economic growth.[54] The dynamics underlying politics in Wyoming, the first territory to gain woman suffrage, were complex. Wyoming women themselves petitioned for the ballot, while legislators seized the same means to embarrass a conservative Republican governor. The resulting victory in 1869 was thus ascribed partly to "conservative, political motives, not progressive, ideological ones."[55] Woman suffrage soon proved so satisfactory that when later applying for statehood, Wyoming informed Congress, "We will remain out of the Union a hundred years rather than come in without woman suffrage."[56] Utah, a territory populated by members of the Church of Jesus Christ of Latter-Day Saints (Mormons), had nearly forty times the number of women as Wyoming, and it, too, enfranchised them in 1869. When debate over polygamy became a national issue, Congress disfranchised Utah women in 1887 through federal legislation.[57]

In Colorado women requested suffrage upon admission to statehood in 1876, but were unsuccessful until an 1893 referendum.[58] Three years later Utah reenfranchised women when it entered the union, and in the same year, Idaho granted suffrage to women through a state amendment. As a result, women voted in four western states for more than twenty years before passage of the federal suffrage amendment. These states' experiences with suffrage provided a testing ground for the concept and influenced women of other states to agitate for the ballot. As advances continued in the West, the next states to grant women full suffrage were Washington (1910); California (1911); and Arizona, Kansas, and Oregon (1912). The addition of Montana and Nevada in 1914 formed a solid block of western states (see figure 3.22). By this time, the

Cartooning for Suffrage

WOMAN SUFFRAGE IN WYOMING TERRITORY—SCENE AT THE POLLS IN CHEYENNE.
FROM A DRAWING BY KENDRICK—SEE PAGE 198.

3.21.
"Woman Suffrage in Wyoming Territory—Scene at the Polls in Cheyenne."

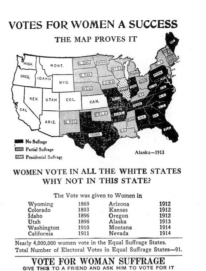

3.20. Map of States Enfranchising Women.

3.22. Harry Osborn, "Two More Bright Spots on the Map."

3.23. Alford, "A Blot on the 'Scutcheon."

eastern states could be redefined as the blemishes on the map (figure 3.23).

The Suffrage Press

Suffrage journals linked women in a political network spanning cities and towns across the nation. The women's press helped strengthen convictions, plot suffrage progress, and consolidate and standardize rhetoric. It was a women's network, or, as one suffrage journal openly proclaimed, a press "edited by women, for women."[59] Periodicals were particularly important at a time when newspapers and magazines provided news, entertainment, and education.

The first American woman suffrage periodical appeared in January 1868, when Susan B. Anthony and Elizabeth Cady Stanton founded *The Revolution* (figure 3.24). Their weekly newspaper relied on funding from philanthropist George Train, whose short-lived enthusiasms characteristically left the woman's rights leaders steeped in debt. Although the paper ceased publication in May 1870, its short life was an important one. Eleanor Flexner pointed out that its existence "gave their movement a forum, focus, and direction."[60] The American Woman Suffrage Association introduced a paper of its own, the *Woman's Journal*, edited by Lucy Stone, Henry Blackwell, and Mary Livermore. Issued weekly, it took a more moderate approach, enabling it to survive from 1870 until 1917, when it became the *Woman Citizen*. For many years it was edited by Alice Stone Blackwell (figure 3.25) and was actively promoted by enthusiastic supporters (figure 3.26). The *Woman's Journal* featured cartoons regularly after 1910, and in 1916 featured a trio of art editors: Blanche Ames, Mayme B. Harwood, and Fredrikke Palmer, who selected and contributed cartoons.[61]

The Revolution.

PRINCIPLE, NOT POLICY: JUSTICE, NOT FAVORS.—MEN, THEIR RIGHTS AND NOTHING MORE: WOMEN, THEIR RIGHTS AND NOTHING LESS.

VOL. II.—NO. 2.   NEW YORK, THURSDAY, JULY 16, 1868. $2 A YEAR. / SINGLE COPY 10 CENTS.

The Revolution.

ELIZABETH CADY STANTON, } Editors.
PARKER PILLSBURY,
SUSAN B. ANTHONY, Proprietor.

OFFICE 37 PARK ROW (ROOM 20.)

TAMMANY PLATFORM UNDER THE INK.

THE Democratic party in National Convention assembled, reposing its trust in the stupidity, disloyalty and lack of discrimination of the people ; standing on the opinions of dead men, who having been under the sod a hundred years, must know more of the vital issues of this hour than the living men of the present, do nevertheless, believe (however unconstitutional the fact may be) that slavery and secession were settled by the war, or the wisdom of the North is resuscitated with the election of Horatio Seymour and Frank Blair, unless all the States be immediately restored to their ancient rights, under the old Union, Constitution and Laws ; in other words, unless the moral world be turned backward on its axis.

Second. Amnesty for all past political offences, especially those of *skin* and *sex*, and the regulation of the Elective Franchise by *all the people* of the States. (*Woman's Right's plank.*)

Third. We demand the payment of the public debt of the United States as leisurely as practicable ; for while the public lands and moneys are concentrated in the hands of the few and the producers pay all the taxes, the commerce and industry of the country will be necessarily crippled, and it must take generations to pay the debt. By this means we make a fixed political issue, furnishing an excuse for heavy taxation, and thus supply the national granary from which our rulers can covertly feast and fatten at the public expense.

Fourth. We believe in equal taxation of every species of property, not only the poor man's bread, but the rich man's bond. (Cheers.) (*Poor man's plank.*)

Fifth. We believe that money that is good enough for the butcher and baker, the pensioner and soldier, is good enough for the bond-holder. (Cheers.) (*Soldiers and workingmen's plank.*)

Sixth. We believe in a tariff for revenue, with incidental protection to domestic industry, *i. e.* " Robbing Peter to pay Paul ;" in the right of the State militia to stay at home in time of peace, in the reduction of the army and navy (of course leaving all the office is in place and pay), in the abolition of the Freedmen's Bureau (the poor whites being now able to furnish their own rations). We are opposed to negro supremacy, and therefore endorse those legislative acts of the republican party which secure equality to the white and black races of the South.

Seventh. We demand the expulsion of corrupt men from office (*vide* N. Y. City Government and State Assembly), and the restoration of the Executive and Judicial branches of the government to their rightful power (though we dare not trust these principles by placing either Chase or Johnson in the White House). That the usurpations of Congress and the despotism of the sword may cease, that the Military may be subordinate to the Civil power, we will play a nice little game in Tammany, by which to exalt New York's most distinguished civilian over the proudest military chieftain of the day, and the ferocious Frank Blair over the smiling Colfax—the said Blair being ready to draw his sword to overthrow by force the reconstruction policy of Congress as soon as he shall be elected.

Eighth. We deny the right of England to imprison American citizens for alleged crimes committed on our soil, beyond her jurisdiction ; and we demand the immediate release of George Francis Train, one of the shining lights of American Democracy, and all our Irish voters now suffering in British jails. (*A bid for a million votes.*)

*In demanding these measures of reform, we arraign the Radical party for its disregard of right, and its unparalleled tyranny and oppression in driving four million slaves from under the protecting wing of the Pharaohs of the South into the Canaan of Suffrage and Self-support. After the most solemn and unanimous pledge to control the logic of events, both houses of Congress have acted on the higher light acquired by time and fair debate, carried our flag to victory and restored the Union by destroying slavery, which they had vowed never to touch. Unfortunately, in this grand shuffle of the cards by East, West, North and South, by some strange deal the ace of spades is always trump. Instead of rebuilding the old Union, they have built a new one ; secured the right of free speech, locomotion, habeas corpus, and trial by a jury of his peers to the black man. They have established tribunals to prevent arbitrary seizures and arrests, and secret star chamber inquisitions, for the new made freedmen, thus giving an unheard of importance to those benighted Africans, and making their political status equal to that of all other citizens. Moreover, they have secured to these people the privilege of learning to read and write, to go to the Post-Office, and telegraph to their friends, to have their private rooms, papers, and letters, and made the Southern Bastile a free home for its people. And to all these Jacobin measures, the Chief-Justice has said, " It is so ordered." These same radicals have waged a greater war, and of course made a greater debt than any nation in all Europe. They have performed the most astonishing piece of legerdemain known in history, in stripping the President of the clothes he made with his own right hand, and rocking the pillars of the republic from the very foundations, and yet leaving the government firmer than before, and the Executive clothed in Constitutional fabrics made by Congress without gusset or seam. If Grant and Colfax are elected in November, there will

be nothing for us to do, but to pick up the chips of our constitutional liberties and meet in solemn Convention to resolve and declare that states where individual rights are held more sacred than Laws, Unions and Constitutions, can only end in a centralized, consolidated government. That is to say, if the black men, being a majority in South Carolina, should so legislate as to deprive all the white men of the right of suffrage, and Congress should interfere for their protection, it would be a flagrant usurpation of power which could find no warrant in the Constitution?

While our hearts are overflowing with gratitude to our brave soldiers and sailors for carrying our flag to victory against a most determined and gallant foe, yet we deplore all those legislative acts secured by their votes, that are the legitimate fruits of their victories.

As to the Public Lands, though we did just what the republicans are doing when we were in power, yet, having been purified by suffering for eight long years' with anointed vision, we now see that the Public Lands should be distributed as widely as possible among the people, and should be disposed of under the Pre-emption or Homestead laws, and sold in reasonable quantities to none but actual occupants at the minimum price established by government.

As calm observers, looking at the heedless world go round, through the loopholes of our retreat, we have been taught many sublime lessons we never could have learned in the whirlpool of power. In closing, we appeal to every patriot (including all the conservative element ; we especially mention them, as their patriotism is doubtful, and excluding the radicals, as theirs is certain) to forget all past differences and unite with us in the great approaching struggle to elect Horatio Seymour and Frank Blair, that the war for the Union, the Constitution and the Laws, may be commenced in earnest.   E. C. S.

THE PRESS ON TAMMANY AND WOMAN'S SUFFRAGE.

Evening Express, July 6th.

A letter was received with great laughter from Susan B. Anthony of the Woman's Suffrage Association, urging the claims of women to participate in elections. The resolution was referred.

Tribune (Editorial), July 7th.

Miss Susan B. Anthony has our sincere pity. She has been an ardent suitor of the democracy, and they received her overtures yesterday with screams of laughter.

Tribune (Correspondence), July 7th.

The speech (Gov. Seymour's) was both heavy and long, and but for the memorial of Miss Susan B. Anthony on behalf of the women of America, its somnolent qualities might have affected the Convention for the rest of the day. But Miss Susan may die in the belief that the democracy agrees with her that the little difficulty of sex *is* insurmountable, and she is probably aware already that the Convention and the wards of Tammany, the Sixth Ward strikers, the rural politicians, and the pardoned rebels, are quiet as fond of universal laughter as universal amnesty, from the derisive cheers which greeted her memorial.

3.25. Alice Stone Blackwell (1857–1950).

3.26. "Newsgirls" Promoting the *Woman's Journal*.

3.24. *The Revolution*, 16 July 1868.

the
WOMAN
VOTER

SUFFRAGE IN 1916

HOW IT FEELS TO BE A JUSTICE

THE GREAT WAR AND
WOMAN SUFFRAGE

IS SUFFRAGE GOING OR COMING?

SEPTEMBER, 1916

Published By the Woman Suffrage Party of New York City

Five Cents a Copy

3.27.
Woman Voter,
September 1916.

3.29. Nina E. Allender sorting cartoon prints.

MARYLAND SUFFRAGE NEWS

Entered as second-class matter December 14, 1912, at the postoffice at Baltimore, Maryland, under the Act of March 3, 1879.

Vol. II, No. 31   SATURDAY, NOVEMBER 1, 1913   Five Cents

A GOLDEN OPPORTUNITY

TABLE OF CONTENTS

DEDICATION

To the poor women without homes, to the little toilers who should be in the schools and playgrounds, to the white slaves in their tragic bondage, and to the children who die, these pages are dedicated! May every woman who is not too idle to have a thought, or too vain to have a soul, or too rich in gold to have a heart, join in the great struggle for women's freedom!

Purity, Liberty, Justice—these we must work for!

ELECTION DAY WORK

Two Strong Arguments in Behalf of Suffrage to Be Presented to the Voters on November 4.

Seeing is believing. Many voters still think that short-haired masculine women are the only ones who wish to vote. The burden of proof lies with the suffragists. We know that perfectly normal, good looking, motherly women desire the franchise, but we must prove it to the satisfaction of the voters. Tomes could be written establishing the fact that the normal woman is the true type suffragist, but the average voter would still remain unenlightened. The presence of one suffragist at the polls constitutes a more impressive argument in refutation of this outworn prejudice than all the written words ever printed.

The approach to a man's reason is usually circuitous. Logic is often vain; visible, ocular proof is what is needed. The best way in the world to prove that the average woman desires the franchise is for the average woman to be in attendance at the polls on election day working for the cause.

Will you be part of the argument?

The Second Reason.

It is also commonly believed that women would be insulted should they venture to go to the polls on election day. Really chivalrous men cherish this preposterous belief still in spite of the fact that it has been refuted thousands of times in the suffrage States. What is needed is local proof, proof right here in Maryland.

It is perfectly obvious even to the most unreasonable mind that if women can go to the polls unmolested to distribute literature, they could go to the polls unmolested to vote. To establish the utter vacuity of this anti-argument, it is essential that the suffragist should go to the polls on election day when the fact will become self-evident that men are as respectful to women at the polls as they are in the drawing-room.

The suffrage movement is a great democratic movement. Victory cannot be achieved through the labors of a few, no matter how assiduous they may be. The suffragists constitute a great non-militant army, and every soldier must be at her post. Nobody else can do your duty for you.

HELP THE CAUSE.—Mention the Maryland Suffrage News When Patronizing Our Advertisers.

3.28. *Maryland Suffrage News,* 1 November 1913.

Regional suffrage papers supplemented the national ones and appeared under titles such as *Woman Voter* (New York City), the *Maryland Suffrage News* (Baltimore), and the *Western Woman Voter* (Seattle). New York's *Woman Voter* (figure 3.27) was the earliest to assign an art editor to manage its numerous illustrations when it appointed Ida Proper in 1912. From her student days two decades earlier, Proper had ties to New York City's art circles and was able to solicit work from leading cartoonists and illustrators, including John Sloan, May Wilson Preston, Anne Goldthwaite, James Montgomery Flagg, and Boardman Robinson. The *Maryland Suffrage News* (figure 3.28) recruited Baltimore cartoonist Harry Osborn and attracted additional cartoonists whose suffrage work was found only on its pages. When Alice Paul established the Congressional Union, she founded a weekly paper, the *Suffragist*, which soon advertised an official cartoonist, Nina Allender (figure 3.29).

The use of suffrage art was integral to a political scheme of celebration, publicity, and persuasion. British artists formed an Artists' Suffrage League in 1907, with the purpose of producing posters and banners for an upcoming suffrage parade. The group's creations were diverse: ornate and intricate fabric banners; colorful, emblematic posters (up to forty by thirty inches); and postcards (figure 3.30). They sponsored poster contests, offering prizes to promote the use of art for suffrage. Another British group, the Suffrage Atelier, designed visual propaganda and offered instruction in cartoon drawing and reproduction (figure 3.31).[62] Posters and postcards produced in England were distributed by American organizations, cited in the suffrage press, and influenced the drawings of American women artists.[63]

"They are no use, Mr. John Bull Chinaman, we're quite grown out of that sort of shoe! Please take fresh measures."

3.30.
"Evolution."

Jane Bull: "No women admitted! No wonder the place is in such a state. High time for a good Spring clean!"

3.31.
Isobel Pocock.

Making Friends with President Wilson.

3.32. William Walker, "Diplomacy."

3.34. Laura Foster, "Rulers of the Nation."

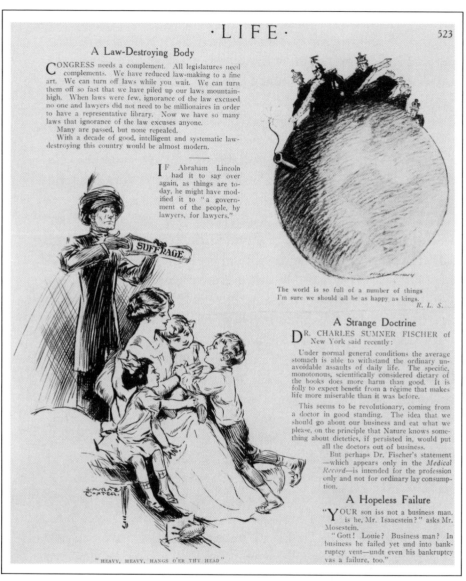

3.33. Laura Foster, "Heavy, Heavy, Hangs O'er thy Head."

Anti-suffrage journals existed, too, beginning with Boston's the *Remonstrance*, published from 1890 to 1920. Suffragists had been ridiculed by popular periodicals for more than fifty years, and humor magazines, notably *Life Magazine*, were unrelentingly unsympathetic, a fact confirmed by statistical analysis.[64] Most of the cartoons opposing suffrage were produced by male cartoonists (figure 3.32), although some notable ones were drawn by a woman, Laura Foster, who employed stereotypes of old-maid suffragists, role reversal, and of unwomanly women (figures 3.33, 3.34 and 3.35). Whether Foster actually opposed the movement at this time is uncertain, for she was later recognized as a suffragist.[65]

The daily press took great pleasure in lampooning suffrage efforts in editorial cartoons, usually drawn by men. Syndicated cartoonist Sara Moore showed some ambivalence and raised the suspicion that the sacred calling of motherhood might be in decline (figure 3.36).[66] The same artist facetiously portrayed a "new masculinism," in which "poor but ambitious young gentlemen" might be given the benefit of home economics instruction in sewing and cooking (figure 3.37).

Turn-of-the-century suffragists, for the most part women highly experienced in public speaking, journalism, and the arts, understood the need to bring woman suffrage to the public's attention. To gain support they employed posters, cartoons, pageants, plays, and public meetings. British suffragists transformed labor's May Day procession into a suffrage parade. In the first massive British parade in 1908, hundreds of well-dressed women clamoring for the vote clustered around colorful ceremonial and political banners.[67] In 1910 the suffrage parade was adopted in New York, engaging

Bye, Baby Bunting
Mother's gone to meeting,
Gone to get her ballot in.
—With apologies to Mother Goose.

3.35. Laura Foster, "In The Political Equality Nursery."

Modern Girls Do
Day Dream, But It
Is Hard to Convince
The Passing
Generation That
The Maternal
Instinct Will Not
Die With It.

3.36.
Sara Moore.

Equal Rights

Why allow women to monopolize the modern privileges?

Why not extend educational advantages to our sons, husbands and fathers?

Why not, ladies and gentlemen, advocate sewing classes for Men?

Every Y.M.C.A. should have a night school where poor but ambitious young gentlemen may learn to make their own clothing.

Working boys can be taught to cut, fit, and sew their own apparel, saving from $25 to $40 on each suit of clothes which they now buy from tailors.

In the absence of domestic science instruction in leading men's institutions, mothers are urged to interest their boys in housekeeping by getting their sons to do housework after business hours.

Instead of allowing selfish daughters to mend, iron, wash dishes and bathe younger children, after they (the daughters) return from store, office or factory, the sons should be permitted to "help mother" every evening.

Both suggestions are part of a movement to revive masculine interest in household economies with the hope of preserving the glorious institution known as the American home.

3.37. Sara Moore, "The New Masculinism."

regiments of women in white dresses, supportive men's leagues, and, of course, great masses of onlookers (figures 3.38 and 3.39). Open-air public meetings, another British practice, were also widely adopted in America. Blending celebration with strategy, Alice Paul's committee staged a suffrage parade in Washington on the eve of President Wilson's inauguration (figures 3.40 and 3.41). The women secured a permit for the parade, but when an unruly crowd began to assault the women, local police failed to intervene. Alice Paul designed effective tactics, and politicians responded. Before the presidential election of 1916, she alerted her peers to their "position of wonderful power, a position that we have never held before . . ."[68] With four million women voters enfranchised, women—if united—could make a difference in the election's outcome.

The Woman's Party had maintained its headquarters in Washington, D.C., from its inception; in December 1916 the National American Woman Suffrage Association, too, finally acquired a Washington "Suffrage House." This action reflected their status as "so solidly housed and so solidly financed that the women would stay until they got the federal amendment they wanted."[69] Carrie Chapman Catt, resuming the presidency of the National American Woman Suffrage Association in 1915, called for a two-pronged attack, her "Winning Plan." The entire organization would work for passage of the federal amendment, while individual states would set respective goals toward resolutions (suffrage states), referenda (where state amendments were likely), and various legislative initiatives.

With the entry of the United States into the Great War, American women refused to postpone the issue of women's political

Cartooning for Suffrage

freedom (figure 3.42). The National Woman's Party established a continuous vigil at the White House gates, some of the women bearing placards demanding a constitutional amendment (figure 3.43). The police arrested nearly five hundred women for loitering and sentenced 168 women pickets to prison.[70] Serving sentences in a workhouse at Occoquan, Virginia, suffragists were housed in deplorable conditions—unsanitary and psychologically oppresive. In protest they adopted the hunger strike—only to be subjected to brutal forced feeding. The National American Woman Suffrage Association dissociated itself from the radical tactics of the Woman's Party, while continuing their own suffrage campaign. They emphasized that women's contribution to the military effort had earned them enfranchisement.

A federal woman suffrage amendment was first introduced to Congress in 1878 and reintroduced in each successive session through 1887. Debate ceased until 1914, when, after a quarter-century of legislative inactivity, revised suffrage strategies and an altered social climate brought victory within six years. By January 1918 the House of Representatives was ready to pass the amendment 274 to 136, but the Senate opposed the amendment in successive votes in September 1918 and February 1919. In May 1919 the House again passed the amendment (304 to 89), and on 4 June 1919 the Senate concurred with a vote of sixty-six to thirty.[71] On 26 August 1920 the Nineteenth Amendment was certified by the Secretary of State, when Tennessee, the thirty-sixth and final state needed, signed for ratification.

Whether radical demonstration or subtle persuasion was ultimately more effective is unknown. For many years antagonism continued between the National Woman's Party and former Na-

3.38. Promoting the March, 1912.

3.39. Suffrage Parade, New York City, 6 May 1912.

3.40. Lore Rogers, Suffrage Parade, Washington, ca. 1913.

Suffrage as a War Measure

SINCE THE WAR BEGAN WOMAN SUFFRAGE HAS BEEN SWEEPING OVER THE CIVILIZED WORLD.

Women are now voters in **Canada**, in **Russia, Norway, Finland** and **Denmark**; they are about to become voters in **Great Britain**; all constitutional liabilities have been removed from them in **Holland**; and government bills to give municipal woman suffrage are under way in **France** and **Italy**.

THE WOMEN OF NEW YORK STATE HAVE NO LESS PATRIOTISM, COURAGE OR ABILITY THAN THE WOMEN OF ENGLAND, RUSSIA OR CANADA.

THEY ASK THE MEN OF NEW YORK TO RECOGNIZE THIS AND VOTE FOR WOMAN SUFFRAGE ON ELECTION DAY.

Where Do New York Women Come In?

During the past four years the women of New York State have made a continuous campaign for Woman Suffrage. By sheer hard work a huge organization has been built up which includes every one of the one hundred and fifty Assembly Districts and extends into most of the polling precincts of the State.

There are over 5,000 women officers in the New York Woman Suffrage Party who are giving most of their time to the work, and more than 500,000 women in the state are enrolled.

During this time, with comparatively little effort, in

CANADA—Five great provinces, Alberta, Manitoba, Saskatchewan, British Columbia, and Ontario, have adopted Woman Suffrage. In the midst of war, and with the votes of her soldiers, Canada has given votes to her women.

UNITED STATES—Since January this year six new states have given presidential suffrage to women: Ohio, Indiana, Michigan, Nebraska, North Dakota and Rhode Island, and Arkansas has given the vote to women in all primary elections.

ENGLAND—The bill to give votes to 6,000,000 English women has passed its third reading in the House of Commons by a vote of 385 to 56. It has the full backing of the British Government and it is promised that there will not be another general election without the votes of women.

3.41. Suffrage Parade, Washington D.C., March 3, 1913.

3.42. "Suffrage as a War Measure."

3.43. Suffrage pickets outside the White House.

tional American Woman Suffrage Association members. Woman's Party supporters felt justifiably slighted when Carrie Chapman Catt accepted public credit for the victory, whereas the National American Woman Suffrage Association accused the Woman's Party of generating negative public opinion and impeding suffrage progress. Following the suffrage victory (figure 3.44), the two groups went their separate ways. Catt of NAWSA organized the League of Women Voters; the National Woman's Party launched a campaign for an Equal Rights Amendment. The struggle had been a long, difficult one (figure 3.45), in which many women's lives had been essentially altered. Some would later acknowledge that they had given their best years to the cause.[72]

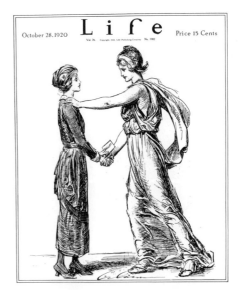

3.44. Charles Dana Gibson, "Congratulations."

3.45. Nina E. Allender. "Every Good Suffragist the Morning after Ratification."

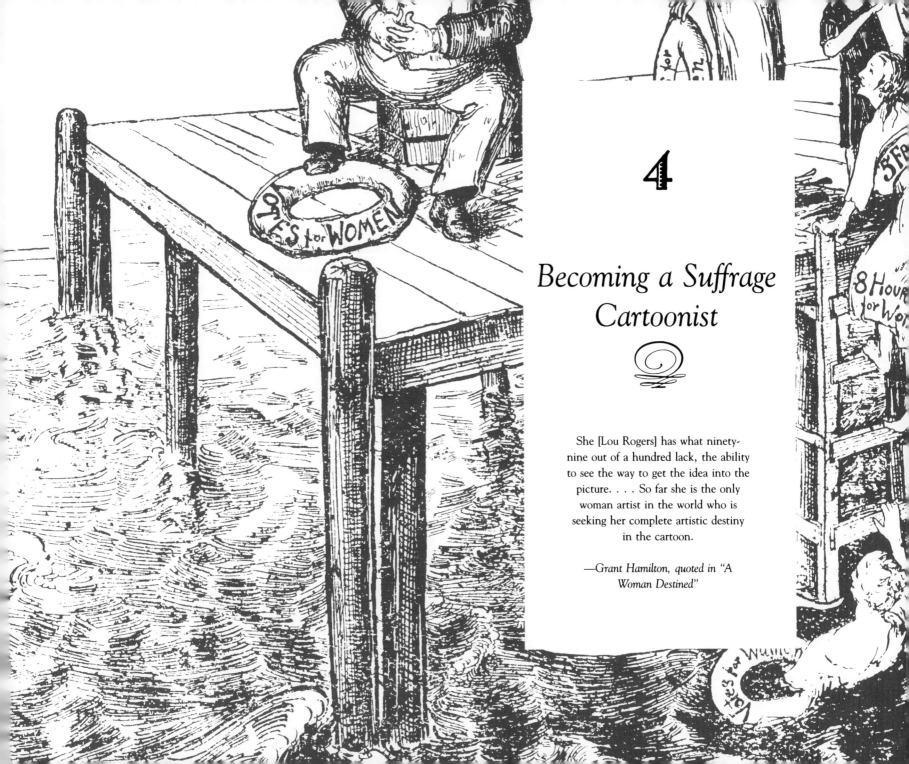

4

Becoming a Suffrage Cartoonist

She [Lou Rogers] has what ninety-nine out of a hundred lack, the ability to see the way to get the idea into the picture. . . . So far she is the only woman artist in the world who is seeking her complete artistic destiny in the cartoon.

—*Grant Hamilton, quoted in "A Woman Destined"*

4.1.
Annie "Lou"
Rogers (1879–
1952).

4.2. Ida Sedgwick Proper (1873–1957).

Suffrage cartoons were produced by a group of American women who perceived the political, social, and psychological ramifications of the women's vote and who chose to focus and dedicate their time, energy and talent to promote this overriding goal. Each conveyed an individual perspective and expectation, but all resolved that art would shape public opinion and influence voters. They put to use the results from many years of art training and experience to promote an idea, to serve a collective group, and to enhance the quality of public life. Viewed against their nineteenth-century upbringing, they often seemed reactionary or rebellious. Yet, these high-spirited women saw themselves as bringing to fruition the highest American ideals. They demanded to see in practice what patriotic doctrines had only preached: equality, citizenship, and political representation.

The suffrage artists who were most prominent and influential included Nina Evans Allender (1872?–1957), Blanche Ames Ames (1878–1969), Cornelia Barns (1888–1941), Edwina Dumm (1893–1990), Rose O'Neill (1874–1944), Fredrikke Schjöth Palmer (b. 1860), May Wilson Preston (1873–1949), Ida Sedgwick Proper (1873–1957), Lou Rogers (1879–1952), Mary Ellen Sigsbee (1876–1960), and Alice Beach Winter (1877–1970) (see figures 4.1–4.8). Their life histories provide the basis for the composite portrait presented below and help to reveal the motivations behind their unusual creative productions.

From available material and the few paintings in museums and private collections, suffrage artists can be seen as women of rich talent, keen ambition, and intense loyalty to the cause. Reconstructing their lives is for the most part neither easy nor completely satisfactory. Few became sufficiently well known to leave written

4.5. Rose O'Neill (1874–1944).

4.3.
Nina Evans
Allender (1872?–
1957).

4.4. Blanche Ames Ames (1878–1969).

4.6.
Cornelia
Barns
(1888–1941).

4.8. Mary Ellen Sigsbee (1876–1960).

4.7. May Wilson Preston (1873–1949).

biographies, and clues to inner motives or the personal meanings of their artistic symbols are virtually unavailable. These are outcomes familiar to those who pursue women's history: lost records, destroyed originals, and indistinct paths. Some of the three dozen women artists who published suffrage cartoons cannot be traced at all, having moved away, changed their names through marriage (some used pseudonyms professionally), or abandoned their art. A few continued to draw or write or were vividly remembered by relatives and descendants.

American Origins

It is sometimes thought that those most intent on social change are discontented radicals, outside the dominant culture, who have little to lose by protest. Nothing could be further from the truth in the case of suffrage artists, among whom the only known European-born, Fredrikke Palmer, was the wife of a Yale language professor. Most, like Lou Rogers, probably the most prolific American suffrage artist, came from long-established American families. Annie Lucaster "Lou" Rogers was the fourth of seven children born to Luther Bailey Rogers and Mary Elizabeth (Barker) Rogers in Patten, Maine (figure 4.9). The siblings, four boys and three girls, formed a close-knit family in the rural lumber town, as she explained in an anonymous autobiographical article. Her images of her childhood remained intense and nostalgic: "In all that woods life—from the winter camps with their vigorous activities to the spring drives of logs with crashing white waters, log-jams, the ringing bing of cant dogs, dams with their roaring sluiceways—we children belonged, not so much looking on as feeling part and parcel of it."[1]

4.9. Luther B. and Mary Elizabeth Rogers, ca. 1875.

4.10. Adelbert Ames, ca. 1865.

The Rogers family was descended from Robert Rogers, who emigrated from England in the 1630s and settled in Newbury, Massachusetts. Rogers's paternal grandfather, Dr. Luther Rogers, migrated "down east" to Maine and helped found the Congregational church, the Patten Academy, and the town library. His two sons fought in the Civil War, where one was killed. Annie's father, Col. Luther B. Rogers, returned to marry and begin a family, but was to suffer the death of his wife. Luther B. Rogers then married Mary Elizabeth Barker, a young teacher at the Academy, just shy of her seventeenth birthday.[2] Barker's father, Annie's maternal grandfather, attended West Point and died in a lumber accident when his children were small.

Another New England woman, Blanche Ames, was born in Lowell, Massachusetts, the fourth of six children (third daughter of four) of Gen. Adelbert Ames and Blanche Butler Ames. Adelbert Ames graduated from West Point, became a General during the Civil War, and served as Governor of Mississippi in the reconstruction years (figure 4.10). Ames's maternal grandfather was Gen. Benjamin Butler, former Governor of Massachusetts, and a one-time Presidential hopeful (see figure 2.31). The family claimed early New England ancestry: Ames (Eames) and Butler clans arrived in the 1630s, and John Howland, linked to the Ames line, was a Mayflower passenger.[3] Nineteenth-century New England had a tradition of strong, intellectual women, and Ames's family was no exception. Grandmother Butler, Sarah Hildreth of Lowell, overcame family resistance to launch an acting career with the New National Theatre in New York City before marrying Gen. Butler.[4] Her daughter, Blanche Butler, received more education than typical of her day, enrolling in the Academy of the Visitation in

Georgetown. She enjoyed reading and painting, and, after marrying Adelbert Ames, must have readily appreciated the artistic talent of her daughter, Blanche.

Ida Sedgwick Proper was a minister's daughter from Bonaparte, Iowa, the fourth of seven children (four surviving girls, two boys) born to Datus Dewitt Proper and Amanda Ellen (Dodds) Proper. Datus Proper enlisted in the Grand Army of the Republic in his teens and after his return from a prisoner of war camp, underwent a religious conversion. In 1866 he married Amanda Ellen Dodds of Chicago and devoted himself to a calling in the Baptist ministry.[5] The Propers traced their heritage to the Palatinate or Rhine Valley in Germany, where the harsh winter of 1708–9 descended on a war-ravaged region. The Johann J. Propper [sic] family joined the approximately three thousand Germans who made the difficult voyage to America, arriving in 1710 and settling along New York's Hudson River. These recent immigrants intermingled with earlier settlers, and Johann's grandson, Peter Proper, married Maria Ostrander, a descendant of an early arriving Dutch-American family.[6] Two generations later, Lewis Wellington Proper, Ida's paternal grandfather, married Mary Sedgwick of upstate New York, a descendant of a seventeenth-century military figure. This colonial ancestor was Robert Sedgwick, a major-general in the Massachusetts militia, whose progeny later included a number of prominent statesmen and writers.[7] Ida Proper's grandparents, Lewis and Mary (Sedgwick) Proper, migrated to the midwest in the 1840s and established their home in Iowa.

Nina Evans Allender was born in Auburn, Kansas, one of two daughters of David J. and Eva S. (Moore) Evans. Allender's maternal grandparents, like Ida Proper's family, joined the western

4.11. Cyrus C. Moore, ca. 1880.

migration and moved from Philadelphia to Kansas in the early years of the territory's settlement. Grandfather Cyrus C. Moore (figure 4.11) was a New Jersey born physician, who took his wife and four young children west by covered wagon to practice medicine in a town outside Topeka.[8] Catherine B. Moore, Nina Allender's grandmother, was born in Pennsylvania and her father (or grandfather), Gen. Bauer, served on Washington's staff during the Revolution, according to family sources.[9] Allender's father, David Evans, had been a school teacher in Oneida County, New York, before migrating to Kansas to become a Superintendent of Schools. Evans, whose last name was common among the New York Welsh community, may have served in the Union forces, as there was a David Evans in the "Fifth Oneida." By 1870 he was a boarder in the Moore household, while Eva, his future wife, was teaching in a remote prairie school. They were married in 1871, while she was still in her teens, and had two daughters, Nina and Kate.[10] In 1881 Eva Evans became a government worker, one of the first such women hired by the United States Department of the Interior. Granddaughter and writer Kay Boyle recounted how Eva and her husband separated, leaving Boyle to wonder: "where Grandma Evans had found the courage to leave Kansas and a grandfather I was never to see and to move with her two young daughters to Washington, D.C." There is evidence that Allender's father, D. J. Evans, also moved to Washington, where he was employed by the U.S. Navy Department.[11]

Mary Ellen Sigsbee, who studied art at the Art Students League of Washington, the Art Students League of New York, and in Paris, also claimed famous and patriotic relatives. Grandfather Lockwood helped found the U.S. Naval Academy at Annapolis and her father, Rear Adm. Charles D. Sigsbee was in command of the USS *Maine* when it was attacked at Havana Harbor. A man of many talents, Charles Sigsbee had published drawings in the *Daily Graphic,* undoubtedly inspiring young Mary Ellen. These five women, seemingly representative of most suffrage artists, claimed multiple generations of American ancestry and a line of male progenitors who offered courageous military service. From common backgrounds emerged shared attitudes, while their individual personalities remained distinctive and unconventional.

Personalities and Life-Styles

In the late nineteenth century, educational and professional barriers were gradually eradicated, avenues for women's achievement expanded, and impressionable young daughters inherited new aspirations and beliefs. Their mothers had come of age witnessing the disruption of their stable community structure as fathers, uncles, brothers, and male companions left home to join the Grand Army of the Republic or, although rare for this group, the Confederate forces.[12] Such women, though proud and patriotic, transformed their anxieties and fears to form the radical belief that women needed more control in shaping their own destinies. In the war's aftermath old ideas seemed outmoded, as the social order became modernized and new technologies emerged. The little girls of the era, born in the 1870s and destined to bring the suffrage crusade to victory, grew up idealistic, talented, and strong-willed. They competed with their brothers and were determined to make something of their own lives.

The life stories of American suffrage artists were distinct from those of their mothers' generation. Most suffrage artists received an extended education, typically attending prestigious art schools and colleges. They became geographically mobile in their occupational pursuits, migrating to large cities, crossing the continent or the Atlantic Ocean. Their family responsibilities were reduced by remaining single, marrying late, or having significantly fewer children. They joined women's collectives whose concerns included politics and self-development, replacing older values of public service and literary appreciation. Feminism and socialism were often substituted for Christianity and a narrow definition of woman's duty.

The most visible suffrage artists, including Allender, Ames, O'Neill, Preston, Proper, Rogers, Sigsbee, and Winter are defined by their births in the 1870s as members of a demographic cohort. Their world views were constructed in the post-Civil War years, and their life-styles were forged in the era of the New Woman. This group shared an outlook by being American-born, white, Protestant, and middle-class in values, and each was in her late thirties to early forties at the time of her primary involvement in the women's movement. Patriotism was strong in families who immigrated to America before the Revolution and whose descendants answered their nation's call during the Civil War. Mothers of suffrage artists were intellectual and pursued self-development through writing, teaching, women's clubs, or even an occupation. Art proficiency became the daughters' dream.

Less apparent than the unbridled enthusiasm and dedication displayed in their suffrage art was the effect of their membership in this transitional generation, vulnerable to historical uncertainties and role tensions. There were few professional role models to guide them, for women had not yet been cartoonists, publicists, or public figures. They were propelled forward by their own cohorts—not drawn by women already enmeshed in the social structure. Guided by their passions and ideals, they were subject to disappointment and disillusionment when goals were not realized as quickly or as fully as hoped. New Women often approached marriage with expectations of a satisfying relationship between equals, and although some remained single or delayed their marriages, at least two were understandably shocked when their husbands left them for other women. Divorce was also becoming a possibility, undergone by O'Neill, Sigsbee, and Allender.[13] Only a small number from this group experienced motherhood, for it curtailed pursuit of their careers unless help with the children could be arranged. Subject to gender discrimination, hardships, and disappointment, women artists nevertheless proved resilient and retained their optimistic faith in personal and social evolution.

American women flocked to big city art centers in the late nineteenth and early twentieth centuries seeking life directions, a career, a relationship, a new life-style, or an ideology. Most sought a mixture of these goals, for the New Woman unabashedly wanted it all. In their teen years these artists had discovered their talents, winning recognition and sometimes money; as young adults they awaited the rewards of the professional artist. Lou Rogers saved her salary from a teaching job to enroll in the Massachusetts Normal Art School in Boston. She followed a pattern typical for Maine women artists, who "gravitated to Boston and New York" by late

He (at the top of his lungs)
  "It seems to me so very queer
  You always screech at me, my dear.
  One would think I could not hear."
She (at the top of her lungs)—
  "I screech at you! Why, Hubby Owl!
  Each time you speak to me you howl!
  And when a thing don't go to suit
  You simply stand around and hoot
  So now! SO NOW! SO NOW!"
A chipmunk sitting in a tree—
  A bachelor laughed happily
  "I am very glad that I am me!"

4.12.
Lou Rogers, "In
the Screech-Owl
Family."

century to earn a living.[14] As Rogers's mother stated in an unpublished memoir: "Her love for drawing absorbed and held her as nothing else did. . . . I tried to dissuade her, to make her realize what a struggle she was up against."[15]

Several years later Rogers moved to New York: "I came to New York without a cent and without knowing a soul. I was unskilled. . . . I was certain of only one thing: I would be a cartoonist." New York, as she understood, was the center of cartooning where she was able to approach newspaper editors and humor magazines with her drawings. Her efforts for employment with a large newspaper failed, however, when the editor reportedly declared "that newspapers had no use for women in this particular line of work and not much use for them in any other."[16] Despite such obstacles, Rogers had become a cartoonist by 1908, evidenced by her whimsical and expressive talking animals in *Judge*. These lacked any social message and instead featured an innocuous husband-wife bird squabble (figure 4.12) or a visually humorous crow (figure 4.13). By 1911 Lou Rogers began submitting cartoons to the *New York Call* and the *Woman's Journal* and became the earliest American woman to produce a series of suffrage cartoons.

Ida Proper, similarly spirited, ambitious, and devoted to women's advance, earned her own money for an art education and traveled from Seattle to New York City in the 1890s. In 1911 after extended study abroad, she returned to the United States firmly allied with the women's cause. At the dock she objected to the usual inspection of a "woman's effects," prompting reporters to inquire whether she was a suffragist. She replied, "No, but I am a feminist."[17] Proper commemorated a suffrage demonstration in an oil painting, "The

Cartooning for Suffrage

End of the Suffrage Parade, Union Square." In 1912 she joined sculptor Malvina Hoffman in the unorthodox act of converting a brownstone on East Thirty-seventh Street into a gallery. The *Evening Sun* announced: "Suffragist Painter and Sculptor Strike Out for Themselves as Exhibitors of Their Work." Reviews of Proper's New York exhibits declared her work, "excellent," "in the spirit of the best kind of decorative painting" and showing "really great qualities."[18] Her reputation was rapidly spreading (figure 4.14).

Greenwich Village, where both Proper and Rogers were active professionally, was a center of art, suffrage, feminism, and socialism. Rogers's determination and rich imagination had lured her there and brought professional accomplishment. Her initial contact with suffrage reveals her idealism ("a recognition of the need to help men and women change their focus a bit"), impetuousness, and inner conviction (instantly "[I] knew I belonged").[19] It is not surprising that Proper and Rogers both joined Heterodoxy, the radical feminist club, or that Proper would pride herself on being a charter member of the group. In the Heterodoxy Club Album presented to founder Marie Jenney Howe, Proper wrote, "My executors are directed to inscribe on my tombstone this single encomium, 'She was a charter member of Heterodoxy.'"[20] Proper's organizational abilities landed her the art editorship of New York City's *Woman Voter*, where she selected monthly cartoons drawn for the paper or reprinted from other sources. Rogers produced several hundred suffrage cartoons, which appeared in *Judge*, the *Woman's Journal*, the *New York Call*, and the *Woman Voter*. She participated in suffrage lecture tours and appeared as a soap-box orator in Times Square.[21] In the chalk-talk tradition of cartoonists, Rogers set up

4.13.
Lou Rogers,
"Sweetheart of the
Corn."

4.14.
Ida S.
Proper,
"The
Moor."

4.15.
Blanche Ames,
ca. 1895.

4.16. Blanche Ames. "Our Answer to Mr. Taft."

her easel at street fairs and lectured on suffrage to the crowds. The *New York Times* acknowledged her efforts in "Suffrage Cartoons for Street Crowds."[22]

Blanche Ames, an art editor for the *Woman's Journal,* came from an influential Massachusetts family and was privately tutored for most of her girlhood. Outgoing, independent, and popular, she was elected president of her class at Smith College (figure 4.15). After graduation she married Oakes Ames (no relation), a Harvard botany professor, and together they raised four children. One daughter, Pauline Plimpton, later described her mother's suffrage involvement: "As to her cartoons, it was a matter of putting her talents to work for a cause. When she believed in something, she threw herself into it heart and soul. . . . Some of her portraits were done on commission, but her cartoons were done for the cause."[23] Ames published cartoons in the *Woman's Journal,* where one attracted the attention of former President Taft, who wrote: "I have before me the Woman's Journal and Suffrage News, of June 5, 1915, with a cartoon entitled Meanwhile They Drown. . . . The implications from such a cartoon are so absurd and unjust to opponents of suffrage that they ought not to aid the cause."[24] The high-spirited Ames responded with a new cartoon in the *Woman's Journal* labeled, "Our Answer to Mr. Taft" in which she reaffirmed her original position (figure 4.16).

Nina Evans, who would become the cartoonist for the *Suffragist,* passed her teen years in Washington studying painting and anticipating a career as an art teacher. However, her plans changed abruptly when marriage was proposed by a charming Englishman, Charlie Allender, who accepted a banking position arranged by her relatives. Not long afterwards, according to the family, Charlie

Cartooning for Suffrage

"flew the coop one day taking another lady along with him, as well as an untold sum of money from the bank, and was never heard of again."[25] Nina Allender was devastated. It was later revealed that Charlie Allender had left England to avoid a prison sentence for embezzlement and forgery. Nina kept the Allender name, hoping to make it respected again, and took a job with the U.S. Treasury Department.

Although Allender worked full time to support herself, she managed to be active in many aspects of the suffrage campaign. She became president of the Stanton Club in Washington, canvassed in Ohio for a referendum, and served the National Woman's Party by traveling to Wyoming. Of her Ohio efforts, Allender wrote to Margaret Foley of Boston: "I never enjoyed any thing more."[26] When Alice Paul organized a massive suffrage parade to coincide with President Wilson's inauguration, Allender declared to Foley: "at last there is something doing in Washington, D.C."[27] It was at Alice Paul's bidding that Allender submitted her first cartoon for the *Suffragist*. She hesitated, insisting that "she painted, and preferred to paint."[28] Her many years of art study led her to resist this possible subversion of her talent. Soon, however, she mastered the cartoon format, was creating weekly cartoons, and earned the title, "Official Cartoonist" of the Congressional Union (figure 4.17).

Disappointed in marriage and having abandoned her art career, Allender redefined her goals to include women's political gains. Relatives considered her chronically unhappy, and yet she could pick up her drawing pen and offer a witty commentary or employ techniques of irony and satire to political advantage. The excitement of the campaign and her friendships with Alice Paul and Margaret Foley were focal in raising her spirits. Family relations

4.17. Nina Evans Allender, ca. 1915.

4.18. Massachusetts Normal Art School Building, built 1885.

4.19. Drawing Class, Massachusetts Normal Art School, ca. 1890.

remained central throughout her life, and she shared a home with her mother for many years and remained close to her sister and nieces.

The Pursuit of Art

In this period, art education for women became readily available at the art academies and schools of design, where women teachers often encouraged girls' efforts and served as potential role models. Lou Rogers entered the Massachusetts Normal Art School in Boston, like other normal schools, an institution founded to prepare teachers (figures 4.18–4.20). The school, whose female students outnumbered the males, reflected a social experiment: the democratization of art education and a concern for the art-teaching profession. As Diana Korzenik explained, "Massachusetts Normal Art School, founded by the state in 1873, revolutionized *who* could study art in this country. As a normal school, it was one of the institutions created as part of a movement to improve the quality of teachers, but as a normal *art* school, it was unique in this country."[29]

Failing to pass her first-year exams, Rogers later criticized its stringent curriculum, asserting that it was not what she expected. She had detested "the musty depths of the school" and "hated the plinths and the dead white casts and the stiff designs for wallpaper."[30] Rogers would pride herself in being a self-taught artist, although she actually resumed her art training fifteen years later at the Art Students League, where she enrolled in George Bridgman's figure drawing class.[31]

The Art Students League of New York, founded by students in 1875, was egalitarian in its policy of admitting female students and

Cartooning for Suffrage

including women on its board. Men and women were enrolled together in all classes except life drawing, which remained segregated until World War I.[32] Young May Wilson Preston, in her teens a founder of New York's Women's Art Club, was reportedly indignant in 1892 when the Art Students League denied her admission to its life drawing classes.[33] That very year, Ida Proper collected money she earned from a library job in Seattle and traveled east to pursue her art education. At the Art Students League Proper studied with William Merritt Chase, John Twachtman, Douglas Volk, and J. Carroll Beckwith, leading painters and illustrators of the day. Her proficiency and promise earned her a fellowship for study abroad, and she chose Munich, one of the leading centers of nineteenth-century art instruction.

In Munich Proper studied at an academy founded by Hermann Obrist, a leader in German Art Nouveau and the Arts and Crafts Movement.[34] When her fellowship ended she returned home for a few years and then moved to Paris. There were thousands of aspiring artists in the Parisian ateliers and academies, where Proper gained exposure to internationally acclaimed teachers. One was Théophile-Alexandre Steinlen, known for an illustration style that was bold and often humorous. Another was an American, Richard Miller, who became her tutor and friend and offered to paint her portrait.[35] Amid the intense competition familiar to the Paris art student, Proper's paintings were accepted by 1908 for the annual salons of both the traditional Société des Artistes Français and the more progressive Société Nationale des Beaux-Arts.[36] Displaying work at the Paris Salon of 1908 was Mary Ellen Sigsbee, who had eloped with artist Balfour Ker and moved with him to Paris. Whether Proper and Sigsbee became friends is not known, as Sigsbee was

4.20. Painting Class, Massachusetts Normal Art School, ca. 1890.

engaged in raising an infant son, in addition to pursuing her art. Three years later both Proper and Sigsbee would return to New York City.

In her teens Nina Evans Allender attended the newly founded Corcoran School of Art in Washington, D.C., and entered the year-end competition.[37] She competed against some very talented girls, who repeatedly outranked the boys for the gold medal prize. The 1889 winner, May Minnigerode, was destined to marry the director of the school, Eliphalet Andrews, and over two decades later would work with Allender on the *Suffragist*. Allender's disastrous marriage of the 1890s was followed by resumption of her training in 1902 at the Pennsylvania Academy of the Fine Arts, one of the first American art schools to provide professional opportunities for women.[38] Nina Allender attended the Academy for four years and with classmates Charles Sheeler and Morton Schamberg participated in Robert Henri's summer art study tour in Europe.[39] During Allender's final year at the academy she may have met a new student, Cornelia Barns. Barns, who lived in Philadelphia, would later contribute to the *Suffragist* with Allender and was a future art editor of *The Masses*. Another art editor of *The Masses*, Alice Beach Winter, studied at the St. Louis School of Fine Arts for five years, moved to New York, took classes at the Art Students League, and married artist Charles A. Winter.

Blanche Ames enjoyed art as a teen, but did not to enter a separate art academy. Instead, she graduated from Smith College in 1899, where she earned a certificate from its art school, in addition to her baccalaureate degree. Ames was no less ambitious than other suffrage artists, for she illustrated her husband's scientific papers on orchids, experimented with color systems in collaboration with her brother, Adelbert, and frequently exhibited her work (figure 4.21). Her solution to combining career with family responsibilities was to furnish an elaborate studio in their North Easton home, and to hire domestic servants to help with the children. Her position of financial security and social opportunity furthered artistic contacts: Ames sat for a portrait with noted Boston painter Edmund Tarbell and traveled to New York to attend the Armory Exhibit of modern art, which included work by May Wilson Preston.

The childhood years of these artists coincided with the founding of the American humor weeklies, *Puck, Judge,* and *Life,* and they entered their teens when newspapers were switching to photoengraving methods to reproduce cartoons. They were familiar with cartoons as popular entertainment, and, as children, they had seen them used more extensively than ever before. Some girls, including Rose O'Neill and Edwina Dumm, were sufficiently inspired by these images to achieve proficiency solely through imitation. O'Neill gained public attention when she won an art contest in Omaha at age thirteen and began drawing cartoons for a local paper. In her teens she moved to New York to further her professional development and in the 1890s became a social and political cartoonist for *Puck.* O'Neill spent much of World War I abroad, where she responded enthusiastically to the propaganda art produced by British suffrage artists.[40] She returned to provide posters, postcards, and banners for the American suffrage cause, many of which featured her famous creations, the Kewpies. Edwina Dumm, trained only through a correspondence course in cartooning, by her early twenties had constructed a portfolio adequate to earn her a position as an editorial cartoonist.[41] Displaying a sophisticated and rich

4.21. Blanche Ames at her easel.

cartooning style, Dumm intermingled suffrage propaganda among other political commentary.

Suffrage as a Mid-Life Focus

The traditional pattern for nineteenth-century women was to move rather abruptly from girlhood to adulthood, with marriage marking the change in status and the assumption of serious responsibilities. The emergence of the New Woman coincided with the early writings of Sigmund Freud, and soon woman's stages would be scrutinized for their psychological significance. It would be theorized that the adolescent discovers who she is, while the young adult blends her sense of identity in an intimate relationship. By middle age, according to Erik Erikson, a woman redefines herself within society, arriving at a sense of *generativity* by passing on her values to the next generation.[42] This endeavor takes on varying forms depending on the historical context; key elements for suffrage artists included a traditional childhood in the 1870s, an autonomous identity made possible in the 1890s, and increasing engagement with women's organizations in the 1910s. Their sense of generativity at mid-life arose partly from a deeply held belief in woman's duty to serve and partly from ideological commitments justifying activism. They resolved to increase opportunities for all women, present and future, and to improve the quality of human life. Earlier suffragists had been devoted to abolition, war service, and temperance, consistent with the focus of nineteenth-century women's clubs, service organizations, and reform societies. Their heirs benefited from professional and educational organizations and embraced ideologies grounded in progressivism, socialism, feminism, and the women's peace movement, and most especially in suffrage itself.

The production of suffrage art and associated activities involved women so deeply as to disrupt many conventional career pursuits. As "ardent suffragists," they demonstrated fervor and passion for the cause, donating time, energy, and talent for suffrage. They received no pay for these efforts—especially remarkable at a time when several of these artists were forced to support themselves and manage family responsibilities. Of the women discussed in this chapter, Lou Rogers, Edwina Dumm, and Rose O'Neill became cartoonists as a career choice. Nearly all the others modified their artistic interests to serve the suffrage cause.

Regional suffrage organizations functioned as networks: recruiting, involving, and motivating those it reached. Pushed by inner idealism and ambition, this group of suffrage artists, by accident or design, found themselves in cities and communities that pulled them further into suffrage circles. It is not by accident, however, that the nucleus of suffrage artists belonged to the same organizations and knew each other personally. Rogers and Proper were among the feminists who joined Heterodoxy; Barns, Sigsbee and Winter were socialists who contributed illustrations to *The Masses*. The five were active in New York City, which housed the headquarters for the National American Woman Suffrage Association; published its own suffrage paper, the *Woman Voter*; and promoted a Woman Suffrage Press.

The political activity of Washington, D.C., attracted the militant wing of woman suffrage and gave rise to the most highly politicized women's art. Forty-year-old Nina Evans Allender was working in Washington and sharing a home with her mother in the 1910s. There Inez Haynes Irwin described a meeting between Nina Allender, her mother Eva Evans, and Alice Paul: "one Sunday a stranger called." After a brief conversation with the petite woman who wore a little purple hat, "mother and daughter looked at each other in amazement." Both had agreed to donate money and their time.

> Their amazement arose partly from the fact that they had not been begged, urged, or argued with—they had simply been asked; and partly from the fact that, before the arrival of this slim little stranger, they had no more idea of contributing so much money or work than of flying.[43]

Out of enthusiasm and zeal Allender produced cartoons that showed a new spirit and interpretation of suffrage. As an admirer explained:

> Mrs. Allender is the first woman artist who has ever won a name in the magazines of the country as a cartoonist. The ability to crystallize a political situation in picture is a gift women artists seem to lack; at least they have left this field to men. Mrs. Allender not only brings to politics quick insight, but also the eye of a feminist. No man could have projected such a series of cartoons on the suffrage situation of the past four years.[44]

Much of Allender's work in the *Suffragist* addressed specific issues and events and reflected the stance of the National Woman's Party. Alice Paul had chosen Allender to be their cartoonist, but the benefits were mutual.

The *Woman's Journal* maintained editorial offices in New York in the early 1910s, but in 1912 returned to Boston, a city with a liberal intellectual tradition (although also the birthplace of the anti-suffrage movement). Blanche Ames was active in the network of Boston organizations: she was treasurer of the Massachusetts

Woman Suffrage League, had lobbied for suffrage at a Republican National Convention, and was president of her local suffrage group. In 1915 Ames became an art editor of the *Woman's Journal*, created cartoons for a special suffrage supplement of the *Boston American*, and had her "Cradle of Liberty" selected for a state suffrage poster.[45] Blanche and husband Oakes wrote letters, marched in parades and from 1913 to 1916 hired a news clipping service to record suffrage progress. These scrapbooks, which contain many suffrage cartoons, may have spurred Ames's own interest in drawing cartoons and have since proved invaluable to scholars.[46] She managed to integrate the roles of society woman and activist, as her local newspaper reported:

> Mrs. Ames is a most charming hostess. She is also an answer to the "antis" who claim that a woman cannot be a suffragist and a homemaker. She had her two youngest children with her, little Miss Evelyn and Master Aymas being interested in the speaker and friendly with all the guests. The two older children attend school in Boston.[47]

In her late thirties Blanche Ames cited in the *Woman's Who's Who* her interests as suffrage and her accomplishments as orchid illustrator.

Ida Proper moved to Denver shortly before the turn of the century, where she opened a studio, joined the Denver Art Society, and exhibited her paintings.[48] Colorado was then one of only four states in which women could vote and her residence there may have been instrumental in shaping her views. However, it was not until a decade later, when she was nearly forty, that Proper is known to have immersed herself in the suffrage cause. For the *Woman's Who's Who* of 1914, Proper described herself as the Captain of the Seventeenth Election Precinct, Twenty-fifth Assembly

4.22. Lou Rogers, "The Gimmicks."

District, and art editor of the *Woman Voter*. She next headed the Art Committee of the New York State Woman Suffrage Association.[49] May Wilson Preston became the first woman member of the Society of Illustrators and in 1915 was identified as one of "a dozen of the most distinguished illustrators in the world."[50] She had been associated with the Ashcan circle through her second husband, James Preston, and exhibited in the Armory Show. In her forties May Wilson Preston was an active member of the National Woman's Party and produced suffrage images in a light-hearted, humorous style for the *Woman Voter* and *Puck*.[51] She also illustrated a humorous book, *How it Feels to be the Husband of a Suffragette* whose author was designated as "Him."

Considering the intense involvement that each of these artists showed in suffrage, it might be anticipated that the conclusion of the suffrage campaign would require some readjustment in their lives. Many artists became allied with other causes, as their lives continued to be characterized by energy, dedication, and achievement. Several joined the effort to counter existing legislation forbidding birth control information—an issue of major concern to women, which had resulted in Margaret Sanger's imprisonment. Lou Rogers and Cornelia Barns became art editors for Margaret Sanger's *Birth Control Review*, where they offered some of their strongest feminist statements. Blanche Ames was a co-founder of the Birth Control League of Massachusetts and became president of the New England Hospital for Women and Children. She wrote a full-length biography of her father in the 1960s after John F. Kennedy criticized him in *Profiles in Courage*.

With the United States' entry into World War I, Ida Proper returned to New York to aid her country, and was soon stationed at Tours with the Army Ordnance Department, one of the first women to serve overseas with the armed forces. She taught art at the University of Mayaguez, Puerto Rico, for three years, performed occupational therapy in Chicago, and became a news editor for *Power* magazine. Her final move was to Monhegan Island in Maine, where she was attracted by its spectacular scenery.[52] By this time she acknowledged her personal record as a "Jack of all trades," and devoted her time to research, lecturing, writing, and gardening. She produced two books: *Monhegan, The Cradle of New England*, a history exhaustively researched in several languages, and *Our Elusive Willy*, in which she argued that William Shakespeare was of royal descent. Responding to a request for biographical notes, she remained exuberant, "It's been a terribly exciting life and I've had a good time even if I have worked like a drag horse."[53]

Lou Rogers bought a small farm in Brookfield, Connecticut, married artist Howard Smith, and published illustrated verses for the *Ladies' Home Journal* about little people called "The Gimmicks" (figure 4.22). She wrote two animal adventure books, based on the tales she loved to tell the nieces and nephews at the family's summer camp in Maine (figure 4.23) and targeted a child audience when she hosted a weekly NBC radio program "Animal News Club" in the 1930s. Nina Allender supported the National Woman's Party in its campaign for the Equal Rights Amendment and served on its council until 1946, when she resigned for reasons of health. Cornelia Barns, although plagued by tuberculosis for much of her adult life, had moved to California with her husband and son, where she drew magazine covers and contributed to a local newspaper. Fredrikke Palmer, when in her sixties and widowed, left New Haven to live in Honolulu, where her son had taken a job

4.23. Rogers family gathering. ca. 1920. Lou Rogers is in back row, standing, third from right.

as a college professor. Edwina Dumm moved to New York City, and launched a successful syndicated comic strip, *Cap Stubbs* or *Tippie,* about a boy and his dog.[54]

With the death of Edwina Dumm in 1990, the last major suffrage artist passed into history. Dumm, Blanche Ames, and Alice Beach Winter all lived into their nineties, remaining alert and articulate. In 1957 Ida Proper died on Monhegan Island, and Nina Allender in Plainfield, New Jersey, both having lived into their eighties. May Wilson Preston, Rose O'Neill and Cornelia Barns had all died in the 1940s. Lou Rogers succumbed to multiple sclerosis in 1952 and was buried in her hometown of Patten, Maine. Outgoing, fun-loving, and an inspiration to her own generation, the public activist disappeared behind the private headstone, which reads: "Annie R. Smith." The life of Blanche Ames, in contrast, remains visible through the creation of a state park, Borderland, which preserves her estate and studio at North Easton, Massachusetts.[55] The lives of all these women, united by vocation and by suffrage at a critical time in women's history, reveal a commonality of purpose, hope, and vision demonstrated through their art.

5

Persuasive Themes

One effective picture in glaring color
or bold black and white may bring
home a political lesson or point a
moral far better than all the oratory of
the platform or all the appeals of
the pulpit.

—*"The Poster in Politics"*

During the last campaign, the direct indorsement of Woman suffrage by every political party in the country amounted to the inauguration of a new national policy.

5.1.
Lou Rogers,
"Another Inaugural Ceremony."

American suffrage art was produced by artists working individually, who appeared less influenced in content and style by each other than by prevailing conventions in the realms of symbolism, cartooning, illustration, advertising, and poster art. Each artist recognized the potential of the graphic form to present a succinct, compelling argument. The suffrage cartoon defined a visual propaganda medium with a single aim: to promote the enfranchisement of women.

The messages within these cartoons parallel the movement's rhetoric and fall into several categories. Some present the argument of justice or rights, expressing women's claim to principles found in the U.S. Constitution: liberty, justice, democracy, and equal representation. A number, using images concentrating on the victimization of women workers, the abuse of child labor, and the pervasiveness of political corruption, reflect the belief that women, if given the ballot, would bring about major social reforms. Others portray woman suffrage as inevitable, riding the tide of progress. Some cartoons present women as moral crusaders and woman's nature as exemplary, pure, and virtuous, frequently employing images of women as loving, nurturing, devoted mothers responsible for children's moral upbringing. Still other cartoons present the argument that women's support and participation in World War I obligated the nation to make them full citizens.

Justice

The dominant nineteenth-century justification for suffrage was the claim to rights, or as Aileen Kraditor described it, the "justice argument."[1] It was based on belief in the inherent equality of all

Cartooning for Suffrage

humanity and the inalienable right to justice. This principle was represented by Justice, the ancient goddess distinguished with a sword, set of scales, and a blindfold to eliminate bias.[2] Her appearance took on varied forms in women's art, depending on the context and message (figures 5.1–5.3). Although her conventional insignia are absent, she retained full classic drapery when depicted by Mary Taylor and Lou Rogers. In both images Justice confronts Uncle Sam, revealing her position of superior authority. She forces him to acknowledge the principle that women have a right to vote by invoking the words of Lincoln's Gettysburg Address and the platforms of major political parties: "During the last campaign, the direct endorsement of Woman suffrage by every political party in the country amounted to the inauguration of a new national policy."[3] Laura Foster's figure of Justice is especially human-like, as she interacts with men and women voters, instead of the symbolic Uncle Sam.[4] She pushes aside mortal men, for as goddess and the principle of justice, she is the highest authority.

In nineteenth-century America, the symbol of Liberty appeared in state seals, on newspaper mastheads, and in the quintessential Statue of Liberty. She was the protecting warrior-goddess Athena/Minerva, who even as Columbia often retained the Phrygian cap. A stars-and-stripes insignia on her robes or headgear, or the inscription "'76," "U.S.," or "Liberty" on her tiara were her identifying marks. Bartholdi's monumental statue, "Liberty Enlightening the World," was erected in New York Harbor in 1886 and itself became the symbol of Liberty.[5] Liberty was the powerful warrior defending her ideals, the queen with sun ray crown, and the mother nurturing her people, as made explicit in Emma Lazarus's poem engraved on a plaque on the statue's pedestal. This latter aspect,

5.2. Mary Taylor, "Are Not the Women Half the Nation?"

5.3. Laura Foster, "Justice—'Make Way!'"

VOTE—WE WILL MAKE IT BIG ENOUGH FOR BOTH BOY AND GIRL.

5.4. Blanche Ames, "The New Cradle."

however, is paradoxical in light of her heritage, as virgin goddess, the armed maiden striving for virtue, her body untouched and pure.[6] The mothering role is ascribed to Charity, a female with nurturing breasts, an image here combined with that of virtuous maiden to meet a hastily constructed cultural mythology.[7] In the twentieth century, moreover, Liberty was finally invoked to assert that American women were entitled to political liberty, to a voice in public policy, and to elect government officials on an equal basis with men.

In a cartoon for the *Boston Transcript*, Blanche Ames combined two liberty icons: Liberty personified and the "Cradle of Liberty" (figure 5.4). Although Liberty is attired in classic drapery, tiara, and bare feet to suggest that she walks on sacred ground her face and physique appear human.[8] As Liberty, her care of the two children is anomalous, but the fusion of authority and the principle of liberty underlie the propaganda value of the cartoon. A woman suffrage amendment is essential to enlarge the liberty cradle, thereby accommodating both of Liberty's children, male and female.

Imbued with ideological significance and blatantly female, the Statue of Liberty proved a natural symbol for woman's suffrage. She additionally embodied the discrepancy between the actual and the potential in Winsor McCay's cartoon sequence (figure 5.5), where she discovers herself representing "a liberty that does not exist."[9] To reaffirm symbolic integrity, McCay's statue becomes the activist, replacing her torch with a placard marked Votes For Women. Lou Rogers exposed the chauvinism underlying the cultural image by parodying Liberty as a stick-legged male scarecrow with short trousers and oversized shoes, holding a shining torch whose flame reads, "Government By Male Citizens" (figure 5.6). Without wom-

Cartooning for Suffrage

5.5. Winsor McCay, "Liberty Awakes."

5.6. Lou Rogers, "Are You Helping this Farce Along?"

Lafayette to Rochambeau: "Does the Republic we fought for deny liberty to its own citizens?

5.7. Nina E. Allender, "The Suffrage Protest in Lafayette Park."

"If that donkey only has 'horse sense!'"

5.8. M. F. G., "The Parting of the Ways."

en's enfranchisement, the image the Statue of Liberty presented was an empty facade, for American women clearly enjoyed no political liberty. Members of the National Woman's Party elaborated this theme in their protests, demanding, "Mr. President, How Long Must Women Wait for Liberty?" Used as a slogan on protest placards, Allender reaffirmed its origin as a national ideal when she chose Lafayette and Rochambeau, Frenchmen who had aided the American struggle for independence, to ask in shocked disbelief, "Does the Republic we fought for deny liberty to its own citizens?" (figure 5.7).

Democracy, too, was also personified and used as a cartoon theme in suffrage art. In an early application of partisan symbols in the women's press, artist M. F. G. depicted the National Democratic Convention's choice of "Votes For Women" (victory) versus an "Oligarchy Of Men" (ruin) (figure 5.8).[10] The caption, "If that Donkey Only Has 'Horse Sense'!" satirized the Democratic Party's obvious inability to discern true democracy. This 1912 cartoon reveals an important shift in suffrage strategy, as suffragists began to petition the Democratic and Republican parties directly. The Congressional Union/National Woman's Party set about blaming the party in power, a strategy borrowed from their British counterparts. Applied to cartoon images by Nina Allender, Miss Democracy cautiously treads an icy sidewalk, her safety in the hands of "Congress," a man whose duty it is to scatter ashes on the ice (figure 5.9). Miss Democracy carries the suffrage amendment and demands, "Will you Make 1918 Safe for Democracy?"

Personifications representing Liberty, Justice, and Democracy were symbolic females who helped the cause of real ones, conveying attributes and meanings consolidated over the centuries. Liberty,

Cartooning for Suffrage

Justice, and Democracy embodied the principles on which the nation was founded and the underlying belief that they were incompletely met until applied to its women.

Expediency

Early woman's-rights leaders were reformers united to address the issues of slavery, women's education, property rights, and temperance. Their rhetoric emphasized transcendent principles of civil rights, and constitutional government. By the 1910s, as the graphic campaign became mobilized, suffragists who had entered adulthood in the period of the New Woman increasingly argued that women needed the ballot for protection and social reform. The male-dominated economic system exploited workers and allowed political corruption, encouraging suffragists to believe that women's participation in government would end such abuses. They focused on issues such as sweatshops, white slavery, poor sanitation, and blatant disregard for on-the-job safety.

As a rationale for suffrage, expediency superseded ideas of justice or rights, but was neither articulated consistently nor uniformly understood. According to Aileen Kraditor: "Some suffragists used the expediency argument because social reform was their principal goal and suffrage the means. Other suffragists used the same expediency argument because the link of woman suffrage to reform seemed to be the best way to secure support for their principal goal: the vote."[11]

The expediency argument was advanced through images of the oppressive conditions of women's labor and subsistence. These images were shaped by established socialist iconography, which had already attracted leading illustrators on both sides of the Atlantic.

5.9. Nina E. Allender, "Will You Make 1918 Safe for Democracy?"

5.10. John Sloan, "The Real Triangle."

5.11.
Lou Rogers,
"Branding His
Mark on the
Future Worker in
the Name of
Legitimate
Business."

Among these American women and men artists, Henry Glintenkamp, Robert Minor, Lou Rogers, Mary Ellen Sigsbee, John Sloan, Alice Beach Winter, and Charles Winter supported both woman suffrage and socialism and supplied images initially appearing in the socialist *New York Call* or *The Masses* and then reprinted in suffrage periodicals.

The tragic fire at the Triangle clothing factory in 1911 served to catapult labor issues into public awareness. Over one hundred and forty-six people—mostly women—were killed in a Saturday afternoon blaze. Many jumped from the eighth floor and above onto the pavement when escape routes collapsed or became blocked by panic-stricken workers.[12] Stunned by the tragedy, suffragists joined protests and attended memorial services for the victims. Compassion and indignation heightened their sense of solidarity with factory workers, and emotions aroused by struggling, impoverished, working women reinforced the intellectual commitment of middle-class women to socialism. Artist John Sloan pointed out that the "Real Triangle" was formed by an alliance of business profit, interest, and rent expense (figure 5.10). The reproduction of Sloan's cartoon in the *Woman's Journal* is especially remarkable considering their later refusal to print Rogers's radical caricature of an ass-eared voter (figure 1.1). Public outrage, a male cartoonist, and a focus on capitalism rather than on men, may have made Sloan's drawing more acceptable to cautious editors.

Nevertheless, it seemed acceptable when Lou Rogers selected the theme of worker exploitation in an early cartoon for the *Woman's Journal* (figure 5.11). She argued that if a class of women appeared "degenerate," it was business greed that ultimately was responsible. In "Branding His Mark on the Future Worker," Rogers portrayed

Cartooning for Suffrage

woman as victimized by the characteristics of her work: unregulated hours, unsanitary conditions, and starvation wages. Worse still was the long-term effect on the future worker, the infant clutched in her arms. Man, the large, domineering, masked villain, and his institutions are the perpetrators of this shocking abuse; defenseless women and children are his victims.

Both Sloan and Rogers symbolized the factory boss/capitalist as an overweight, top-hat adorned male. Three decades earlier, Thomas Nast had portrayed corrupt politics as a fallen figure blocking the advance of Business (a woman) beside the gate of prosperity.[13] Sloan's three-way partnership suggests a sinister pact has caused the workers' deaths. Rogers's factory boss, exaggerated in size to suggest his power over woman's fate, threatens the woman directly with steel daggers. If long hours, unsafe conditions, and tedious factory work dehumanized and debilitated the woman worker, women's enfranchisement was the needed corrective, countered suffragists. In Mary Taylor's cartoon, the woman worker slumps at her sewing machine exhausted from overwork (figure 5.12). The conditions of labor have diminished her happiness and well-being, determinants over which she has no control.

Suffragists challenged child labor practices as another social perversion. In Alice Beach Winter's cover for *The Masses* (figure 5.13), the forlorn expression and sad eyes of a child evoke immediate sympathy. The dark shawl reveals her as an impoverished, immigrant girl, one who has no choice but to work, and the stark factory silhouetted behind her symbolizes the dismal conditions of her labor. Mary Taylor(?) portrays a young girl shackled by child labor in a haunting and ironic image (figure 5.14). She has juxtaposed a mistreated child with the words of the Declaration of Independ-

5.12. Mary Taylor, "No Vote Means No Remedy for Long Hours and Short Pay."

5.13. Alice Beach Winter, "Why Must I Work?"

5.14. "Where the Mother's Vote Is Needed."

What Are You Going To Do About It?

5.15. Fredrikke S. Palmer, "Child Labor."

ence to make a political appeal: "Where the Mother's Vote Is Needed." Fredrikke Palmer's "Child Labor" (figure 5.15) interprets the suffocating consequences of profit, greed, indifference, ignorance, poverty, and luxury in an imaginative analysis. She has placed the little girl in an insect's web, marking it as fantasy, but the all-too-apt analogy raises the penetrating question: "What Are You Going To Do About It?"

These examples of child-labor abuse have chosen little girls as the victims, seemingly ignoring the plight of young boys. The appeal may depend on the stereotype of girls' vulnerability and the greater urgency to protect their purity. It is additionally consistent with the fact that women artists represented girls more frequently in pro-suffrage art than did men artists.[14] Partly ideological in offering a statement concerning the young girl's hampered opportunities, women artists, having been girls themselves, additionally identified more closely with female childhood.

Inevitability

Societies and individual consciousness are elevated through time, argued those steeped in Marxist dialectics. Karl Marx predicted that social organizations would progress to higher forms, so a government run by both men and women seemed historically advanced. Women's mental enlightenment and greater self-realization would be achieved as human nature and civilization evolved toward higher levels. Discussions of progress and social evolution paralleled concern for the future of the human race, including considerations of eugenics and women's fitness to be mothers. Ideas of enlightenment and higher consciousness have both social and biological

Cartooning for Suffrage

connotations. In Darwinian evolution, mind is the highest form of organic life. This is the message expressed in "The Tail of the Comet" by Lou Rogers, which reflects on woman suffrage and the resulting elevation of human consciousness (figure 5.16).

A popular strategy in suffrage propaganda was to portray victory as inevitable and therefore obviate any possibility of halting its advance. Such images focus on the inevitable triumph of suffrage and celebrate a victory judged to be necessary, unavoidable, and well deserved. In "Up! For This is the Day" (figure 5.17) an angel of righteousness unfurls her proclamation to a small group of young women. Borrowing a text from the Book of Judges, the celestial herald recalls Nike, the Greek winged goddess of victory, or an angel secularized with an American flag. The trumpet of glory is a familiar symbol in religious and secular literature, and the phrase "Now press the clarion to thy woman's lips" inspired some suffrage art directly.[15] She is the allegorical herald, drawing on righteousness and inevitability to aid women's crusade for the ballot. The juxtaposition of a symbolic female with images of real women adds an additional dimension, that of otherworldly females empowering actual women.

The force of progress was assumed by suffragists to be automatic and irreversible, for they had witnessed amazing feats of technology, transportation, and communication during their own lifetimes. They saw the coming of women's enfranchisement as but another step in the inevitable march forward. In a cartoon by Mary Taylor (figure 5.18), progress is symbolized as a train (the woman's vote), thundering along toward the helpless Anti (a small dog). No one can easily stop a train—least of all a yapping dog. A similar message is conveyed in Laura Foster's cartoon, "The Steam Roller" (figure

5.16. Lou Rogers, "The Tail of the Comet."

5.17. Mayme B. Harwood, "Up! For This is the Day."

Persuasive Themes

5.18.
Mary
Taylor,
"An
Inevitable
Fatality."

5.19. Laura Foster, "The Steam Roller."

5.19). The machine is driven by a trio of women representing Equal Suffrage and the West, whose collective mission propels them forward and crushes the opposition in their path.

Woman's Uniqueness

Lacking a well-consolidated ideology, suffragists espoused different ideas and ideals, which nevertheless all converged on the demand for the ballot. There had been the historical splits of the 1870s (the American association versus the National association) and the splits of 1913, when the foundation was laid for the National Woman's Party. Conflict and incompatible views were integral to a movement that Lisa Tickner perceived as grounded in paradox: the attempt to show the vote as so significant as not to be denied and yet so trivial as to create no essential alterations in the social system.[16] Its aims could not be expressed in a comprehensive and coherent belief system.

For the turn-of-the-century public, questions of biological gender differences came to overshadow the theological consideration of woman's sphere. Suffragists now argued that women should vote on account of the distinguishing attributes of the female mind. In challenging political discrimination based on gender, suffragists insisted that innate differences justified their need for the vote. Whereas nineteenth-century suffrage advocates condemned male dominance and political inequality, twentieth-century feminists discovered a new rationale from pseudoscientific claims of female uniqueness, how women's virtues and experiences would improve society (the expediency argument). This new emphasis on women's abilities, interests, and experience—women's differences—was superimposed on, rather than substituted for, the earlier accent on shared humanity. The two assumptions were not fully compatible, as Nancy Cott recognized. On the one hand, suffragists upheld "the rights that women (like men) deserved" and on the other hand, they asserted "the particular duties or services that women (unlike men) could offer society."[17] Endorsing both propositions struck a precarious balance.

Suffrage imagery was grounded in an historical setting and particular world view. Within that setting certain metaphors and social models were understood or even assumed. In retrospect, it is recognized that some uses perpetuated unfortunate stereotypes, such as the view that women are natural housekeepers. Nevertheless, ascribed to woman's sphere, housekeeping provided images that could be used to suffragists' political advantage.[18] Experience in combating household soil and disarray prompted the analogy of the pure, clean, and honest influence that women would contribute to the city and nation. Government was merely public housekeeping.[19] A suffragist with broom in hand (or mop, pail, and scrub brush) became a popular cartoon motif.

"From Force of Habit She Will Clean This Up" states a cartoon by Lou Rogers (figure 5.20). Wearing her housekeeping apron and armed with mop and pail, a diminutive and dainty worker is ready to tackle the enormous problems created by men. At one level the image attests to women's competence and skills. What limits the image from a modern perspective, though, is that it appears to accept, rather than to challenge, a particular division of labor. But not all suffrage housekeepers fit the same mold. Cornelia Barns's figure is strong and angular, ready to restore order to social disarray (figure 5.21). Her new broom (the vote) will eliminate prostitution, child labor, and the need for charity institutions, while birth con-

5.20. Lou Rogers, "From Force of Habit She Will Clean This Up."

5.21. Cornelia Barns, "The New Voter at Work."

5.22. May Wilson Preston.

5.23. Fredrikke S. Palmer, "Justice Handicapped."

trol, legalized through women's legislative interests, will allow the new voter to remove civic disgrace.

The woman's vote was generally expected to elevate virtue through enhanced government standards. Woman, as morally pure, would steadfastly resist temptation and corruption. Woman would reject tainted money and power, as May Wilson Preston proposed (figure 5.22), a contrast with male corruption and greed that leave "Justice Handicapped" (figure 5.23). Fredrikke Palmer's mother figure is brightly lit, to signify her inherent goodness, as she tries to place justice on the scales of society. Jack Sears symbolized gender differences in integrity as a full, meaty ear of corn (the Woman's Vote) compared to its remnant, the cob (Boss Rule Politician) (figure 5.24). Women combating corruption served as a prevalent and convincing suffrage image, but the assertion that women were inherently pure was paradoxically the same one that men had long used to justify separate spheres. On the other hand, if the social system is the source of corruption, wouldn't women entering the world of politics (or business) be subject to the same influences responsible for male depravity and unscrupulousness?

Notions of women's separateness were implicit in themes of motherhood. Mother and child appear in cartoons such as "Justice Handicapped" (figure 5.23) and "Branding His Mark" (figure 5.11). Blanche Ames, a suffrage artist with four children of her own, employed the image of the devoted mother, with the caption "Double the Power of the Home—Two Good Votes Are Better Than One" (figure 5.25). Ames presented an irreproachable, caring mother, who cuddles her young infant and amuses her two older children. The representation draws on many symbols: the interior of the home, the cat, the knitting, the cupboards and stove. The rooms

Cartooning for Suffrage

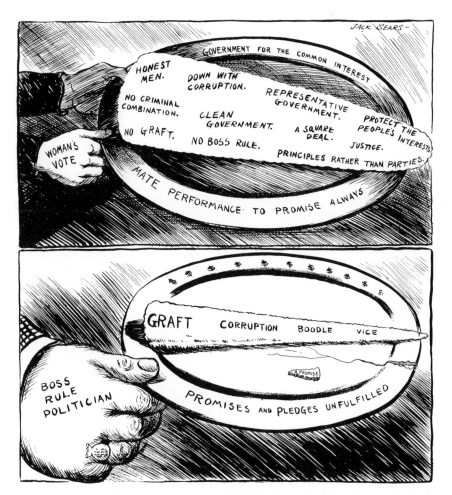

5.24. Jack Sears, "The Corn or the Cob—Which?"

5.25. Blanche Ames, "Double the Power of the Home—
Two Good Votes Are Better Than One."

5.26.
Rose O'Neill,
"Give Mother the
Vote."

*The War-monster:
"Hurry up, woman,
and rear thy sons; I
must have more
food for my
powder!"*

5.27.
Fredrikke S.
Palmer, "War and
the Mother."

appear tidy and welcoming, an appearance emphasized by the sign reading, *God Bless Our Home.* As to the little boy and girl, their roles are surprisingly conventional. The boy is larger than the girl and is actively reading from the book on mother's lap; the girl stands by attentively, but passively, a toy dangling idly from her hand. The image projects a view of the true, wholesome, American woman, who shows no dissatisfaction with her role in the home but will strengthen society's virtue by doubling her middle-class husband's vote. The argument from motherhood continues in a parade of Kewpies, bearing a banner marked *Votes For Our Mothers* (figure 5.26). The work is by Rose O'Neill, originator of the Kewpie doll, who repeated this image in magazine illustrations, postcards, and suffrage fliers. It offered a new twist: children demanding their mothers' votes.[20] O'Neill's explanatory caption was

> Our food, our health, our home, our schools, our play are all regulated by man's votes—
> > Isn't it a funny thing
> > When father cannot see
> > Why mother ought to have a vote
> > On how these things should be?[21]

Mothers, not fathers, had the clearest view of the children's welfare.

With the outbreak of the war in Europe and America's imminent involvement, pacifism was cited as a further rationale for women's enfranchisement. Women were held to possess instincts to protect children, which naturally included a reluctance to send them to battle. With mothers as voters, war would cease. In "War and the Mother" by Fredrikke Palmer (figure 5.27), a woman withholds her children from the impatient war monster who declares, "Hurry up, woman, and rear thy sons; I must have more food for my

Cartooning for Suffrage

powder." The pillar and vine in the setting reinforce the image of a stable, protecting home, which is woman's province. Lou Rogers's character, Motherhood of the World (figure 5.28), smashes the sword of war in "If She Had Her Way." In an earlier cartoon (figure 5.29), Rogers maintained that the woman's vote will be used to destroy war machinery. Rogers labeled this image the New Woman, the pacifist with a ballot.

But pacifist claims were ultimately overshadowed by persistent assertions that women's historical contribution to the war effort was a compelling argument for enfranchisement.[22] In "A Lost Argument," Edwina Dumm drew Uncle Sam, recruiting master, confronted with the cliché, "Women have no right to vote; Do they go to war?" (figure 5.30). Yet trained, devoted women have volunteered for service to their country, eager to work as clerical workers, munitions workers, Red Cross volunteers, farm workers and navy recruits. The bullets and ballots association was lost; women were now going to war. In figure 5.31, a suffragist challenges Uncle Sam's position with evidence of war service, demanding, "Is it not Enough?" Women have contributed to the work of the Red Cross, and practiced food saving and thrift; they have kept the home fires burning and displayed sacrifice, patience, love, courage, and patriotism. The ballot could be transformed into an award for services rendered, an expedient and well-deserved "war measure."

A further cartoon strategy consolidates the association between patriotism, the war effort, and suffrage. Nell Brinkley, creator of the wide-eyed, long-eyelashed, syndicated Brinkley Girl, offered an allegorical trio as her three graces (figure 5.32). Juxtaposed in front of a gigantic American flag, Suffrage, Preparedness, and

5.28.
Lou Rogers, "If She Had Her Way."

5.29.
Lou Rogers, "She Will Spike War's Gun."

5.30. Edwina Dumm, "A Lost Argument."

5.31. Nina E. Allender, "American Woman: Is It not Enough?"

Any man who loves and reveres his mother and his country should idolize, if he worship at all, the three graces Suffrage, Preparedness and Americanism. —Nell Brinkley.

5.32. Nell Brinkley, "The Three Graces."

Americanism are identified by their respective costumes: the suffrage sash, the military-style outfit, and the stars, stripes, and hat of Columbia. The caption reads: "Any man who loves and reveres his mother and his country should idolize, if he worship at all, these three graces, Suffrage, Preparedness, and Americanism."

Historically late images for the suffrage campaign include a soldier and suffragist, marching hand in hand (figure 5.33). In this new rendition of gender spheres, he bears a rifle on his shoulder, and wears a sash marked Patriotism; she carries an American flag and wears a Universal Suffrage sash. It is the patriotic suffragist who personifies ideal American womanhood.

5.33. Laura Foster, "Hand in Hand."

6

Countering the Antis

The only real argument against
suffrage for women is the Anti,
herself. That there could be a woman
with no desire for political freedom in
her soul and with so little self-respect
she does not object to being classed
with idiots, the insane and the
criminal almost makes one doubt that
women are prepared for the ballot.

—*Dorothy Dix, "Why is an Anti?"*

Suffragists targeted the anti-suffragist, or "anti," as a subject for verbal and visual caricature. Portrayed as vain, illogical, and misguided, her credibility was diminished through ludicrous caricatures that concomitantly intensified suffragists' feelings of righteousness and solidarity. Suffragist and anti-suffragist struck a complementary relationship, each defining herself implicitly against an image of the other.[1] Each side sought to assign positive attributes of womanhood to itself, ascribing unworthy motives and traits to the other side. As a result, cartoon and poster art relied less on the actual situation than on fabricated images to establish and define its propaganda issues.

Cognitive scientists emphasize that images provide a vision of the world that regulates behavior in profound yet subtle ways.[2] These images are not faithful representations, but part myth, part invention, and part exaggeration, what Daniel Boorstin termed a *pseudo-ideal* of substitute meaning and value: "It is synthetic, believable, passive, vivid, simplified, and ambiguous."[3] Some images are seized ready-made, as when British anti-suffragists caricatured the suffragist using two existing models, "the domineering and nagging wife" and "the embittered spinster."[4] Originating in practices of humorous illustration, the images were superimposed on the suffragist. Tickner credited these antis with an initial pictorial advantage by thus challenging the womanliness of the suffragist. Soon anti-suffragists on both sides of the Atlantic raised the suspicion that any woman who demanded a political voice must be either lacking a man for good reasons (the spinster) or be undesirable as a life companion (the domineering wife).

Suffragists, in turn, caricatured the female anti as egocentric, shortsighted, and a detriment to her gender. The anti was portrayed

Cartooning for Suffrage

as entrenched in an outmoded past and intent on perpetuating an obsolete social structure. After all, anti-suffragists were typically members of the middle and upper class, whose identities were based on social definitions they were reluctant to abandon.[5] Opposed to the idea of woman suffrage from the start, antis formed their own societies as the suffrage movement grew stronger. The Massachusetts Association Opposed to the Further Extension of Suffrage to Women, a group of women, was formed in 1895.

Anti-Suffrage and Its Alliances

Although the most powerful suffrage opponents were men, it was the woman adversary who most antagonized suffrage supporters and seemed most incomprehensible. The woman anti, the threat from within, was the one artists sought to exploit and ridicule. She was depicted as the frivolous woman—the self-centered, irresponsible individual who exploits the benefits of society without offering her labors in return. May Wilson Preston portrayed Madame Anti as a woman of pampered status and limited vision (figure 6.1). Preston's caricature contains exaggerated gestures (her finger movements and the tilts and pivots of her head) and unflattering fashion accessories (her oversized hat).[6] Blanche Ames demonstrated the shortcomings of anti-suffrage character by contrasting types in "Two Pedestals" (figure 6.2). She portrayed the anti-suffrage woman as frivolously attired, focused on self, preoccupied with fashionable pets, and poised on the flimsy pedestal of "Sham Chivalry." The pro-suffrage woman, in contrast, arose from a sturdy foundation of equality and justice and is a mother devoted to her children. There is no question who will contribute more to society.

6.1. May Wilson Preston, "Madame Anti Makes her Annual Report."

Which will the Voters Choose for Women on Nov. 2nd?

6.2. Blanche Ames, "Two Pedestals."

United We Stand.

6.3. Cornelia Barns, "Anti-Suffrage Meeting."

"I am Utterly Opposed to Woman Suffrage."

6.4. Van Loon, "Anti Suffragist."

Suffrage artists cast the male anti in a similar visual mold: self-centered, well-to-do, an American dandy. Stereotyped as socially nonproductive, he was occasionally a factory boss or liquor trafficker. Cornelia Barns's "Anti-Suffrage Meeting" (figure 6.3) shows a cigar store with a quartet of socially privileged men. They wear fashionable attire: high-button shoes, vests, and straw hats. Their slouched postures, vacuous facial expressions, and lack of political commitment is highlighted by the ironic caption: "United We Stand." Van Loon's anti is a loner walking at a brisk pace, his downward gaze and narrowed focus reveal his preoccupation with himself (figure 6.4).[7] The anti's smart clothing and accessories (top hat and walking stick) disclose his comfortable life-style; he is a man convinced that he needs no justification for his views.

The most ambitious visual attack on the opposition was Ida Proper's "Anti-Suffrage Parade," a four-panel construction in which fifteen characters, joined by the chains of dogma, domination, indifference, selfishness, and tradition, march forward (figure 6.5). Each figure represents a social type, literary figure, or famous individual known to take a stand against suffrage. Proper portrayed the anti-suffrage male as dogmatic, outdated, and unscrupulous. Women antis were pampered, immature, and illogical. Caricature, satire, and allusion exposed the opposition as preposterous and untrustworthy.

Some of the images reveal the ways that those with vested interests—politicians, bosses, and brewers—impede political change. These three sport rounded bellies (their interests well compensated), two puff cigars, and each wears a hat. "Let women rock the cradle but leave the 'rocks' to us," asserts the senator, carrying a placard reading They Would Take Our Jobs. The boss, too, is

Cartooning for Suffrage

ANTI=SUFFRAGE PARADE

6.5. Ida S. Proper, "Anti-Suffrage Parade."

6.6. Blanche Ames, "Anti-Allies and the Dog."

If the Anti-Suffrage Cause Ever Looks at Itself in the Glass.

6.7. Fredrikke S. Palmer, "Mrs. Jekyll and Mr. Hyde."

concerned with the elevation of women's power, protesting simply, "They would 'boss' us." The brewer, who offers $50,000 to promote anti-suffrage, falls back on the cliché, "woman's place is in the home." A loss of male dominance, political power, and business interests govern the concerns of each.

Females are included among four real individuals in the parade. Ida Tarbell, a well-known journalist who disputed women's claim to the ballot, joins the procession with a placard marked It Would Unsex Woman. Her pockets bulge with money from her magazine articles on "The 'Business' of being an Anti," a parody of Tarbell's recent book title, *The Business of Being A Woman*. Mrs. Gilbert Jones, one of the organizers of New York City's League for the Civic Education of Women (affiliated with the New York State Association Opposed to Woman Suffrage), carries a banner reading We Want Chivalry. An enormous pointed hat obscures her face, while she lets it be known that "Her Hat is in the Ring." Jones is escorted by clergyman Lyman Abbott, whose costume includes gaiters for "those who may get cold feet," while affirming that "Women are Angels." His anachronistic views are signaled by the magazine he carries, *Retrospect*, formerly *Outlook*. Abbott recently had been selected as a spokesman against suffrage in a *Ladies' Home Journal's* "Both Sides" feature.[8] Edmund Bok, editor of the *Ladies' Home Journal*, clutches a headless dress form marked Bok's Perfect Lady. It proclaims, "Undesirable Women Would Vote."

Some figures are symbolic or fictional: Priscilla Jawbones, Rebecca Wiggin, Richard Barry-Bey, and Mr. Standpat. Priscilla Jawbones, a dour-faced old maid (a gag figurehead from *Life* magazine), carries her scythe marked *Life* Otherwise Known as Dead. Rebecca Wiggin of Sunnybrook Farm, a storybook character and the only child in the parade, declares sweetly, "It would be the dearest thing in life to me—but an awful care."[9] Richard Barry-Bey, in turban and harem pants, advances views attributable to "11th Century Authorship," symbolizing all outmoded ideas. His bauble fears being eclipsed by a certain sphere, that of the woman voter. A frail-looking, ineffective, elderly man, Mr. Standpat, wears a sandwich board that reads Votes fur Wimmin Is Agin the Constitution of U.S.

The remaining participants in Ida Proper's parade include a middle-aged gentleman reading *Behind the Times*, a stern-looking matron who is concerned that "Election Day—Tuesday—is always Ironing Day," and two fashionably dressed young women who have no time in their busy social schedule. "We don't need the ballot," contend these belles, whereas the matron argues, "It takes 10 minutes to vote. I haven't the time." The views of the procession are unrealistic, unsubstantiated, and out-of-date. When all the reasons against suffrage are given and their motley adherents exposed, it is a parade of folly.

The Brewer's Association in Proper's parade reflects a suspected tie between anti-suffragists and the liquor interests. In "Anti-Allies and the Dog," Blanche Ames juxtaposed three male adversaries: the boss, the vicious interests, and the liquor interests (figure 6.6). Joined by a female anti, they engage in a tug-of-war to stop woman suffrage. The horse of progress, on which Suffrage is seated, seems unlikely to be seriously impeded. Significantly, the woman anti is portrayed as merely misguided; she stands highly illuminated by the street lamp, in contrast to shadowy male figures, inherently corrupt.[10] The theme of the woman anti cavorting unknowingly with male liquor interests inspired another effective cartoon, "Mrs.

The Brewer: Have no fear, my dear, I can afford to pay your bills.

The Anti: I always knew that indirect influence was enough.

6.8. Ida S. Proper, "Beauty's Garden."

6.9. Laura Foster, "Looking through a Glass, Darkly."

6.10. Lou Rogers, "Latest Addition to the Junk-Heap."

6.11. Lou Rogers, "In the Land of Extinct Volcanos."

Jekyll and Mr. Hyde," by Fredrikke Palmer (figure 6.7). As the Anti gazes into the mirror, her secret partnership with the liquor interest is revealed. She is a slender, well-dressed woman; Mr. Hyde is a grotesque old man. The contrast between them preserves the greater innocence of the woman, who fails to recognize the identity of Mr. Hyde/liquor. "If the Anti-Suffrage Cause Ever Looks at Itself in the Glass," clarifies the caption. Ida Proper also explored this theme, sketching a female anti linked arm in arm with a brewer (figure 6.8). "Have no fear, my dear, I can afford to pay your bills," he assures her. Other specious arguments from the antis appear on various flowers: "[Women] would meet undesirable people at the polls," "It would destroy chivalry," "It would unsex her," that "Woman's place is in the home," and so on. She is blinded by trust and endorses anti-suffrage uncritically. Liquor manufacturers and dealers viewed all women as temperance crusaders who, when given the vote, would endanger their profits. For this reason they held a vested interest in stopping the campaign and worked for its defeat.[11] Paradoxically, the Eighteenth Amendment ushered in prohibition before the suffrage amendment was ratified.

The female anti, though susceptible to men's corrupting influence, remained a potential subject for conversion to the pro-suffrage cause. Laura Foster sketched a suffragist and an anti-suffragist as physically similar, each using a different viewing glass through which to see the suffrage question (figure 6.9). Prejudice colors the anti's perception; corrected vision should let their political views mesh. The suffragist offers, "Try this glass sister."

Suffragists, seeking to expedite social change, cited progress and evolution as firmly on their side, arguing that anti-suffragists were politically anachronistic. Lou Rogers illustrated this concept by

Cartooning for Suffrage

relegating the distraught turtle of anti-suffrage to the Junk Heap of the Ages (figure 6.10), the dumping ground for outmoded ideas, including the rights of kings, religious intolerance, and the assertion that the world is flat. Another metaphor chosen by Rogers was that of geological extinction (figure 6.11), where the anti inhabits a desolate landscape of volcanoes individually marked: Suffrage Is Not a Natural Right, Women Don't Know Business, Women Would Lose Their Influence, and Bad Women Would Out-Vote Good Ones.

Suffragists challenged anti-suffrage propaganda as unsubstantiated, prejudiced, outmoded, and swayed by vested interests. Furthermore, the antis' actions revealed a major contradiction: These women violated the very principles they claimed to uphold. One delightful example shows an anti-suffrage woman hastening to the train station to attend a lecture on "Why Women Should Stay at Home" (figure 6.12). Ida Proper (figure 6.13) featured the deserted headquarters of an anti-suffrage society, where a rough-looking man announces, "They ain't at home. The ladies have gone to Michigan to tell the ladies there to stay at home."

The Debate over Woman's Sphere

By 1910 "Woman's Place is the Home" was a worn cliché, convincingly satirized by suffrage cartoonists. Fredrikke Palmer raised the question of just what would happen if men kept women home and excluded them from public places—the church, school, workplace, and volunteer agencies (figure 6.14). Lou Rogers investigated the significance of home as a refuge for working women when snarling hounds of starvation wages, broken laws, intolerable hours, cold, hunger, and discouragement threatened her safety and health

6.12. Jessie Banks, "Anti Suffragist off to Lecture on 'Why Women Should Stay at Home.'"

They ain't at home! The ladies have gone to Michigan to tell the ladies there to stay at home.

6.13. Ida S. Proper, "Gone to Michigan!"

But when the hounds of Starvation Wages, Broken Laws, Intolerable Hours, Cold, Hunger and Discouragement pursue her, where is her place and what is her protection?

6.15. Lou Rogers, "Woman's Place is at Home."

6.16. Jessie Banks, "Woman's Place Is in the Home. We're Going Home."

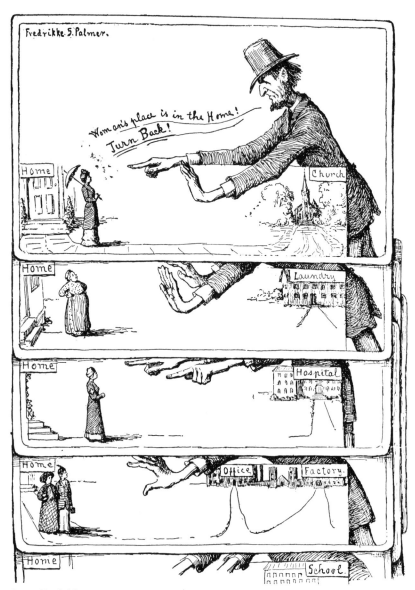

6.14. Fredrikke S. Palmer, "If The Anti Were Large Enough."

(figure 6.15). "Where is her place and what is her protection?" demanded Rogers.

Suffragists claimed that women's work outside the home had already redefined her sphere and thus the ballot would not alter social divisions. By 1900 the census classified nearly five million women as breadwinners.[12] If one-fifth of all adult women already worked outside the home, having the ballot could hardly change her sphere. Whether women belonged in the home or wanted to remain in the home was largely irrelevant.

"Woman's Place is in the Home" agreed one New York suffrage group, tongue in cheek. The Empire State Campaign Committee urged a 24-hour strike of all women.[13] Those who worked outside the home would stay home for a day, and all others would refrain from any activities outside the home. Critics writing in major New York newspapers complained that the proposed strike would disrupt routines and commerce. Journalists bestowed so much attention on it that protest organizers abandoned the plan; they had already made their point. Artist Jessie Banks gleefully pointed out the potential magnitude of women's absence from each occupation: 153,000 domestics, 51,000 teachers, 100,000 seamstresses, and so on (figure 6.16). Commerce would come to a standstill without a female work force, for as the accompanying article announced, "Woman's Place [is] in the World."[14]

For Lou Rogers, modern woman's transformation was already so complete as to be impossible to undo. Any attempt to reverse the course would be comparable to placing the proverbial square peg in a round hole (figure 6.17). Rogers's illustration cited the major forces altering woman's sphere as increased knowledge and gains in business skills. Knowledge and work experience have remolded

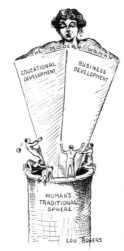

6.17. Lou Rogers, "Fitting A Square Peg into a Round Hole."

First Suffragist: "What a noise they make!"
Second Suffragist: "And that's all!"

6.18. Nina E. Allender, "Exploding Opposition."

6.19. Lou Rogers, "No, She Does Not Need my Sword."

The anti-suffragists tell us that women have so many privileges they do not need the vote.

6.20.
M. F. G., "A Striker's Wife."

and redefined the modern woman's identity. Because woman has evolved beyond her historic sphere to an expanded social position, it is obvious that the ballot is requisite to her modern role.

Antis remained dedicated to woman's pedestal and place in the home, the politics of states' rights and indirect influence, and insisted that women neither desired nor needed the ballot. Nina Allender symbolized each argument as a firecracker (figure 6.18), each bursting with a loud bang. One suffragist remarks, "What a noise they make!" and the other replies, "And that's all." The theoretical foundation of anti-suffrage has vanished with a little smoke and a big bang.

Major Arguments against Suffrage

Antis repeated their arguments so often that they could be readily anticipated. In 1885 Daniel Livermore formulated nine common assertions in his chapter "Prominent Objections Refuted."[15] Alice Stone Blackwell later wrote a pamphlet "Objections Answered" for the National American Woman Suffrage Association which refuted unfounded claims. Approximately thirty objections to suffrage were specified, reducible to four major concepts: women don't need the ballot, women don't want the ballot, women don't deserve the ballot, and women would be harmed by enfranchisement.

In Blackwell's commentary on the vote as unnecessary, she considered the objections that "Women are represented already by their husbands, fathers and brothers" and "If the laws are unjust, they can be corrected by women's indirect influence."[16] Several cartoons probe these themes, including Lou Rogers's voteless woman shown at the mercy of the savage beast, Exploitation (figure 6.19).

The female figure clutches the only available instrument of defense—a small broom of silent influence. A sword marked The Vote could defend her adequately, but the male voter/spectator withholds this, claiming, "No, she does not need my sword." The sword has a rich heritage as symbol, the weapon of righteousness and glory in the hands of Justice, Athena, or Nike. Here, the weapon of goddesses is usurped by the male and used to reaffirm his masculinity. Another drawing, by artist M.F.G., portrays a small, dark, and bare apartment, where deprived of resources and political voice, an impoverished striker's wife comforts her children (figure 6.20). "The anti-suffragists tell us that women have so many privileges they do not need the vote," declares the caption.

An ironic contrast between a sturdy housewife and the male weakling who proposes to take care of her was offered by Anne Goldthwaite (figure 6.21).[17] The housewife tells the suffragist canvasser, "He says he can take care of me good enough—besides the polls is too rough for ladies." Antis often asserted that women did not need the ballot because their views are already represented in the votes of their men folk. Lou Rogers challenged this logic in figure 6.22, inquiring, "If a man represents the women of his household how can he represent himself?"[18]

Antis argued that because most women were not actively campaigning for the vote, they obviously didn't want it. Of course, they continued, it would be granted promptly if the majority of the women really wanted it. Antis advanced the arguments that: "The majority [of women] are opposed to it," "Women are already over-burdened," and "Whenever the majority of women ask for suffrage, they will get it."[19] Blanche Ames symbolized the anti's position on the issue by depicting a male figure withholding a life

"No. He ain't for wimmin votin'. He says he can take care of me good enough—besides the polls is too rough for ladies."

6.21. Anne Goldthwaite.

6.23. Blanche Ames, "Meanwhile They Drown."

6.24. Eloise Valiant, "—But He Can Fight!"

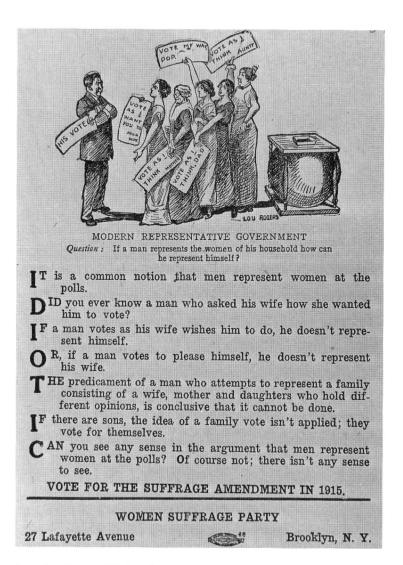

6.22. Lou Rogers, "Modern Representative Government."

154

preserver (the vote), while in the water below, women and children are tossed by turbulent waves: white slavers, disease, filth, and sweatshop labor (figure 6.23). The male voter proclaims, "When *all* women want it, I will throw it to them," while his female companion, Anti-Suffrage, passively accepts his view.

The fact that women do not defend the nation in war or enforce its civilian laws appeared to justify the opinion that women were undeserving of or unqualified for enfranchisement. Women simply were not and should not be full citizens. Blackwell consolidated these claims: "If women vote, they ought to fight and do police duty" and "Men, by the nature of their occupations, know more about business than women, and hence are better fitted to run a city or a state."[20]

The argument linking citizenship and willingness to fight was readily contested. Eloise Valiant drew a woman energetically working beside her dozing spouse (figure 6.24). Lazy and nonproductive, his worth as a citizen is nevertheless upheld by the claim "But He Can Fight." Women had a basic involvement in national security, argued Lucy Stone, who pointed out that "Some woman risks her life whenever a soldier is born into the world."[21] Lou Rogers incorporated Stone's theme into "Arms Versus the Army" (figure 6.25). When a swell-chested soldier asserts, "But madam, you cannot bear arms," the suffragist clutching her infant, retorts, "Nor can you, sir, bear armies."

A further arena of suffrage debate clustered around the harmful consequences of women voting. Antis feared the decline of society, should women participate in elections. Before 1920 many polls were located in saloons, forging an image of the undesirable men whom women would encounter if permitted to vote. Opponents

He: But, madam you cannot bear arms
She: Nor can you, sir, bear armies.

6.25. Lou Rogers, "Arms Versus the Army."

6.26. Edwina Dumm, "Well! Well!"

6.27. Katherine Milhous, "Votes for Women."

asserted that voting women would be "unsexed," an epithet hurled at nineteenth-century women for deviant behavior such as public speaking, the pursuit of higher education, or wearing bloomers. Blackwell summarized these unsubstantiated claims: "It will destroy chivalry," "It works badly in practice," and "It will turn women into men."[22]

Edwina Dumm likened the anti-suffrage campaign to the overprotective mother withholding some object from a young child (figure 6.26). Ohio (a middle-aged man) would indeed bestow the eagerly sought gift (equal suffrage), were it not for intervention from the anti (her mother). The anti presents no reason, just reiterates that "It's very injurious."

In figure 6.27, Katherine Milhous proclaimed, "It doesn't 'Unsex' her to do this," and portrayed five acceptable occupations for women: cleaning lady, nurse, factory worker, shopkeeper, and waitress. In the final frame, in which a woman deposits a ballot, is the reminder, "But this—is another story." The energy and strength required to earn a living or complete her household chores is womanly—the act of voting is not.

Antis feared losing the respect and social privileges gained through chivalry, the noble and generous courtesies extended by gentlemen to the fair sex. But chivalry, too, could be redefined. Wouldn't the highest act of chivalry be to offer a gift of "Votes for Women"? asked Lou Rogers. In "American Chivalry in Perfect Flower," a male presents a flower pot with an oversized bloom: the vote.[23]

Antis asserted their claims from the time the women's vote was first proposed. This provided an early advantage, because constant repetition creates the ring of truth, and refuting it is viewed as "protesting too much." As greater numbers of politically active

Cartooning for Suffrage

women formed a testing ground, the arguments against suffrage could be evaluated. The claim that equal suffrage "works badly in practice" inspired Lou Rogers's image of the anti and the walnut (figure 6.28). The fact that no state or country ever repealed women's enfranchisement (the nut) overwhelms the tiny anti with her small nutcracker. Suffrage experience has failed to support the anti's dire predictions.

Considering that women had voted and run for election, the arguments against suffrage (and the larger "woman question," as it was called) appeared shortsighted and ludicrous. Suffragists challenged these claims as illogical and untrue, speculating that female antis could be converted and their distorted vision cleared if given an accurate presentation of the facts.

6.28. Lou Rogers, "A Nut She Doesn't Try to Crack."

7

Classical Symbols and Metaphors

To date the Woman's Movement is lacking an established symbol. Some cartoonists picture the suffragist as a stern-faced woman armed with a brick or a "Votes for Women" banner, while others draw society girls, ribboned and bannered, smiling their way to victory.

—J. E. Murphy, *"Famous Characters of the Cartoonists"*

7.1. Lou Rogers, "His Mistake."

A well-defined array of symbols existed long before the suffrage campaign, constituting the distinctive attributes of the modern cartoon. Major symbols included Uncle Sam and Columbia, the donkey and the elephant, the goddesses of Justice and Liberty, and top-hatted men of wealth and influence. Embellishing the lexicon of cartoon symbols were captions, titles, and internal labeling common to turn-of-the-century cartoons. Some cartoonists perceived the need for a fresh character to represent women and their political advances—one that would facilitate communication from artist to audience through a recognized image.[1]

The role of symbols in visual imagery had been understood by Freud, who theorized that underlying jokes and dreams were symbolic alterations, combinations, and compromises. Freud believed that meanings were consolidated and sharpened during joke construction, a technique transforming complex ideas through allusion, analogy, metaphor, and substitution. Compounding several ideas into a single image helps overcome resistance and enhances the symbol's power to influence the viewer.[2]

Gombrich applied Freud's framework to cartoon symbolism in "The Cartoonist's Armoury," where he discussed the various devices and techniques.[3] He pointed out that symbols are derived from diverse sources: cultural conventions, natural metaphors, and impromptu creations. Cultural symbols, some originating in antiquity, take their meaning from familiar settings and associations, particularly folk tales, mythology, ancient history, and Bible stories. The modern cartoonist continues to modify or update key details, such as the setting, attire, or even the gender of an established figure. By imposing recognized characters or relationships on a

Cartooning for Suffrage

current situation, the viewer identifies motifs of good and evil, heroism and villainy.

Male voters often regarded women's demand for the ballot as a destructive or unsettling challenge to the social order. Women artists, in turn, satirized men's astonished reactions as women stormed the political citadel, fostering images of suffrage as an intrusion or invasion for which classically derived figures were often impressively well suited. One cartoon by Lou Rogers compared twentieth-century woman to the genie from *Arabian Nights*, ecstatic upon her release into the world (figure 7.1). The genie has been imprisoned in the "Urn of the Centuries" and now uses modern education as the catalyst for her escape—much to the chagrin of her unthinking accomplice.

In efforts to block women's political advance, some men resembled the Roman hero Horatius, who single-handedly defended a bridge against an Etruscan invasion (figure 7.2). A Virginia congressman, Charles Carlin, was dubbed Horatius in Allender's satirical rendition, where his raised pinkie, cobweb-covered shield, and propensity to smoke on duty undermine his dignity. The cartoon refers to an incident in 1916 when a Congressional vote on the suffrage amendment was delayed through controversial maneuvers. The House Judiciary Committee began by considering the amendment in subcommittee, as was proper. But when the bill was presented for the full committee's vote, the process was suddenly accelerated, the waiting period ignored, and the amendment was defeated. Outraged suffragists demanded a revote, counting on support previously pledged. When the amendment was in fact reconsidered, Representative Carlin outmaneuvered the women by

7.2. Nina E. Allender, "Horatius at the Bridge."

7.3.
Lou Rogers, "A Modern Woman's Task."

7.4.
Lou Rogers, "The Woman Behind Columbus."

recommending indefinite postponement of all proposed constitutional amendments.[4] The status quo was preserved and Carlin was cast as the Roman hero.

The social changes sought by turn-of-the-century suffragists were revealed in polarized metaphors of confinement versus release, defense versus invasion, defense versus assault, and stability versus instability. The destruction of antiquated patriarchal institutions as necessary to women's political advance, was illustrated in Lou Rogers's analogy between the blinded and enraged strongman Samson demolishing the columns of the temple and "A Modern Woman's Task" (figure 7.3). Suffragists insisted that the structure of taxation without representation was unjust and should not stand, and Rogers's allusion to a Bible story confers a sense of righteousness on the movement. She asserts that women have gained considerable power and strength (the giant woman figure), which to be effective, must be directed against social obstacles (outmoded institutions). Allender, in turn, accuses men of anachronistic defense strategies, of being warriors from antiquity who fear the loss of privilege and tradition.

Heroic Women

Heroic women provided an impartial set of images for suffrage art. In their suffrage parades, British artists carried colorful banners commemorating Jane Austen, Susan B. Anthony, Marie Curie, George Eliot, Joan of Arc, Florence Nightingale, Lucy Stone, and Mary Wollstonecraft, among others. Images of famous women writers, scientists, and philosophers provided role models and Susan B. Anthony and Lucy Stone were favorites for American suffrage cartoons. Individual women could not match the recognizability of presidents

George Washington, Abraham Lincoln, Theodore Roosevelt, and Woodrow Wilson and rarely conveyed the symbolic quality needed to inspire. In banner, sculpture, parade and pageant, Joan of Arc alone matched the prototypic female hero.[5] She inspired twentieth-century suffragists and was a personified symbol: virginal warrior, wearer of saintly armor, and possessor of sacred dagger.

Another significant woman was Queen Isabella of Spain, who encouraged and financed Columbus's voyage (figure 7.4). She appeared in a cartoon designed for Columbus Day in 1912, portrayed as obscured, distant, and vague. Columbus dominates the frame, seated upon a large throne and bearing a crown marked King of Discoverers. Underlying this graphic are two concepts: that important women have been overlooked by history and that the participation of modern women in politics would help restore their factual place.

Another cast of cartoon characters came from nineteenth-century fiction (figures 7.5 and 7.6). Young Eliza from Harriet Beecher Stowe's *Uncle Tom's Cabin* appeared wearing an academic gown and mortar board while racing across the icy waters to seize the vote. In Nina Allender's cartoon, the Senate is depicted as the villainous Simon Legree, jealously guarding the Constitution for himself. Eliza pursues Legree/the Senate in order to obtain justice for women. In "Madame Defarge—1918 Model, or Tale of Two Parties" (*A Tale of Two Cities*), Madame Defarge represents a different sort of influential female, shrewd and politically savvy. She knits the Senate record (inactivity on suffrage) revealing that the Senate's failure to recognize women's political demands will shape the outcome of the coming elections. Although neither Eliza nor Madame Defarge share many traits with their namesakes, each

7.5. Nina E. Allender, "A Modern Eliza."

7.6. Nina E. Allender, "Madame Defarge—1918 Model, or Tale of Two Parties."

7.7. Nina E. Allender, "The Wise Women of the West Come Bearing Gifts."

7.8. Rollin Kirby, "Pauline Revere."

character's fundamental roles and motivations were familiar to turn-of-the-century readers, allowing them to serve symbolically.

Another cartoon technique consists of placing women in men's roles. For example, figures of suffragists replaced the three Biblical kings in Allender's "The Wise Women of the West" (figure 7.7). They arrive in Washington with gifts of loyalty, power, and courage, and, like the wise men, seek the celestial star over the Capitol. They rely on modern methods and have forsaken camels for an automobile, but the cartoon's biblical text heightens a sense of woman's righteous mission. Paul Revere and Hamlet likewise underwent gender changes to serve woman's cause. In a newspaper cartoon by Rollin Kirby, used also as a suffrage flier, Pauline Revere brings news of the western elections, that enfranchised women voters were preparing to show their influence (figure 7.8). She is portrayed as a serious figure, the solitary rider on a mission of destiny across the desolate landscape, dressed in the outfit of a revolutionary minuteman. Hamlet, in the famous scene where he contemplates the death of his companion Yorick, is represented by a woman wearing Shakespearean costume and academic gown (figure 7.9). Rogers's rendition features a feminist philosopher confronting Ridicule, or "the grinning skull of dead jests." She remains vital and strong, whereas men's ridicule has been relegated to the graveyard, the skull in fool's cap.

Gallant Men

The attributes and needs of women were projected graphically against a social structure created and perpetuated by men. Waged between a dominant and subjugated group, the struggle could be altered by cooperation or by force. Because unlike other social "minorities" women necessarily coexist within men's society, male gallantry and chivalry were compelling metaphors for granting woman political rights. While trying to provide models that encouraged men to support the cause, women artists sometimes inadvertently perpetuated a stereotype of female helplessness.

A courteous gentleman, Sir Walter Raleigh, inspired Edwina Dumm's cartoon in which Ohio plays the gentleman to suffrage (figure 7.10). Just as Raleigh once laid down his coat to the Queen of England in a courtly gesture, Ohio offers the coat of equal suffrage to expedite woman's advance through the mud of prejudice, ignorance, and discrimination. The woman appears confident and well dressed, signifying the status that the woman's movement merited. The state of Ohio, unfortunately, proved less gracious than the cartoon figure by defeating the referendum. Ohio would not enfranchise women for two more years. A president offers another example of cartoon chivalry, proclaiming: "I go for all sharing the privileges of government who assist in bearing its burdens, not excepting women" (figure 7.11).[6] Under an arch bearing the words of Lincoln ("Fit to Bear the Nation's Burdens, but not its Highest Privileges"), Lou Rogers presented womanhood emerging from a small, dark passage. If Abraham Lincoln, symbol of patriotism, democracy, and human rights acknowledged women's claim to full citizenship, shouldn't his successors complete the political act that he had verbally endorsed? Nina Allender cleverly juxtaposed Lincoln's image with Woodrow Wilson's (figure 7.12) creating a visual parallel between Woodrow Wilson's opportunity to liberate American women and the events commemorated in *Emancipation*, a statue in Washington by Thomas Ball. Wilson, however, rejects the appeal of American women and loses the

"Alas, Poor Yorick. I knew him well," meditates the *feminist philosopher over the grinning skull of dead jests."*

7.9. Lou Rogers.

7.10. Edwina Dumm, "A Modern Sir Walter?"

"I go for all sharing the privileges of government who assist in bearing its burdens, not excepting women."—Abraham Lincoln

7.11. Lou Rogers, "If Lincoln Were Alive."

7.12. Nina E. Allender, "Great Statues of History."

opportunity to be women's liberator. He is immortalized in his refusal; both ironically become "Great Statues of History."

Wilson appears ludicrously as fairy godmother to Cinderella, where he carries a shining wand that holds the magical power to transform the ragged sister (disfranchised women) into the fair maiden in glittering gown at the ball (figure 7.13). In what for 1915 was clearly a fairy tale, the smiling Wilson takes two cages of mice (the House and Senate) and a large pumpkin (the constitutional amendment) and announces, "The pumpkin shall be a coach; the mice will be horses to pull it; and YOU shall go to the polls!"

In 1916 the Republicans, meeting in Chicago, selected Supreme Court justice and former governor of New York Charles Evans Hughes as their presidential candidate. The Democrats nominated Woodrow Wilson for a second term. On the day before the G.O.P. convention, the formation of the Woman's Party was announced by the Congressional Union. Its representatives promptly informed the Resolutions Committee that women voters would be enormously influential in the coming election. The national press reported that the women "neither begged nor threatened the men on those committees." Instead they

> calmly announced to the rather bewildered politicians of the old parties that four million women were going to vote this year in twelve states, having ninety-one electoral votes, twenty-four United States senators and something like seventy representatives in Congress; that they wanted the full privilege of the franchise extended to all the women of the land, and that any party that stood in the way of votes for women throughout the land would, in their humble opinion, make a most disastrous mistake.[7]

Republican candidate Hughes was the first to endorse a suffrage plank, inspiring a cartoon by Mary Taylor, "None But the Brave Deserve the Fair" (figure 7.14). As Hughes gallops along the road to success, candidate Wilson remains at a standstill. Hughes's image is conflated with that of the medieval knight in shining armor, although in this unlikely portrait he wears a top hat and coat and rides the G.O.P. elephant. The Republican plank, though favoring "the extension of Suffrage to women," weakened the measure by assuring each state the right to decide the issue. The Democrats hastily added a suffrage plank, endorsing "extension of the franchise to the women of the country by the States."[8] They, too, proved reluctant to challenge states' rights.

Patriotic Emblems

The images derived from popular political symbols and slogans evoked rich associations linking the suffrage campaign to cherished American values. The personifications and emblems used in suffrage art include Uncle Sam, Columbia, Old Glory, the American Eagle, and the Liberty Bell. One approach was to substitute women for or juxtapose them with the conventional male figures, suggesting that the suffrage campaign was no different in philosophy and ideals than the patriotism on which the nation was founded. Another technique was to portray symbols of the government or political parties as the agents responsible for responding to women's petition for the ballot. Use of Columbia and the hastily constructed Pauline Revere provided female renditions of patriotic figures. Another image created for suffrage was a "Spirit of '76," with an all-women fife-and-drum corps. Several cartoonists produced versions, such as Nina Allender's 1915 example subtitled "On to the Senate"

Fairy Godmother Wilson: "The pumpkin shall be a coach; the mice will be horses to pull it; and YOU shall go to the polls!"

7.13. Nina E. Allender.

7.14. Mary Taylor, "None But the Brave Deserve the Fair."

7.15. Nina E. Allender, "'The 'Spirit of '76.' On to the Senate!"

7.16. Clara Reynolds, "The Liberty Belle."

(figure 7.15). It advocated a constitutional amendment (the flag) and characterized the movement with Enthusiasm and Faith (beating the drums). A set of illustrations by Howard Chandler Christy called "Liberty Belles" offered a pun adaptable for suffrage. Clara Reynolds's "Liberty Belle" (figure 7.16) is a modern woman who wears a fashionable riding habit and sits astride her pure white horse. She clutches a Votes for Women banner set prominently against a large emblem, the American Liberty Bell. The image compounds aspects of Joan of Arc, Paul Revere, and the spirit of Liberty to gain its effectiveness.

As the campaign became more politicized, conventional symbols, especially of the Democratic and Republican parties, grew more prevalent in suffrage art. In 1915 suffrage strategy was complicated by a new issue—the Shafroth-Palmer Resolution. Senator John Shafroth proposed a federal amendment that would require each state to decide the suffrage question by ballot, whenever a sufficient number of voters demanded it. Many suffragists saw this amendment as a partial victory, and indeed the National American Woman Suffrage Association supported it initially.[9] Nina Allender, however, responded to its inherent weakness in an incisive image of the Democratic donkey, or Sixty-fourth Congress, at the crossroads (figure 7.17). "But I can't get the old dear to take both roads at once," protests the suffragist. The Shafroth road for state-by-state decision is winding and circuitous, whereas the Anthony road, which proposed that the federal amendment enfranchise all women, is direct and efficient. Though in principle both proposals would improve the status of women, Allender's graphic metaphor reveals that one cannot travel in two directions at once and that the Anthony amendment is obviously preferable.

In a number of suffrage cartoons Uncle Sam appears as the government's agent. Lou Rogers drew him holding up an ear trumpet, symbolizing the suffrage message as still poorly received (figure 7.18). Though masses of women agitate for vote reform, it is the twelve equal suffrage states that will enable him to hear their appeal. "Keep It Up, Girls; He Isn't Stone Deaf!" they assert.

The act of feeding is associated with nurturing, nourishing, and domesticating and is thus perceived as woman's duty or as maternal. In Grace Jones's cartoon (figure 7.19), the suffragist, in goddess-like apparel, seeks to tame a national emblem, the eagle. Her classical profile and drapery lend authority, as does her command over the animal kingdom (the wild bird that eats from her hand and accepts her pole as its perch). A related cartoon features a donkey (the Senate) awaiting his meal of votes (figure 7.20). Allender has juxtaposed the popular wartime food conservation slogan "Food Will Win the War" with the suffrage question, implying that unless the donkey cooperates with the women's issue, the election feeding may be seriously curtailed.

Natural Metaphors

Another major class of metaphors, though grounded in culture, appears so closely linked to cognition and independent of specific referents that Gombrich considers them natural or *physiognomic* metaphors (for example, a response to an angry face or to a "dark, huge, frightening monster"). It is the use of these potent metaphors that for Gombrich gives the political cartoon its unique power—the ability to "mythologize the world" of politics.[10] A strong image commands our feelings and beliefs and appears direct, originating

Suffragist: "But I can't get the old dear to take both roads at once!"

7.17. Nina E. Allender, "The 'Anthony' and 'Shafroth' Suffrage Amendments."

7.18. Lou Rogers, "Keep It Up, Girls; He Isn't Stone Deaf!"

7.19. Grace Jones, "Taming the American Eagle."

7.20.
Nina E. Allender,
"Food Will Win
the War."

7.23. Rollin Kirby, "Until Women Vote."

170

in our earliest childhood experiences of the world. Nast's cartoon of Columbia attacked by the Tammany Tiger, for example, arouses perception of helplessness and victimization. Suffrage art used metaphors of darkness, bondage, physical abuse, imprisonment, and drowning to evoke ideas of adversity; and symbols of escape, rescue, light, warmth, growth, abundance, accomplishment, and forward movement for victory or triumph. These metaphors color the suffrage cause as beneficial and just, its opponents as offensive, loathsome, and evil.

Without the ballot, women were shown as imprisoned, enslaved, and victims of oppressors. In "Tearing off the Bonds," Lou Rogers portrayed a woman whose release is brought about by the spirit of one million women voters, who, by proving women competent in the political realm, destroy obsolete restraints (figure 7.21). The force of suffrage is again the draped goddess with classic profile. In a more modern setting, even the college graduate finds herself shackled should she attempt to enter society alongside her male classmates (figure 7.22). H. Park's title, "Handicapped," was borrowed from a British suffrage poster, where the image of a woman drifting at sea in a boat without a sail was a 1909 contest winner.[11] Radical cartoonist Rollin Kirby symbolized the New York State Legislature as a factory boss with bullwhip in hand, driving women workers into his cannery (figure 7.23). The state senate had recently decided to increase the work limit for women and children from sixty to seventy-two hours a week (written out by the whip). The politician/boss (they need not be distinguished) is shown as a wild-animal tamer, subjecting workers to his whims.

Countering symbols of oppression and confinement (women without the ballot), enfranchisement was represented by images

7.21.
Lou Rogers,
"Tearing off the
Bonds."

7.22.
H. Park,
"Handicapped."

When women cannot vote the ship of state is like the
steamship "Titanic" with only half enough life boats.

7.24. Card, "Votes for Women to the Rescue."

7.25. Lou Rogers, "Getting Her Pigs to Market."

such as a rescue ship, efficient machinery, steps and ladders, or a torch. In "Votes for Women to the Rescue" by Card, a large rescue boat appears in a treacherous, monster-infested sea (figure 7.24). The *Ship of State* occupies an area plagued with sweatshops, fire traps, and major social evils (white slavery, child labor, impure food, gambling, saloons, social disease, smallpox, and diphtheria). Without the women's ballot, the *Ship of State* must be compared to the *Titanic*, lacking the provisions to avoid disaster. Only the modern steamer, *Votes for Women*, provides an alternative to the ill-equipped large vessel or the small, drifting craft called poverty. Lou Rogers offered the analogy of a primitive pig farm (figure 7.25), for without the vote, the farmer must run after each pig to secure her objective (effective legislation). Chances of success using a heavy club are small; the ballot, in contrast, would supply the means to move her products from home to government directly: the pigs slide down the chute efficiently. In "The Next Rung" by Blanche Ames, votes for women is a rung on a ladder rising from a dark abyss into the sunlight (figure 7.26). The young suffragist gradually emerges from ignorance and greed, overcoming the demons of Injustice and Prejudice. The ladder's rungs consist of education, property, professions, business, votes for women, and true democracy. Enacting a classic metaphor, she has been plunged into darkness but ascends into light. The ladder aligns women with the force of progress. "The light shineth in darkness; and the darkness comprehended it not" proclaims another cartoon based on the light/dark metaphor (figure 7.27). The biblical quotation used by Nina Allender was applied to the effort to enlighten Congress; Votes of Women radiates from a torch held by the ethereal

7.26.
Blanche Ames,
"The Next Rung."

"The light shineth in darkness; and the darkness comprehendeth."

7.27. Nina E. Allender, "A New Light on the Situation."

A NEW RECRUIT TO THE ANIMAL KINGDOM OF COURSE THE SYMBOL OF THE WOMAN'S PARTY WILL BE A "DEER"

WOMAN'S PARTY

DONKEY ELEPHANT MOOSE

7.28. John McCutcheon, "A New Recruit to the Animal Kingdom."

SAHARA OF HUMAN ASPIRATIONS

WOMAN SUFFRAGE

POLITICAL FADS

LOU ROGERS

7.29. Lou Rogers, "Winning Out on the Long Endurance Test."

angel of suffrage, while men stand complacently in their Committees on Expediency.

The Search for a Suffrage Symbol

Newspaper cartoonist J. E. Murphy had commented on the need for suffragists to construct an accepted symbol of suffrage.[12] The clearest American model of cartoon symbolism was the work of Thomas Nast, master of fabricated imagery. After formulating a symbol, Nast would incorporate it skillfully and systematically, giving it a seemingly natural association. But women did not establish a unitary, identifiable symbol for the suffrage movement. The ballot box stood for all elections, not just the women's vote, and the "little deer," which John McCutcheon proposed, was just too cute, devoid of strength and conviction (figure 7.28).[13]

Only one suffrage artist, Lou Rogers, attempted to develop a complete bestiary of symbols. She selected the camel as her symbol of woman suffrage, a turtle as anti-suffrage, a cat as indirect influence, adding an inanimate tin can as political contempt. As she explained in a 1913 interview, "I chose the camel because it is obviously The Animal, on account of its endurance, its age-old reputation for carrying enormous burdens, etc., besides its being the water wagon of the animal kingdom.[14]

Rogers depicted her camels in desolate landscapes, on hillside paths, and on cliffs overlooking the water's edge. In an early example, the suffrage camel, with Arab woman rider, trots across the Sahara of Human Aspirations, leaving the bones of political fads behind (figure 7.29). The camel, turtle, cat, and tin can appear involved in a lively struggle in "Progressing in Spite of Themselves" (figure 7.30). As the camel gallops up the hillside "to higher levels," it is countered by the turtle and cat. The turtle assures, "We'll stop 'er before she reaches the top," words that reveal that the camel, of course, is female. One of Rogers's most effective camel images shows the extermination of the cat, a "moral nuisance." Rogers takes advantage of the fact that camels can kick, as well as march, juxtaposing the camel's action with the cat's known aversion to water. Cast into Lake Michigan, the terrified cat commemorates the Illinois legislative decree that gave women presidential suffrage (figure 7.31). The cat was the most flexible symbol in the trio, given its array of postures and expressions. It can hiss, scratch, climb, and plausibly enter government offices through a subterranean coal chute, as depicted in another cartoon by Rogers (figure 7.32).[15] Rogers's anti-suffrage turtle acts appropriately—plodding along, no progress anticipated—for its path is a circle (figure 7.33). It is prevented by its tether from changing its route, the way anti-suffragists sought "social betterment."

To be effective, a pictorial symbol had to be either culturally grounded, as were Uncle Sam, Columbia, and the elephant and donkey, or constitute an appropriate natural metaphor, as do light, darkness, and monsters. Though Rogers understood the camel as an image of determination and survival, it bore little relation to women's self-image or experience, had no natural enemy or oppressor, and did not interact with distinctive predators or prey. Rogers's camel, moreover, did not set spontaneous goals for itself and was dependent on its trainer, a tiny woman whose presence confuses the imagery. Camels and turtles are poor candidates for anthropomorphizing, as we rarely project emotion onto them. Also, Rogers tended to show animals engaged in undomesticated, inborn

7.30. Lou Rogers, "Progressing in Spite of Themselves."

7.31. Lou Rogers, "Ridding a State of a Moral Nuisance."

7.32. Lou Rogers, "Using the Back Way."

behavior patterns, unlike the cartoon donkeys and elephants of the day who danced, chatted over fences, and sat in the schoolchild's desk. Rogers may have been influenced by Thomas Nast's experiment with the camel as his initial symbol for the Democratic party, but others discovered that the camel seemed better suited as a symbol for prohibition.[16] Fused with natural metaphors and reminiscent of Aesop's fables, the suffrage bestiary failed to provide the women's movement with its desired symbol. Other artists failed to incorporate these symbols, and Rogers herself abandoned them after a half-dozen published cartoons. They were too inflexible, restrictive and narrow—and did not produce an image adequate to women's collective vision.

7.33. Lou Rogers, "En Route for Social Betterment."

Cartooning for Suffrage

8

Women's Imagery

It would be impossible for any man to
have done Mrs. Allender's work.
A woman speaking to women,
about women, in the language
of women.

—*Inez Haynes Irwin,* The Story
of the Woman's Party

When American women artists first picked up their pens and brushes for suffrage, they encountered a tradition dominated by smiling Gibson Girls and the memories of Nast's avenging Columbia. Their task was to convert this pictorial language into a form that would enhance female representations and provide images to expound suffrage doctrines. They sought techniques of satire, parody, and burlesque that would attack the social world of man and his institutions; challenge male dominance in politics, and defy demagogic protection of men's sphere. It would expose the exploitation and subjugation of women, address women's issues as significant, and reveal female social experience as distinctive. Presenting issues from a woman's viewpoint, and allying women with justice and might would promote identification with the movement, strengthen allegiance, and inspire confidence in imminent victory. Women artists were forced initially to rely on masculine conventions that were alternately incorporated, modified, and rejected in suffrage cartoons. To fulfill their own objectives, it was inevitable that the iconography and style of women's cartoons would lead in new directions.

Representations of Women

Women sought to portray themselves as competent and deserving would-be voters, although this was at odds with the customary stereotyped representations that men's art offered. Stereotyping, according to social scientists, accentuates, simplifies, and redefines characteristics, molding perception of its objects. During periods of social upheaval, moreover, emerging stereotypes help define a group and its positions of status and worth. Sociologist Teresa Perkins suggested that the complexity of social relations broadened the range of women's images, while protest against women's subordinate status would itself contribute to new stereotypes.[1] In fact, the popular press retaliated by depicting the suffragist or "suffragette" as unattractive, selfish, and rowdy. She ignored her husband (whom she must have had difficulty obtaining), neglected her children, and disrupted the affairs of her community. Portrayed as outlandish and repulsive in the humor magazines, these suffragists belong to the category of grotesque women. They contrasted sharply with other images, such as men's views of ideal women.

The ideal nineteenth-century American woman was, to the European eye, "beautiful, self-reliant, fashionably dressed but competent in housework, desirable but innocent, and above all enjoying a freedom unknown elsewhere in the world."[2] But where the sixteenth-century goddess/continent on her armadillo was voluptuous and sensuous (figure 2.5), late nineteenth-century woman was delicate and pure. "Womanliness came to mean sexlessness," observed William Wasserstom.[3] Popular culture maintained the boundaries of womanhood and fashioned an image of the ideal where female passivity and helplessness were commended—powerful women were an aberration.

For the turn of the century, new schemes were devised to classify women. In *The American Eve*, Ernest Earnest distinguished four types: the titaness, the college girl, the office girl, and the Gibson Girl.[4] The titaness was powerful, more goddess-like than real, whereas the student, worker, and Gibson-style companion were subordinates in the male hierarchy. Three of the four roles designated by Earnest were specifically called "girl": the college girl, office girl, and Gibson Girl, for not surprisingly, male artists preferred drawing young models, who were at the peak of physical attractiveness, lacked wisdom and matronly authority, and remained clearly subordinate. They fulfilled men's fantasies without arousing their fears. Another attempt to categorize men's images of women includes an interpersonal dimension. Author Judith Fryer suggested that men regarded the *temptress* as possessing "alluring yet frightening sexuality," in contrast to the *American princess*, who was "never threatening to men," and "beautiful and innocent." Less positive from men's perspectives were images of the *Great Mother*, an archetypal figure who was "powerful" and "manipulative and destructive." In visual representations she occasionally cropped up as a mother-in-law or raving suffragist. Turn-of-the-century writers also probed aspects of the *New Woman*, who superficially appearing free and equal, was judged by Fryer to be "a caricature."[5]

In popular art of the late nineteenth and early twentieth centuries, Martha Banta identified three female types: the beautiful charmer, the New England woman, and the outdoors pal.[6] Most traditional was the charmer—idealized, alluring and sophisticated. As intellectual interests emerged, she became the New England woman; acquiring athletic skills, the outdoors pal. The dual aspects of brain and brawn were often combined in the New Woman, whose spirited disavowal of social restrictions led the next generation to admire and imitate her. Even the science of the day could no longer assert that woman's physique was fragile and unhealthy and her brain inappropriately small.[7] The New Woman, widely featured and debated in the popular press, developed her mind (like Banta's New England woman and Earnest's college girl), exercised her body (like the outdoors pal), and became economically self-sufficient taking what to her seemed a glamorous job (the office girl). Sensual, intellectual, and active, turn-of-the-century woman

Cartooning for Suffrage

abandoned the pious, retiring stance of true womanhood for freedom, adventure, and control.

Suffrage artists endeavored to cultivate positive, realistic images
of woman, of her enhanced potential in society, and a previously
unacknowledged sense of power. It was neither her body (temptress,
athlete, Gibson Girl) nor her intellectual prowess (New England
woman, college girl) that predominated, but interpersonal strengths
and political competencies. Her will appeared strong, her manner
assertive. Admirable roles included those of the nurturing mother,
dutiful housewife, and faithful helpmate. She provided skilled service as a teacher or nurse and was a reliable worker. Occasionally
she appeared as belle, compellingly feminine, or as Amazon warrior, with phenomenal strength. As modern woman, she entered
the new century of social and psychological disquietude, challenging barriers and beliefs.

The New Suffragist

Nineteenth-century male cartoonists represented the woman's
rights advocate as a virilized, unattractive, old maid dressed in
bloomers.[8] The public accepted this stereotype—a representation
that remained virtually unchanged for over half a century. As late
as 1952, an American author, commenting on a photo of suffrage
leaders, wrote "Improbable as it seems, many of the granite-faced
feminists were married . . ."[9] The stereotype had molded his
perceptions.

That around 1910 the public was becoming more sympathetic
to the women's vote is evident in the changing characterization
of the suffragist.[10] Boardman Robinson of the *New York Tribune*
explored the transformation in a cartoon, "The Type has Changed"

8.1.
Boardman
Robinson, "The
Type Has
Changed."

8.2.
Nina E.
Allender,
"Our Hat in the
Ring."

(figure 8.1). A slender, good-looking, young woman adjusting her fashionable hat replaced the stout, dour-faced, masculinized agitator.[11] The young woman represents the New Woman (with traces of the charmer), who now rallies under the suffrage banner. In Robinson's image, however, the pretty young suffragist seems paradoxically passive in her posture, gaze, and inactivity. Only a ribbon pinned to her chest identifies her political sympathies.

Suffragists credited Nina Allender with forging an up-to-date, positive image, what admirers dubbed the "Allender girl." Allender's suffragist was attractive and energetic, with a single-minded commitment to women's political advance. In "Our Hat in the Ring," she appears stylishly dressed, her skirt shortened above the ankles, her manner more wholesome than sensuous (figure 8.2). Her serious face reflects her determination to win the struggle, and she assumes a hands-on-hips posture of assertiveness and confidence. May Wilson Preston's suffrage figure is a self-assured, commanding soapbox orator (figure 8.3). Slender and fashionably attired, apparently a society woman, she too rests her hand on her hip. The pedestal, once limiting, is transformed into a platform or political accessory from which to sway the crowds.

Representations of suffragists in other cartoons offer a range of figure types. Fredrikke Palmer's suffragist possesses a matronly figure and is tastefully dressed as she offers flowers to the political parties (figure 8.4). By symbolizing suffrage victories as flowers, voting is redefined as a womanly activity, and she is able to challenge the parties without violating her sphere. Lou Rogers created a housewife suffragist presenting her Thanksgiving harvest of four more states (figure 8.5). It is a wholesome image of competence and

8.4. Fredrikke S. Palmer, "A May Basket for the Parties."

8.3.
May Wilson
Preston, "Votes for
Women."

8.5. Lou Rogers, "Ready to Serve."

Mrs. Sam—I'm too big for this.
Sam—I need meat and potatoes.

8.6. Lou Rogers, "A Simple Case of Common Sense."

Mrs. Sam: "It is Terribly Humiliating to Me, Sam, to Have You Go to Europe in Last Century's Hat."

8.7. Lou Rogers.

determination, which, represented by an undistinguished-looking housewife, promotes everywoman as suffrage crusader.

In these images drawn by women, the variations in age, attractiveness, and activity parallel the diversity found in women themselves. Allender's and Preston's figures enter a political arena and gaze across the frame (broad horizons, future orientation). Palmer's and Rogers's figures confront the viewer face on, an appeal made between equals. As the image of the suffragist underwent transition, women artists extended the boundaries more forcefully.

The Ancillary Female

It is an irony of history that Uncle Sam eclipsed the figure of Columbia at the very moment when suffragists were seeking symbols of the female aspect of the nation and of themselves. Columbia, a female symbol born with her nation, rarely appeared as a suffrage image (for an exception, see figure 1.24). In contrast, Uncle Sam, who represented the masculine government, was a common figure. He served as an escort or husband in some women's images, and suffrage figures were shown to challenge his authority. A "Mrs. Sam," was even created for suffrage cartoons, including one by Lou Rogers in which she is tired of her unappetizing political diet (figure 8.6).[12] This Mrs. Sam, a stocky, matronly woman, hair drawn back tightly into a bun, was a suitable adjunct to her male partner. Her inferior status is linked to poor nutrition, because Sam alone has access to the vote (meat and potatoes). In another cartoon by Rogers, Mrs. Sam chides her husband for wearing an antiquated crown marked Divine Right of Men-Folks to Rule the Women-Folks (figure 8.7). Although her face is healthy and reveals

Cartooning for Suffrage

strength of character, she is, somewhat paradoxically, the prototypic nagging wife. Edwina Dumm's Mrs. Sam nags as well, in
"Fashion Hints from Darkest Russia" (figure 8.8). Mrs. Russia's
equal suffrage bonnet distresses Mrs. Sam, who grumbles, "And to
think you let her get it first." Mrs. Sam is a stout, strong-minded,
older woman, who openly displays her aggravation over her husband's suffrage policy. Although her image fails to elevate the status
of women, it offers human emotion (indignation) as a response to
an actual event: the enfranchisement of Russian women. Laura
Foster selected Susan B. Anthony, drawn in a realistic style, as
the suitable mate for Uncle Sam (figure 8.9). The humanizing
force of women's influence is made clear by softening the portrayal
of Sam with a rounded face, smile, and affectionate gaze. Anthony
appears self-assured and determined, her detachment reflecting her
preoccupation with the women's struggle.

With Uncle Sam symbolizing the male government, there remained a need to represent American women. Rogers, Dumm,
and Foster struggled to find a new female symbol, choosing not
goddesses, but worldly and imperfect companions for Uncle Sam.
Perhaps these depictions of jealous and nagging women could re-
assure men that suffrage would amplify women's natural voices and
not transform them into viragoes.

The term womanly furnished implicit messages underlying both
pro-suffrage and anti-suffrage art. As Lisa Tickner explained:

> In all this [definition and prescription] "womanliness" was a complex
> construct, full of contradictions and capable of being exploited to
> surprisingly diverse ends. It is easily seen as a restrictive concept
> that constrained women's opportunities and regulated their spheres
> of action; but at the same time it provided them with a strong sense

8.8.
Edwina Dumm,
"Fashion Hints
from Darkest
Russia."

8.9.
Laura Foster,
"Uncle Sam and
Aunt Susan."

8.10. John Bengough, "On the Road to Victory."

Suffrage: "Shall I try a new record or stick to the double disc?"

8.11. C. D. Batchelor, "An Important Choice."

of identity, restored them to socially valued responsibilities, and gave them the moral authority to pursue an actively regenerative role.[13]

For woman suffrage to be accepted, the movement had to maintain an image of the womanly.

Women Portray Women

There were a number of male cartoonists who were strong advocates of suffrage: John Bengough, Harry Osborn, C. D. Batchelor, Boardman Robinson, and Charles Winner, among others. Each contributed graphics directly to the women's press lending male authority to legitimize women's goals. Their suffrage art was noticeably different from women's, most often restricted to the political issue of securing the ballot through depictions of energetic suffragists, campaign activities, and parades. For the suffrage campaign in Ohio, John Bengough featured an automobile decorated with slogans, driven by a suffragist who runs down her opposition (tiny antis and liquor representatives) (figure 8.10). C. D. Batchelor portrayed Suffrage (a woman) deciding her convention strategy (state action, federal action, or both), while an elephant and a donkey wait to base their strategies on her announcement (figure 8.11). In both cases the women are solitary, expressionless, and separated from everyday life. Each reflects woman-as-symbol, placed in a political setting.

Women artists, in contrast, did not separate the issue of enfranchisement from questions of social reform, life-styles, and concepts of womanhood. They viewed the suffrage campaign as embedded in a social context and linked to far-reaching transformations. After all, most women artists were pathbreakers in their profession. They were trained in newly founded (or recently opened to them) art institutions, and most had encountered discrimination first hand in the exhibition hall or academy. Women painters were considered novelties, and women cartoonists more so. In 1902 Kate Carew was touted as "the only female exponent of the funny side of life," whereas *Cartoons Magazine*, which featured articles on a conspicuous number of women cartoonists (including Lou Rogers, Nina Allender, and Edwina Dumm), may have been astonished that they existed at all.[14]

In promoting the suffrage campaign, women projected their convictions onto a variety of female roles: mothers, wives, workers, professionals, reformers, activists, and dreamers. Suffragist figures drawn by women could not be mistaken for Gibson Girls—they were too responsible, dedicated, and competent. They were constructed in a range of ages, body shapes, fashions, and social statuses, although their skin was always white. Suffrage artists drew these women characters to advance specific arguments. Women who were attractive and feminine were used to allay fears of the unwomanly. Gentle mothers devoted to children, husband, and friends needed the ballot to better fulfill their duties. The wage earner, a New Woman respected for her freedom, required the ballot for self-protection.[15] Because women contributed their labor to society, they had earned the right to vote. The twentieth-century militant and progressive woman would use the ballot to build a better society. Socially and psychologically unlike her predecessors, the progressive woman was the last to emerge and the least common. To be a citizen in society, she needed the ballot as her instrument of self-interest, self-protection, and fulfillment.

8.12.
Fredrikke S.
Palmer, "Will
Congress Heed?"

"That child needs a woman to look after her."

8.13. Nina E. Allender, "Come to Mother!"

Manifesting different needs for the ballot, three characterizations of women dominate, in order of historical emergence: (1) traditional women, (2) wage-earning women, and (3) militant and progressive women. Within woman's established sphere, traditional woman was represented as passive, pious, and demure, a true woman for whom motherhood was the only possible vocation. An image by Fredrikke Palmer presents the plight of a nurturing, yet powerless, mother, two small children at her side (figure 8.12). Her arm is immobilized by the heavy ball and chain of disfranchisement, and she is universalized by classical drapery that transcends the suffrage context. Her resolute gaze conveys conviction and power, and her maternal role assures her womanliness. Nina Allender's cartoon, "Come to Mother," bridges the gap between home and politics by portraying Congresswoman Jeannette Rankin, the first woman in Congress, as the nurturing mother looking after the little girl Suffrage Amendment (figure 8.13). Allender seeks to lessen the contradiction between politics and woman, but its effect is double-edged: celebrating the congresswoman's public role at the expense of reminding the viewer that as a woman she is intrinsically different. Rankin embodies the principle of motherhood in government as does a symbolic figure drawn by Lou Rogers (figure 8.14). Rogers's more forceful image gains power from motherhood and applies it to diminish the corruptibility of the little boy/candidate. "Are your hands clean, son?" she demands. The image confronts men with female authority, yet softens its thrust through the more palatable metaphor of age guiding youth.

Women could offer political statements from the home without appearing unfeminine. A domestic setting by Allender shows the

Cartooning for Suffrage

1918 elections being heated on a stove and stirred with a spoon labeled Women's Votes (figure 8.15). By delaying his mealtime, the man (Senate) risks spoiling the food (elections). Another Rogers cartoon depicts a suffrage vacuum cleaner, powered by women voters, dislodging filthy little creatures or "Old Fogie Notions About Suffrage" (figure 8.16).

Nina Allender selected a formal dance as a setting to suggest that the ballot is the "ladylike" accessory to gain men's favor (figure 8.17). The western, voting woman is surrounded by male suitors, whereas the eastern woman can not figure out why the lady with the fan (votes) is getting all the attention. Voting is not unwomanly, but a new-found power with which to captivate gentlemen. Women can alter politics and their places in it from within their traditional spheres.

Some images portray women as productive workers in society, to whom the right to vote should unquestionably be given. Turn-of-the-century women fit various occupational categories, some qualifying them particularly for enfranchisement. According to the 1900 census, women wage earners generally were employed in five main categories: 40 percent in domestic and personal services (maids, nurses), nearly 25 percent in manufacturing (textile mill workers); 16 percent in agriculture, 10 percent in trade (saleswomen, stenographers, clerks), and 9 percent in professional services (teachers, musicians, artists).[16] The diligence and devotion that women demonstrated as workers, equipped them to participate in public affairs. Not only did women share in the drudgery of society's labor and therefore deserve a voice in its governance, but women needed the vote to alter the conditions by which they earned their daily wages.

8.14. Lou Rogers, "Transferring the Mother Habit."

Suffragist—"If he doesn't stop talking and come in his dinner will be spoiled!"

8.15. Nina E. Allender.

8.16. Lou Rogers, "Rushing the Growlers."

"Born to Nurse.
And to soothe and
to solace, to help
and to heal the sick
world that leans on
her."

8.18.
Marietta Andrews.

Why is the lady with the fan getting all the attention?

8.17. Nina E. Allender, "The Wall-Flower."

8.19.
Nina E. Allender,
"They Shall Not
Pass?"

Nursing, a calling within women's sphere, was classified as a service occupation rather than as a profession during this era. Suffragists appropriated it to promote a womanly image of idealism, purity, and service, illustrated by Marietta Andrews's cartoon of a nurse standing on the deck of the ship beside a life preserver, symbol of her occupational aim (figure 8.18). That the nurse's patriotic contribution was acceptable when the ballot was denied her in return seemed inconsistent and ironic. Nina Allender elaborated the theme, adopting a slogan used by the French at Verdun, "They shall not pass," when portraying the Senate halting an army of nurses as they try to march along the Path of Political Freedom (figure 8.19)

Women had been encouraged to become public school teachers in America for nearly a century. The profession was considered well suited to middle-class women, who nevertheless received one-half to two-thirds the salary of a man. Nineteenth-century women, including several mothers of suffrage artists, often taught school in their late teens before they married. The significance of the teaching role was a blend of authority with the womanly. Allender's teacher looms over her reluctant student, the Democratic donkey at his desk (figure 8.20). She appears confident and assertive (hand on hip), whereas he struggles to memorize the lesson that four million women voters demand the national enfranchisement of women. Allender underscores her point with a quotation from Wilson: "Most of the pupils of most of our universities systematically resist being taught." The donkey is unteachable.[17] Rogers's image, in contrast, is a grotesque caricature of the teacher, who borrows the power of the Great Mother (figure 8.21). She represents to each man his nightmare when he has failed to remember a sig-

—President Wilson at the Berea College Meeting, Washington D.C., 24 February 1915.

8.20. Nina E. Allender, "Colleges and Colleges." *Most of the pupils of most of our universities systematically resist being taught.*

8.21.
Lou Rogers, "Still Teaching Him."

"The farmer's wife is his partner in burdens: why should she not be his partner in privileges? The National Grange believes she should. It has just passed a resolution declaring emphatically and unanimously for equal suffrage."

8.22. Lou Rogers, "Why Can't She Vote Too?"

8.23.
Lou Rogers,
"Welding in the
Missing Link."

nificant lesson, in this case that democracy is government by *all* the people. In both cartoons the voter/politician is a little boy dominated by his teacher—one legitimate source of women's power over men.

If women share in the labor of society, why not in the governance? "The farmer's wife is his partner in burdens; why should she not be his partner in privileges?" asked Lou Rogers (figure 8.22). Her female figure appears androgynous: strong and muscular, even if she must use two hands to carry her share of the weight. Suffragists further believed the woman worker would bring the values of the home into the public sphere. Rogers symbolized this by depicting a metalworker forging the link between home and government (figure 8.23). Her worker is strong and skilled and might be accused of usurping a man's job, but this accusation is diminished by reference to the home and by the incongruous feminine gown from which her muscular arms protrude. Men and women are equal in their contribution but bring different values to society; the ballot should belong to both.

Suffrage images of militants and progressives encourage a rethinking of gender roles and society. The images present modern woman as unique in history and recognize the social forces that shape her qualities. Cornelia Barns, in a powerful image, argued that control of woman's body was itself a social issue (figure 8.24). A distraught, pregnant housewife, accompanied by her husband and five small children, might have limited her family or timed it differently if allowed medical knowledge on birth control. In denying her information about her own body, society must accept the blame.

Cartooning for Suffrage

Modern-thinking women were forced to cook the meals, wash the clothes, mind the baby, feed the animals, and clean the house before tackling the concepts of political economy, downtrodden women, or suffrage. In figure 8.25, Laura Foster shows a woman attempting systematic research, with her typewriter on the kitchen table (symbol of her conventional sphere). The split frame reveals how the social division of labor has provided men a circumscribed occupation and left women unending chores. Suffrage was only one of the changes sought by women, contended the same artist in another cartoon (figure 8.26). "Dreaming Dreams" offers visions of new occupations for women: combat duty, police work, operating heavy farm equipment, fighting fires, and jury duty. It is a call for new role definitions that will permit women to follow individual inclinations. Society must provide new options.

These militant and progressive images are precursors to contemporary feminism, for they combine the goal of personal liberation with an awareness of social forces discovered through consciousness-raising. Replacing the nineteenth-century social reformer, the twentieth-century feminist is bent on restructuring an unjust and restrictive society. Her images are increasingly subversive, for she seeks not only the ballot but comprehensive social change. She understands the interrelationship of political, social, and psychological emancipation.

8.24. Cornelia Barns, "We Accuse Society!"

8.25. Laura Foster, "Man Works from Sun to Sun, But Woman's Work is Never Done."

8.26. Laura Foster, "Dreaming Dreams No Mortal Ever Dared to Dream Before."

9

Suffrage, Art, and Feminism

Feminism is that part of the progress
of democratic freedom which
applies to women.

—*Beatrice Forbes-Robertson Hale,*
What Women Want

Suffrage graphics were produced by dozens of American women, who viewed suffrage issues from alternate perspectives, and who used diverse art techniques and forms to achieve suffrage aims. Several questions emerge in attempting to understand the origins and functions of this art. What features characterized suffrage cartoons as art by women? Why did women's art assume the forms and styles that it did? What influenced these women to become cartoonists for the suffrage cause? What was the relation between their artwork and twentieth-century feminism? Although it is not easy to find answers to these questions, an examination of the issues they raise helps uncover important aspects of women's history and leads to an appreciation of suffrage cartoons as feminist art.

Suffrage Cartoons as Women's Art

The image of the suffragist changed, not surprisingly, when women took up the drawing pen (and typewriter) on their own behalf.[1] They refashioned the image of the suffragist into a younger, more vigorous woman of deep inner conviction. Much of this image shift was credited to Nina Allender, who drew the suffragist as young, slender, and energetic—a woman of competence and intense dedication to the cause. As an anonymous colleague wrote:

> She [Nina Allender] gave to the American public in cartoons that have been widely copied and commented on, a new type of suffragist—the young and zealous women of a new generation determined to wait no longer for a just right. It was Mrs. Allender's cartoons more than any other one thing that in the newspapers of this country began to change the cartoonist's idea of a suffragist.[2]

Allender promoted her suffragist representation through repetition and exposure in numerous cartoon situations over a period of years. Other women artists, though less consistent, further enlarged the suffragist image. Lou Rogers portrayed her as everywoman—a mother, housewife, and worker (see figure 8.5). Fredrikke Palmer gave her maturity and wisdom (see figure 8.4), and Edwina Dumm added obstinacy and persistence (see figure 1.17). They portrayed a suffragist who was robust, sensual, and believable, replacing what Marshall Davidson described as the "bloodless, sexless, and purified versions of the species" so often found in popular images of women by men.[3] Representations of women by women were too complex to be reduced to simplified social types.[4]

In examining the characteristics of women's suffrage art, it is instructive to compare their work with suffrage art by men. Three early works by men, which may have served as prototypes for women's cartoons, are of particular interest. The depictions are realistic, drawn with heavy black lines and a mixture of precise detail and stylized elements. A 1913 cartoon by John Sloan for *The Masses*, "She's Got the Point," depicts a suffrage rally (figure 9.1). It focuses on a well-dressed suffrage orator, reputedly based on Sloan's wife.[5] Instead of reinforcing the inherently pro-suffrage imagery, however, the caption restructes the scene to impugn suffragists' motives. A wife tells her husband "You'd better be good, Jim, or I'll join 'em." Weakened in its propaganda value by the caption—which may have been added by the editors—Sloan's cartoon did not offend suffragists, who reprinted it in the *Woman Voter*. Sloan's treatment of the figures, moreover, differs considerably from Nina Allender's slender, attractive, young suffrage orator who appeared on the cover of the *Suffragist* (figure 9.2). Specifically, Allender reveals more of the speaker's body, letting it dominate the picture and affirming power and control through her

"You'd better be good, Jim, or I'll join 'em."

9.1. John Sloan, "She's Got the Point."

9.2.
Nina E.
Allender,
"The Summer
Campaign."

9.3. John Sloan, "The Return from Toil."

Women Come to Washington to Demand Democracy at Home.

9.4. Nina E. Allender, "Supporting the President."

gestures and posture. The crowd in Allender's cartoon contains men and women intermingled; a second suffragist helps by distributing suffrage propaganda. Women are working collectively to achieve the common goal of suffrage. The endorsement of suffrage is not weakened by glib humor; it is a serious portrayal of women as political.

Groups of women are featured in several cartoons, including ones by John Sloan and Nina Allender (figures 9.3 and 9.4). Sloan's well-known drawing, "The Return from Toil," portrays six young women walking along a city street at the end of a work day.[6] Their clothes are stylish, their manner carefree, and their camaraderie is shared; nevertheless, their gazes are neither reciprocal nor parallel, implying a rather transient association. Nina Allender's line of middle-class women is about to board a train for Washington, D.C., in "Supporting the President." By placing the suffragists' heads and feet in similar positions, Allender depicts a collective purpose, the individual subordinated to the social whole. These women are serious, dedicated, and energetic.

Woman's place is a theme explored in a number of suffrage drawings. Maurice Becker's "Woman's Proper Sphere is the Home" appeared in *The Masses* and shows a stout working-class woman walking down a public street (figure 9.5). With a bulky load upon her head, she passes a top-hatted, wealthy gentleman, who strolls by leisurely. As a man, he occupies the public arena freely, even when his activities reveal no apparent purpose. The woman enters a public setting only to pursue her livelihood, and she also must carry her infant, a symbol that her domestic domain has intruded into the public sphere. Allender, too, examined the theme that "Woman's Place is the Home," but emphasized the conflict between

Cartooning for Suffrage

women's duties beyond the home, where her wages are earned, and responsibilities to her family (figure 9.6). Allender's shawl-clad immigrant mother glances back at her home and six children, from whom she is torn by her factory job. A drawing by Mary Ellen Sigsbee shows home not as abandoned, but as transformed into a dismal site of labor in which all available hands must participate (figure 9.7). The work is menial and meaningless, and the compensation insufficient to satisfy their needs for security and comfort. Not an idyllic refuge, the home has taken on the most dehumanizing aspects of the marketplace.

The struggles in women's lives were often portrayed with greater compassion and intensity by women artists, whose cartoon characters appear cast from different molds. Sloan's figures of working class women, according to art historian Patricia Hills, express "pure, simple innocent spontaneity" and seem "removed from political struggle."[7] Despite efforts to present a sympathetic portrayal of women and their plights, Sloan's representations remain idealized and hollow. Becker's figure, invoked to satirize the notion of "woman's sphere," reveals the obsolescence of a domestic role, and remains a symbol where feelings and character are concealed. The identification between women artists and their cartoon counterparts increases the credibility of their figures and projects an image that is more complex, yet accessible. Allender's suffragists are attractive, educated, and purposeful. Allender and Sigsbee portray the working-class mother as caring and responsible, augmenting their portraits with dilapidated slums and large broods of children. These women artists, unlike the men, have highlighted the deficiencies of the home, the scope of women's domestic responsibilities, and the possibilities of women's collective action.

9.5. Maurice Becker, "Woman's Proper Sphere Is the Home."

9.6. Nina E. Allender, "Woman's Place Is the Home."

9.7. Mary Ellen Sigsbee, "Woman's Place Is in the Home."

Your little daughters some day will make as good citizens as your sons. See to it that they receive equal justice.

9.8.
Fredrikke S. Palmer, "When Will Their Independence Day Be?"

Women's suffrage art often depicted young girls, a feature whose presence offers an extended view of the vote—that political power would affect all women, from infancy to old age. Just as social discrimination begins at birth, a woman's right to the ballot could restructure the social world for a young girl (figure 9.8). Men drew girls, too, in their pro-suffrage graphics, but less frequently, and rarely with the same message. Men typically approached the suffrage question as an issue affecting adult women.

Although most suffrage cartoons portrayed white, middle-class women, several women artists extended this range. Radical women artists grasped the diversity of women's experience and represented social classes, ethnicities, and even races. For socialist women, including Lou Rogers, Mary Ellen Sigsbee, Alice Beach Winter, and Cornelia Barns, the worker formed the core of society. The sweatshop conditions under which women and children were forced to work challenged the fundamental workings of male-dominated democracy and its neglect of humanitarian ideals. Suffragists asserted that improved labor conditions, an aspect of social progress, would be established with the woman's vote.

Cornelia Barns and Nina Allender interpreted the handicaps faced by immigrant women sympathetically in their portrayals of babushka-adorned women (figure 9.9). This wave of new immigrants, however, aroused fears in the native-born population, and would soon lead to immigration quotas. Many suffragists insisted that enfranchising women of a more "desirable stock" could help offset the immigrant vote. In the hands of radical socialist artists, in contrast, immigrant women were represented as an exploited group who had a special need for the vote.

Women of color are seldom found in suffrage art, a fact reflecting the attitudes of most suffrage leaders, who, often prejudiced themselves, feared losing the potential support of white Southerners. Boardman Robinson exposed the movement's racial prejudice in his cartoon titled "Just like the Men" (figure 9.10). Yet Alice Beach Winter and Mary Ellen Sigsbee included blacks in some of their published illustrations (figure 9.11). They depicted realistic females who lacked the exaggerated physical characteristics then in vogue among cartoonists. These cartoons, however, offer no specific call for suffrage and portray blacks only in low status positions (children, domestic servants).

Although most women artists sought to redefine women's roles in their suffrage art, the range of effective propaganda arguments was limited. Artists recognized the importance of creating visual images and types of women that would be acceptable to the public. This partly explains the preponderance of domesticity, femininity, and motherhood themes in suffrage art. It was a battle, explained Lisa Tickner, between the suffragist and her opponent over who could be seen as "womanly."[8] Both claimed traditional feminine strengths for themselves and attacked the character of their rivals. Some suffrage images of women reflect society's traditional expectations so closely that it is difficult to see them as dynamic political art. When Nina Allender's society belles volunteer to be "The President's Valentine," one wonders just what they intended to offer in exchange for the vote (figure 9.12). Nor did the suffragist willing to sweep and scrub the halls of Congress elevate woman's vocation, even if the metaphor is useful.

The challenge was to create images conveying an overall sense

9.9. Cornelia Barns, "One Man—One Vote."

Votes for WHITE women.

9.10. Boardman Robinson, "Just Like the Men."

9.11. Alice Beach Winter, "Puzzle: Find the Race-Problem."

9.12. Nina E. Allender, "The President's Valentine."

of femininity but also reflecting traits or activities leading to a reconsideration of woman's sphere. In redefining rôles, Lisa Tickner claimed that a balance was needed between familiar, acceptable patterns for women and new, unaccustomed portrayals: "if the boundaries of womanly decorum were to be extended in this process and not just confirmed, other figures had also to be deployed, in less familiar roles but with feminine grace and dignified mien."⁹

One collection of acceptable, alternative images contained symbolic personifications. Females embodying Victory, Wisdom, Justice, and Liberty enhanced belief in women's inherent goodness and power while sanctioning political values and goals. Their use not only advanced women's claim to the ballot but also suggested that gender-appropriate traits needed to be reconsidered. Cartoonists also selected cultural heroes, transforming male figures into females, and forcing a reexamination of their characters. Women as Hamlet, Samson, the Wise Men, and Paul Revere convey the notion that women can be rulers, thinkers, patriots, and heros. These females with male traits are considered androgynous, a fact that modifies their psychological nature as well as their social position.

Another way cartoonists established role-discrepant behavior as tolerable was to have the action carried out by those given greatest role flexibility, for example, the very old, the very young, the unassimilated, or the eccentric. Character types are important in cartoons, and people are more willing to appreciate humor when the characters are "children, animals, 'primitive' races and 'sub-humans.'"¹⁰ Remoteness created by age (for example children or old women), distant historical periods and cultures, and social classes furthers the acceptance of contradictory elements in suffrage images. As an example, Nina Allender selected a little girl to

Cartooning for Suffrage

depict an aggressive confrontation between a suffragist and the government (figure 9.13). Throwing snowballs is not a ladylike action, but carried out by a little girl in a pretty dress and hat, it appears cute. Similarly, stacking boulders to block a man's path is not a feminine means of protest, but performed by a goddess, it becomes an acceptable symbolic gesture (figure 9.14).

Depictions of cartoon women—crusaders, patriots, moralists, rebels, martyrs, workers, mothers, or suffragists—defined a position relative to the male social structure. They represented unequals and subordinates, whether they supported or challenged men's endeavors. Men, in turn, consistently dichotomized individual women as virtuous/corrupt, good/evil, and powerful/weak. Women, in contrast, understood the underlying conflict or tensions, and depicted them in popular images of women and portrayals of women on stage. Marina Warner has described the ambivalence latent in such images: "the disorderly woman inside the virtuous freedom fighter. The rhetoric of justice tips over easily into the dramatics of insubordination."[11] These tensions define the complexities of character and the unification of seeming opposites found in a whole being.

As suffragists examined woman and her sphere, they tried to portray her as inherently capable, as contributing unique virtues to society, and as limited by her environment—thereby countering claims that she had little inherent ability or interest in politics. Some speculated that if gender differences arose as a result of the social system, they were neither innate nor immutable. An emphasis on social determinants of behavior ultimately would undermine time-honored beliefs in woman's distinctive character. It would later be seen that the social barriers separating women from

Judiciary Committee: "Wha' jer goin' to do next?"

9.13. Nina E. Allender, "December 16, 1915."

9.14. Lou Rogers, "Forcing Him Out of the Rut."

9.15. Nell Brinkley, "When Poverty Comes in the Door Love Flies Out The Window."

9.16.
Mary Ellen
Sigsbee, "The
Easiest Way."

the political and economic domains of men might be the source of her claim to moral purity.[12] The issue recalled what Kirk Porter identified as the "keynote" of suffrage philosophy: "No one can possibly say what is woman's natural sphere until she has the same liberty as man has to develop and seek her sphere by natural processes."[13]

If adverse social conditions reduced women's potential and the quality of life, oppression was not only a distressing situation to be alleviated, but a link in a causal social chain. Poverty lessened the fullness of life, claimed Nell Brinkley in "When Poverty Comes in the Door Love Flies Out the Window" (figure 9.15). Mary Ellen Sigsbee examined the conditions that lead a young girl to prostitution: no job, inexperience, and promises of a rewarding life-style (figure 9.16).

Wealthy women enjoyed societal privileges in addition to material luxuries. Although legislation forbade dissemination of birth control information, some techniques of family planning were known to the upper classes. As a result, those who could least afford a large family were most likely to have one. Lou Rogers acknowledged this fact in a cartoon for the *Birth Control Review* (figure 9.17), where Mrs. Poor Patient complains, "If you're rich, the law don't count." Some women activists sought an egalitarian society, where rich and poor, immigrant and native-born, and diverse racial and ethnic types had similar opportunities.

Forms and Styles of Suffrage Art

Most suffrage cartoonists appear to have had little, if any, experience in drawing cartoons prior to suffrage. The small number who had experimented with cartooning include Lou Rogers, Laura

Cartooning for Suffrage

Foster, Sara Moore, Nell Brinkley, Rose O'Neill, and Edwina Dumm. The rest were painters, illustrators, and amateurs, who in seeking an effective propaganda medium selected the cartoon form. It is perhaps paradoxical that most American suffrage cartoons appeared in suffrage journals and thus reached an audience already sympathetic to their views. They were not widely distributed to the public.

The use of suffrage cartoons by American women coincided with the establishment of a magazine that influenced them greatly. *The Masses*, a New York City socialist magazine published by an impressive set of intellectuals, offered social commentary and illustrations setting high aesthetic standards. John Sloan headed its committee of art editors, encouraging high quality graphic reproductions and a bold, uncluttered look. The magazine soon influenced the styles of individual artists and the format of other publications. Some cartoons in the suffrage press were reprinted from *The Masses*, and the suffrage press's use of art editors probably originated with the magazine. *The Masses* supported women ideologically and welcomed women writers and artists to its staff of editors. Alice Beach Winter, one of the art editors, specialized in child portraiture, capturing the experience of slum children and contrasting the worlds of rich and poor (figure 9.18). Art editor Cornelia Barns drew several ironic portrayals of male voters (figure 9.19). She exhibited technical freedom (even reversing the conventional figure-ground relationship), economy of detail, and wonderfully ludicrous figures. Also published in *The Masses* was a drawing (figure 9.20) by Mary Ellen Sigsbee of a young girl and an old man titled, "The Question Why Are We Here." It was later reprinted in the *Woman's Journal*.

Mrs. Poor Patient—"If you're rich, the law don't count."

9.17. Lou Rogers.

"He ain't got no stockin's, he's poorer nor me."

9.18. Alice Beach Winter.

9.19. Cornelia Barns, "Voters."

The Masses' aesthetic philosophy was anticipated by an important development in the graphic arts, the emergence of the so-called Ashcan school. These early twentieth-century painter/illustrators advocated independence and freedom of expression in art and organized new associations and societies as alternatives to the national academy.[14] Ashcan artists were instrumental in reassessing the relation of realism to aesthetics. As leader Robert Henri explained, "It takes more than love of art to see character and meaning and even beauty in a crowd of east side children tagging after a street piano or hanging over garbage cans."[15]

By altering their definition of art, without believing that they were necessarily perverting their talents, artists were free to use their work in the interest of social causes. An ideology, a technique, and a visible school of practitioners permitted the adoption of a bold new cartoon style, evident in *The Masses.* In *Art for the Masses,* Rebecca Zurier characterized this style as "an extraordinarily vivid, textured line that looks as if the artist had reached out with a black crayon and drawn directly on the page."[16] The use of the lithographic crayon, in a style reminiscent of Daumier, was integral to the magazine's message: "The crayon line took on political significance as a stylistic rebellion against bourgeois illustration; it affirmed a graphic tradition of social protest."[17]

Editor Max Eastman moved *The Masses'* offices to Greenwich Village, where its advocacy of socialism, feminism, birth control, and other radical causes appealed to feminists and suffrage artists. There were strong links between its artists, theorists, and the suffrage movement. Max Eastman himself was the head of a Men's Suffrage League, and his sister, Crystal, was a major feminist theorist and member of Heterodoxy.

The visual conventions that suffrage artists adopted in their cartoons stemmed from two separate traditions: the fine arts' arena of drawing and painting, and the craftsmanship of the newspaper cartoonist-illustrator. British suffragists emphasized these traditions by organizing two separate groups of artists. Members of the Artists' Suffrage League were fine artists who applied their abilities to banners, posters, and postcards. The Suffrage Atelier attracted women associated with the arts and crafts tradition of printing and the decorative arts, and also contributed posters and cartoons for suffrage.[18] In the United States, artists individually forged links with suffrage papers, which accepted a wide range of styles and talents. Work by graduates of the nation's finest art academies appeared alongside that of amateurs and young girls.

Certain characteristics and limitations inherent in the cartoon make it difficult to appreciate and interpret suffrage illustrations. Cartoons' messages exist at various levels, they are open to multiple interpretations, and they may be accepted for more than one reason. One may laugh at the suffragist or with the suffragist, depending on one's orientation, and suffrage scrapbooks, including those assembled by Blanche and Oakes Ames, contain both pro- and anti-suffrage art. "Mother Goose as a Suffragette," a set of nonsense verses illustrated by staff artists of the *Brooklyn Daily Eagle*, was adopted by the campaign, and suffragists eventually published them as a booklet.

The modern cartoon as an art form lacks a clear, artistic "original." The artist may submit a drawing on a scrap of paper (with parts pasted over) or as a large-scale, polished work. The caption, if present, may be altered by the editor and, in any case, will look different when set in type. Early twentieth-century cartoons were

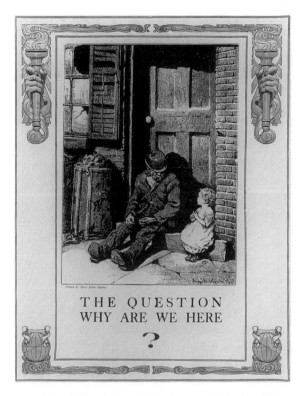

9.20. Mary Ellen Sigsbee, "The Question Why Are We Here."

sometimes reproduced in a large, easy-to-read size, as in *The Masses*, or reduced to a two-inch space on a page of *Judge*. Lou Rogers drew originals for street crowds in a size large enough to entertain, although her published forms never exceeded twelve inches. It is difficult to distinguish some designs intended for newspaper cartoons from those intended for posters.[19] When designed for photographic reproduction, a cartoon has no true or intended size. Many were drawn larger than the reproduced size, but were additionally adapted to another format. British artists produced a number of suffrage designs in both poster format (up to sixty by forty inches in size) and postcards, suggesting their suitability as either. American suffrage artists published a few works as posters, and some small, printed fliers. Some large, poster-sized original drawings by Blanche Ames and Nina Allender, which remarkably have survived, were actually published as cartoons.

The Influences of Ideology

The experience of turn-of-the-century women artists exposed and sensitized them to cultural biases and discrimination against women. Most sought to support themselves through their art and thus experienced the struggles to obtain a rigorous education and to become economically self-sufficient. The position of artist required talent, ambition, and dedication; launching an art career necessitated training and money. They had to exhibit and sell their work to support a studio, which was particularly difficult in an unfamiliar city or country. In the struggle, views of oneself, of women, and of society were expanded.

Social impediments for the nineteenth-century woman artist included reservations about women entering a profession, restricted art opportunity (segregated classes, no exposure to nude models, exclusion from inner circles), and the secondary status of the "lady artist." The latter was linked to an implicit distinction between men's art, which was large scale, bold, and used oils, and women's art, which was generally small scale, delicate, and used watercolors. Most women artists had contemplated issues of career, marriage, and professional name. Some, like May Wilson Preston, discovered associations or professional opportunities closed to them, and joined societies of women artists seeking mutual support. Forged as a result was what Paula Gillett described for England as "the strong link between the feminist movement and the first organization of women artists."[20]

Suffrage artists, like suffrage leaders, came from middle-class, Protestant, established American families. The women saw themselves primarily as patriots motivated by indignation, not as radicals or rebels. Born in the 1870s, their childhoods spanned a period of rapid cultural transition. While being trained in the social duties expected of young girls, they learned to accept the doctrine that men and women had separate spheres (figure 9.21). They believed that women had a mission to enhance the quality of life—a concept that some would invoke later as license to surmount intellectual, social, and political barriers. There were some, however, who even as young girls resented rigid gender divisions. Lou Rogers, despite a rather idyllic childhood in the Maine woods, grew up envying her four brothers. As her mother later recounted, "Annie was born with a grievance, namely, being a mere girl when she would so much rather be a boy. She consoled herself with dressing in her brothers' clothing and taking a boy's part in all their games."[21] As these women experienced the rapid technological and social changes

9.21. "A Happy Home."

JOSH.—*Yes, my darter's goin' to graduate this year an' she's busy now preparin' her valedictory.*
HIRAM.—*What's a valedict'ry?*
JOSH.—*That's the kind of a dress they wear when they graduate.*

9.22. Charles J. Taylor, "An Unpardonable Mistake."

in the world around them, they came to view social structures as changeable, and were determined to promote social and political reform. The late nineteenth century marked the founding of women's colleges and of art schools open to women. Educational and professional options kindled personal ambition, in turn, replacing older feminine virtues of modesty and selflessness. By the time the 1870s-born women reached early adulthood, society was rapidly replacing the ideal of true woman with that of the New Woman. The image of the New Woman, an individual of "independent spirit and athletic zeal," was featured and exploited in the popular press of the 1890s (figure 9.22).[22] The professional woman artist, who extended her "womanly" talent of painting to new levels, was now admired for her perseverance and spunk. Suffrage artists who had originally internalized the nineteenth-century notion that women had a social obligation to help others, were ready to work for a social goal of momentous import, over advancing their own careers. Thousands of women saw it as their social duty to join the suffrage cause as volunteers—canvassing, speaking, traveling, writing, drawing, or using other professional skills.

In their thirties and forties at the time of suffrage activities, these artists had already completed their art education and chosen their life-styles and careers. The similarity of their ages suggests that maturity and life experience proved beneficial to the cause, perhaps reflecting Erik Erikson's idea of *generativity*, the middle-aged person's contribution to the next generation and to society.[23] United in a social movement, the organized campaign for the ballot, suffrage artists were participants in women's collectives that generated encouragement, support, and enthusiasm. As suffrage leaders solicited contributions for women's publications and forums, these

Cartooning for Suffrage

artists transformed their personal achievement goals into service for the collective mission. Their art took on new significance.

Suffrage Art and Feminism

In the second decade of the twentieth century, the American women's movement adopted the term *feminism*. The shift in vocabulary was significant, broadening objectives, intensifying militant fervor, pluralizing female possibilities, and allowing men to participate.[24] The word *feminism*, applied to beliefs underlying the advocacy of woman's rights and woman's emancipation, originated in France and made its way to England around 1895.[25] It remained politically imprecise, identified with a spirit and an attitude more than with a specific program of action. To its advocates, it was a higher-order concept, "not synonymous with the struggle for the ballot or with the demand for equal wages."[26] " 'Votes for Women,' is near and insignificant compared with the stretches that lie beyond that simple, first step," wrote Heterodoxy member Edna Kenton. "Many women of this generation will stop short, in their path to self-realization, with their enfranchisement, calling it a good fight won, and the battle ended."[27]

Beatrice Forbes-Robertson Hale, who also belonged to Heterodoxy, summarized the relationship by stating that "enfranchisement is only a branch of the tree of Feminism."[28] For Heterodoxy's founder, Marie Jenney Howe, the major goals of feminism had three aspects: the women's vote, a means of economic self-support, and the social "revaluation of outgrown customs and standards." Howe recognized the final goal as including a "changed psychology" and "new consciousness in women."[29] In short, the concept of

9.23. Lou Rogers, "Breaking into the Human Race."

feminism transcended strictly political aims. It urged a social position of equality and a psychology of inner development.

Feminism was an ideology loosely linked to radical life-styles, and was therefore popular among the activists, writers, and artists of Greenwich Village. Its role in that community was explained by June Sochen, "Village feminists, however, saw the vote only as a modest stepping-stone to the larger goal: a cultural re-orientation that would give all human beings an equal opportunity. Acting counter to the beliefs of most of their contemporaries, they saw feminism as the value system that would accompany the new socialist order."[30] As residents of Greenwich Village, members of Heterodoxy were eager to describe the principles and merits of feminism. In 1914 they organized a mass meeting on "What Feminism Means to Me," and several days later held a second meeting, titled "Breaking into the Human Race." The meeting's title had been used by Lou Rogers some time earlier as the caption to a cartoon (figure 9.23). At the meeting, the following topics were scheduled for discussion:[31] (1) The Right to Work, (2) The Right of the Mother to Her Profession, (3) The Right to Her Convictions, (4) The Right to Her Name, (5) The Right to Organize, (6) The Right to Ignore Fashion, and (7) The Right to Specialize in Home Industries. Each of these topics emphasized women's autonomy in areas such as careers, homes, beliefs, attire, and names, but there was no specific session addressing the issue of the ballot.

The new feminism reflected a reconsideration of goals and differed sharply from the nineteenth-century woman's rights movement. As Mari Jo Buhle noted, because it was "increasingly doubtful that women could alter public life sufficiently to meet their own inner needs, Feminists chose to wage their battles elsewhere—

Cartooning for Suffrage

within the interstices of private life. In redefining the ultimate goal as self-realization rather than advancement, Feminists drastically altered the teleology of woman's mission."[32] The major shift, then, was from the social to the personal aspects of feminism. Coupled with this change toward inner psychology was the recognition of diversity in women's backgrounds, personalities, and beliefs. Nancy Cott noted the complexity of twentieth-century feminist goals and demands, suggesting three core components of feminism:

> First is the belief in what is usually referred to as sex equality but which might be more clearly expressed in the negative, as opposition to sex hierarchy. . . . Second, feminism . . . presupposes that women's condition is socially constructed, that is, historically shaped by human social usage rather than simply predestined by God or nature . . . [Third] Feminism posits that women perceive themselves not only as a biological sex but . . . as a social grouping.[33]

Feminism expanded its objective (external and internal), offered a theory explaining woman's nature as socially constructed, and stressed the importance of collective action or empowerment. The distinction between equal political rights for both sexes and characteristic gender differences was maintained. "Feminism asks for sexual equality that includes sexual difference,"[34] asserted Cott. The new women's movement abandoned nineteenth-century claims to an inherent female nature and began to see most women's traits as socially constructed. In the transition, as Buhle recognized, faith in the "collective advancement of women" was weakened.[35]

By the close of the suffrage campaign, women's art reflected the new values of feminism, broadened its targets, and attempted to restate the significance of the movement. All three of Cott's com-

9.24.
Mary Taylor,
"Equal Rights."

9.25. Cornelia Barns, "Waiting."

ponents of feminism are found in cartoons. An example of the first, equality, appears in Mary Taylor's graphic in which the Liberty Bell proclaims equal rights (figure 9.24). The second component, the belief that social forces shape woman's nature, is depicted in figure 9.23 by Lou Rogers. Her cartoon uses confinement in a dark prison cell to represent woman's social condition, a condition that blocks full human development. An example of the third component, that women perceive themselves as a social group, is seen in "Waiting" by Cornelia Barns (figure 9.25). Women carry the ancient torch of enlightenment and bring nurturance (their babes in arms) and determination to this timeless setting. Women's strength and empowerment result from an unending assemblage of women. Two related aspects of feminism, the insistence on the personal psychology of a new consciousness and a recognition of the essential differences among women, were harder to capture in single images. A few ethnic women and women of color were portrayed (see figures 9.6, 9.9 and 9.11). The theme of inner development is evoked in Allender's post-suffrage cartoon, "The Thinker" (figure 9.26). These aspects, would become more central when the second wave of feminist theorists appeared in the 1970s.

For three-quarters of a century American women struggled to become a part of their nation's political system. Framed against the forces of modernization, technology, industrialism, progressivism, and national and international wars, women organized a political campaign that established solidarity, built networks, and helped them rediscover themselves. When the Nineteenth Amendment was ratified in 1920, suffrage organizations were delighted to find themselves obsolete. But in their initial struggle was the foundation for a more comprehensive feminist ideology. Its uncompleted tasks became the focus of a few, including Crystal Eastman, who in 1920 wrote: "Men are saying perhaps 'Thank God, this everlasting woman's fight is over!' But women, if I know them, are saying, 'Now at last we can begin.'"[36]

9.26. Nina E. Allender, "The Thinker."

Chronology Chart

Date	Women's History	Cartoon History
1431	Joan of Arc burned at stake	
1494		*Das Narrenschiff* by Sebastian Brant
1515		Invention of etching
1568		Dutch pictorial propaganda
1580		America symbolized as female or male (Amazon, goddess, or Indian)
1593		*Iconologia* by Cesare Ripa
1603		Illustrated edition of *Iconologia*
1630s	Anne Hutchinson urged women's public expression	
1646	Margaret Brent demanded a voice and a vote	
1709		*Moral Emblems* (English-language edition of *Iconologia*)
1748		Word "caricature" used in English
1760s		Liberty figure represents American struggle
1776	Abigail Adams urged her husband to "remember the ladies"	
1776	New Jersey constitution specified property and residence as voting requirements	

Date	Women's History	Cartoon History
1777		Columbia as symbol of America; Richardson edition of *Iconology*
1787	U.S. Constitution ratified with no mention of sex	
1790	"On the Equality of the Sexes" by Judith Sargent Murray	
1792	*A Vindication of the Rights of Women* by Mary Wollstonecraft	
1795		Invention of lithographic process
1807	New Jersey revoked the right of women to vote	
1813		Brother Jonathan figure created
1830s	Uncle Sam figure created	
1831		*La Caricature* founded
1832		*Le Charivari* founded
1840	Women delegates denied seating in Anti-Slavery Convention	
1840	*Women in the Nineteenth Century* by Margaret Fuller	
1841		*Punch* founded
1843		Word *cartoon* redefined
1848	Convention at Seneca Falls; New York women granted property rights	
1850s	Woman's Rights Conventions held	

Appendix A

Date	Women's History	Cartoon History
1857		Currier & Ives partnership formed
1862		Thomas Nast joined *Harper's* magazine staff
1866	American Equal Rights Association formed	
1867	Kansas referendum	
1869	National Woman Suffrage Association formed; American Woman Suffrage Association formed; suffrage granted women in Wyoming & Utah Territories; *The Revolution* founded	
1870	*Woman's Journal* founded	
1874	Woman's Christian Temperance Union (WCTU) founded	
1876		*Puck* founded
1878	Federal woman suffrage amendment first discussed in Congress	
1887	Utah women disfranchised	
1881		*Judge* founded
1881	WCTU endorsed woman suffrage	
1883		*Life* founded
1884	Belva Lockwood ran for president of U.S.	
1890	National American Woman Suffrage Association formed; General Federation of Women's clubs formed	

Appendix A

Date	Women's History	Cartoon History
1890s		Photoengraving used; Rose O'Neill active cartoonist
1893	Colorado women enfranchised by referendum	
1895	Mass. Ass'n. Opposed to the Further Extension Of Suffrage To Women formed	
1896	Utah granted statehood and reenfranchised women; Idaho granted woman suffrage by state amendment	
1908		Art Exhibit by the Eight marked beginning of Ashcan School
1908	Artists' Suffrage League formed in England; British suffrage parade	
1910	Washington State granted suffrage to women; suffrage parade in New York City; *Woman Voter* founded	
1911		*The Masses* founded
1911	*Maryland Suffrage News* founded	
1912		"Modern Woman" page added to *Judge*; *Cartoons* magazine founded
1913	Suffrage parade in Washington, D.C.; *Suffragist* founded	
1914	Congressional Union formed	
1915	Shafroth Amendment proposed	
1916	National Woman's Party reorganized	

Date	Women's History	Cartoon History
1916		Edwina Dumm hired as editorial cartoonist
1917	*Woman Citizen* replaced *Woman's Journal* and *Woman Voter*; National Woman's Party pickets arrested	*The Masses* ended
1918	Suffrage Amendment passed House	
1919	Suffrage Amendment passed House and Senate	*Puck* ended
1920	Nineteenth Amendment signed; League of Women Voters organized	
		Cartoons magazine ended
1922	National Woman's Party proposed Equal Rights Amendment	

Artists' Biographies

Allender, Nina Evans (1872?–1957)

Born in Auburn, Kansas, where her father served as superintendent of schools. Resided in Washington, D.C. after 1881 when mother employed by U.S. Department of Interior. Attended Corcoran School of Art and Pennsylvania Academy of the Fine Arts. Official National Woman's Party cartoonist; numerous examples in the *Suffragist*. Married Charles Allender from England, who deserted her. References: Boyle, *Words*; Corcoran Gallery; Kansas Historical Society; Pennsylvania Academy of Fine Arts; Radcliffe.

Ames, Blanche Ames (1878–1969)

Born in Lowell, Massachusetts, where family owned woolen mills; father Civil War General, former Governor of Mississippi. Artist and illustrator, attended Smith College, active Massachusetts Suffrage Association. Cartoons published in *Woman's Journal* and *Boston Transcript*. Married Oakes Ames, a botany professor at Harvard. Children: Pauline, Oliver, Amyas, and Evelyn. References: Crane, *Blanche Ames*; *National Cyclopedia*; *Notable American Women*; Radcliffe; Smith; *Woman's Who's Who*.

Andrews, Marietta Minnigerode (1869–1931)

Born in Richmond, Virginia; father served as major in the Confederate Army. Studied at Corcoran School of Art, D.C., in Paris, and Munich. Created paper silhouettes and wrote books. National Woman's Party; cartoons in the *Suffragist*. Married art teacher Eliphalet Andrews; two children, Eliphalet Fraser and Mary Lord. References: Andrews, *My Studio Window*; *Dictionary of Women Artists*; *New York Times*.

Andrews, Esther

Illustrator active in New York City about 1910. Contributed illustrations to *Woman Voter*. References: Eastman, *Enjoyment of Living*; *New York City Directory*.

Banks, Jessie

Active in New York City; contributed illustrations to *Woman Voter*. References: *Who Was Who in American Art*.

Appendix B

Barns, Cornelia Baxter (1888–1941)

Born in Flushing, New York, and moved to Philadelphia, where father was theater impresario. Attended Pennsylvania Academy of the Fine Arts. Active in California after 1920. Cartoons published in *Birth Control Review, The Masses, Suffragist,* and *Woman Voter.* Married Arthur Selwyn Garbett, a music critic from England. Child: Charles. References: *City Life Illustrated;* Pennsylvania Academy Fine Arts; Zurier, *Art for the Masses.*

Barnhart, Nancy Elizabeth (1889–1964)

Born in St. Louis, Missouri. Studied at Smith College, Art Students League of New York, and in Paris. Illustrator; honorable mention in 1915 suffrage poster contest, cartoon in *Woman Voter.* References: *Illustrators of Children's Books, New York Times,* Smith.

Batchelor, Clarence Daniel (1888–1978)

Born in Osage City, Kansas and attended Chicago Art Institute. Cartoonist at various times for *New York Daily News, New York Journal, New York Mail, New York Post, New York Tribune.* Pulitzer Prize for cartooning. Contributed suffrage art to *Woman Voter.* References: Hoff, *Editorial and Political Cartooning; World Encyclopedia of Cartoons.*

Bengough, John Wilson (1851–1923)

Born in Toronto, attended Ontario School of Art. Cartoonist for *Toronto Globe;* founded humor magazine, the *Grip.* Advocate of woman suffrage, prohibition, and single tax; contributed suffrage cartoons to *Woman's Journal.* References: Charlesworth, *Canadian Scene; Dictionary Canadian Biography; World Encyclopedia of Cartoons.*

Brinkley, Nell (1888–1944)

Cartoonist and illustrator, self taught, worked for Hearst publications, International News Service. Married Bruce MacRae, Jr. References: *Current Biography; Dictionary of Women Artists;* Robbins and Yronwode, *Women and Comics.*

Card

Contributed cartoons to the *Woman's Journal* and *Femina*. Possibly Boston area.

Carter, Robert (1875–1918)

Born in Chicago. Cartoonist for *New York American*, *New York Sun*, *Philadelphia Press*, *Progressive Globe*. Suffrage cartoons reprinted in *Woman Voter*. References: *Cartoons Magazine*; *World Encyclopedia of Cartoons*.

Coppinger, May

Contributed illustrations to the *Woman's Journal*.

Dumm, Edwina (1893–1990)

Born Frances Edwina in Upper Sandusky, Ohio; father was a newspaperman. Took correspondence course in cartooning and was hired as editorial cartoonist on *Columbus Monitor*, where she endorsed suffrage through her cartoons. Professional comic strip artist. References: Caswell, "Edwina Dumm"; Robbins and Yronwode, *Women and Comics*.

Emmons, Marion D.

Contributed cartoons to *Maryland Suffrage News*.

Fitzpatrick, Daniel Robert (1891–1969)

Born in Superior, Wisconsin, attended Chicago Art Institute. Cartoonist for *Chicago Daily News*, *St. Louis Post-Dispatch*. Pulitzer Prize for cartooning. References: Hoff, *Editorial and Political Cartooning*; *World Encyclopedia of Cartoons*.

Foster, Laura (Monroe)

Cartoonist and illustrator active circa 1905–1919. Published extensively in *Life*; pro-suffrage cartoons found in *Judge*. Added Monroe to signature in 1919. Reference: *Judge*.

Gelletly, May Florence (1886–1955)

Possibly the cartoonist who signed "M.F.G." in *Maryland Suffrage News*. Studied Maryland Institute, Art Students League. Reference: *Dictionary of Women Artists*.

Goldthwaite, Anne Wilson (1869–1944)

Born Montgomery, Alabama, daughter of Confederate artillery captain, lawyer. Studied at National Academy of Design and Académie Moderne, Paris; taught at Art Students League of New York. Suffrage art in *Woman Voter* and participated in Exhibition Committee of artists who donated share of sales to suffrage. References: *Dictionary of Women Artists; Notable American Women.*

Harwood, Mayme B.

Cartoonist and one of the art editors for the *Woman's Journal.*

Jones, Grace

Published cartoons in the *Woman's Journal.*

Kirby, Rollin (1875–1952)

Born in Galva, Illinois, freelance illustrator, cartoonist for *New York Mail, New York World.* Pulitzer Prize for cartooning. Suffrage cartoons reprinted in *Woman Voter, Suffragist,* and as suffrage flier. References: Hoff, *Editorial and Political Cartooning; World Encyclopedia of Cartoons.*

McCay, Winsor (1869–1934)

Born in Spring Lake, Michigan, self-taught artist. Comic strips, pioneer in animation, and syndicated editorial cartoonist. Suffrage art reprinted in *Woman's Journal.* References: Canemaker, *Winsor McCay; Who's Who in Art; World Encyclopedia of Cartoons.*

Milhaus, Katherine (1894–1977)

Born in Philadelphia, where she attended the Philadelphia Museum School of Industrial Art and Pennsylvania Academy of the Fine Arts. Worked as author and illustrator. Suffrage post card for Pennsylvania Limited Equal Suffrage League. References: *Dictionary of Women Artists.*

Minor, Robert (1884–1952)

Born in San Antonio, Texas. Cartoonist for *New York World, New York Call, San Antonio Gazette, St. Louis Post-Dispatch.* Active in Communist Party. Cartoons reprinted in *Woman's Journal, Woman Voter.* Married Mary Heaton Vorse, Lydia Gibson. References: Garrison, *Mary Heaton Vorse;* Hoff, *Editorial and Political Cartooning;* Schwarz, *Radical Feminists; World Encyclopedia of Cartoons.*

MKall (?)

Illegible signature on several cartoons in *Maryland Suffrage News.*

Moore, Sara

Born in Detroit and returned at age 16. Reporter for the *Detroit News,* cartoonist and writer for *New York Mail,* "Cartoonettes," McClure Syndicate, *Chicago Tribune.* Sent to England to observe British suffrage activities. Married Frank G. Eastman; children: Philip Moore and Paul Glover. References: *Detroit News;* Logan, *Women in American History;* Ross, *Ladies of the Press.*

Morse, Grace A.

Cartoons in *Woman's Journal.*

Neall, Josephine W.

Designed suffrage calendar for 1912.

Osborn, Harry (died 1915)

Family home in Darlington, Wisconsin. Cartoonist for *Baltimore News,* religious and social themes. Suffrage art for *Maryland Suffrage News.* References: *Cartoons Magazine.*

O'Neill, Rose Cecil (1874–1944)

Born in Wilkes-Barre, Pennsylvania, and raised in Nebraska. Father was a book dealer; mother had taught school. Won children's art contest at 13 and began weekly cartoon series for *Omaha World Herald.* Illustration and cartoons appeared in major magazines; Kewpies marketed as popular doll. Joined British suffrage movement; contributed posters and postcards, some with Kewpie themes, to American suffrage cause. Married Gray Latham, Harry Leon Wilson. References: *Dictionary of Women Artists; Notable American Women.*

Palmer, Fredrikke Schjöth (born 1860)

Born in Norway; studied art in Christiania (Oslo) and Berlin. Cartoonist and art editor for *Woman's Journal;* active in Hawaii in 1920s. Married A. H. Palmer, professor at Yale University; Children: Erik Schjoth, Harold S. References: *Dictionary of American Painters; Dictionary of Women Artists; Who Was Who in American Art.*

Park, H.

Cartoons in *Woman's Journal.*

Plummer, Ethel McClellan (1888–1936)

Illustrator and cartoonist, suffrage poster. Married Jacobsen, Frederick Humphreys. References: *Dictionary of Women Artists; Rubinstein, American Women Artists.*

Preston, May Wilson (1873–1949)

Born in New York, studied at Oberlin and Art Students League of New York Illustrator associated with the Ashcan school. Active in National Woman's Party, contributed to *Woman Voter,* and illustrated *How it Feels to be the Husband of a Suffragette.* Married artist Thomas Henry Watkins and artist James Moore Preston. References: *Dictionary of Women Artists; Notable American Women;* Rubinstein, *American Women Artists.*

Proper, Ida Sedgwick (1873–1957)

Born in Bonaparte, Iowa. Father was minister. Sold drawings while in her teens; attended Art Students League of New York and awarded fellowship for study in Munich. Studied and exhibited in Paris. Member of Heterodoxy; stationed with U.S. Army at Tours, France. Art editor of *Woman Voter,* where she contributed some of her own work. References: Farnsworth Art Museum; Maine State Library; Ness and Orwig, *Iowa Artists;* Schwarz, *Radical Feminists; Woman's Who's Who; Women's History Sources.*

Reynolds, Clara

Cartoonist whose work appeared in *Judge.*

Robinson, Boardman (1876–1952)

Born in Somerset, Nova Scotia, spent childhood in Wales. Enrolled Massachusetts Normal Art School, Académie Colarossi and École des Beaux-Arts. Cartoonist for *New York Tribune,* and *The Masses.* Instructor at Art Students League of New York Suffrage art in *The Masses, New York Tribune,* and *Suffragist.* Married Sally Whitney, former student of Rodin and later member of Heterodoxy. References: *Cartoons Magazine;* Christ-Janer, *Boardman Robinson;* Hoff, *Editorial and Political Cartooning; Who's Who in Art; World Encyclopedia of Cartoons;* Zurier, *Art for the Masses.*

Rogers, Lou [Annie] (1879–1952)

Born in Patten, Maine and studied briefly at Massachusetts Normal Art School and Art Students League of New York. Cartoonist published in *Judge, Ladies' Home Journal, New York Call, New York Tribune, New Yorker Volkzeitung, Suffragist, Woman Citizen, Woman Voter, Woman's Journal.* Member of Heterodoxy. Married artist Howard Smith. References: Art Students League, *Cartoons Magazine,* "Lightning Speed"; M. Rogers, "Down East"; Schwarz, *Radical Feminists;* Showalter, *These Modern Women.*

Sigsbee, Mary Ellen (1876–1960)

Born in New Orleans to Navy family. Published drawings and paper dolls in her teens; became painter, newspaper and magazine illustrator. Studies at Art Students League of Washington and Art Students League of New York, and in Paris. Published in *The Masses, New York Evening Journal, Woman's Journal,* and suffrage fliers. Married artist Balfour Ker, artist Anton Otto Fischer. Children: David Ker and Katrina Sigsbee Fischer. References: *Dictionary of Women Artists;* Fischer, *Anton Otto Fischer.*

Sloan, John (1871–1951)

Born in Lock Haven, Pennsylvania, grew up in Philadelphia. Studied at Pennsylvania Academy of the Fine Arts and joined art staff of *Philadelphia Inquirer, Philadelphia Press.* Ashcan artist, art editor of *The Masses;* contributed to *New York Call;* instructor at Art Students League of New York Suffrage art in *Woman Voter, Woman's Journal,* and *The Masses.* Married Anna "Dolly" Wall, an advocate of socialism, woman suffrage, and birth control; married art student Helen Farr. References: Brooks, *John Sloan; World Encyclopedia of Cartoons;* Zurier, *Art for the Masses.*

Sykes, Charles H. (1882–1942)

Born in Athens, Georgia, attended Drexel Institute. Cartoonist for *Life, Philadelphia North American,* and *Philadelphia Public Ledger.* Suffrage cartoons in *Woman Citizen* and *Woman's Journal.* References: *World Encyclopedia of Cartoons.*

Taylor, Mary

Artist active in Baltimore, contributed to *Maryland Suffrage News.*

Valiant, Eloise F.

Artist active in Baltimore, contributed to *Maryland Suffrage News.*

Van Loon, Hendrik Willem (1882–1944)

Born in Rotterdam, the Netherlands, educated at Harvard, Cornell, and Munich. Artist, author, and lecturer; Associated Press Correspondent in Washington. Possibly contributed cartoons to *Suffragist*, attributed to "Frederick" Van Loon. References: National Woman's Party Papers, *Who Was Who in American Art*.

Weed, Clive (1884–1936)

Born in Kent, New York and grew up in Philadelphia. Studied Pennsylvania Academy of the Fine Arts and in Paris. Cartoonist for *New Republic, New York Evening Sun, New York Tribune, Philadelphia Record, Philadelphia Press,* and *Philadelphia Public Ledger*. Contributed cartoons to *Suffragist* and *Woman Voter*. Reference: *World Encyclopedia of Cartoons*.

Winner, Charles H.

Born in Perrysville, Pennsylvania, and attended Pittsburgh Art School. Cartoonist for *Pittsburgh Post;* suffrage art to *Woman's Journal* and *Woman Citizen*. Married. References: *Cartoons Magazine*.

Winter, Alice Beach (1877–1970)

Born in Green Ridge, Missouri; studied at St. Louis School of Fine Arts and Art Students League of New York Paintings and illustrations of children, served as art editor of *The Masses*. Cartoons in *The Masses* and *Woman Voter*. Married artist Charles Winter. References: Del. Art Museum; *Woman's Who's Who;* Zurier, *Art for the Masses*.

Young, Arthur Henry "Art" (1866–1943)

Born near Orangeville, Illinois, grew up in Wisconsin. Studied at Art Students League of New York, Academy of Design, Académie Julian. Newspaper cartoonist for *Chicago Evening Mail, Chicago Inter-Ocean;* freelance cartoonist; contributor to *The Masses*. Married Elizabeth North. References: *Current Biography;* Hoff, *Editorial and Political Cartooning; World Encyclopedia of Cartoons;* Young, *Art Young*.

Journal articles and unpublished sources are given full citations in the Notes. Published books are listed in the Select Bibliography.

Chapter 1

1. [Lou Rogers], "Lightning Speed through Life," *Nation* 124 (13 Apr. 1927): 397.

2. Ida Proper's *End of the Suffrage Parade* was executed in oils; Gertrude Boyle's *Woman Freed*, a sculpture, appeared as an illustration in Boyle, "Art and Woman's Freedom," *Suffragist* 8 (1920): 62–63.

3. Lisa Tickner, *The Spectacle of Women*, 22, depicts the display and distribution of suffrage designs. Some were reproduced in American suffrage periodicals and their familiarity is suggested by continued existence in American collections including the Library of Congress and Schlesinger Library.

4. In keeping with nineteenth-century usage, the term *woman suffrage* or *woman's rights* is used when referring to the movement.

5. Marietta Minnigerode Andrews, *My Studio Window*, 296–97.

6. For discussions of women cartoonists see *City Life Illustrated*; Trina Robbins and Catherine Yronwode, *Women and the Comics*; and Rebecca Zurier, *Art for the Masses*.

7. The aggressive tone of much humor is discussed in Sigmund Freud, *Jokes and their Relation to the Unconscious*, 102–105, 199–200; Ernst Gombrich, "The Cartoonist's Armoury," in Gombrich, *Meditations on a Hobby Horse*, 142; and Martin Grotjahn, *Beyond Laughter*. Graphic art critics have offered sharp, penetrating titles, such as Frank Getlein and Dorothy Getlein, *Bite of the Print*; Mary Campbell and Gordon Campbell, *The Pen, Not the Sword*; Ralph E. Shikes, *Indignant Eye*; Stephen Hess and Milton Kaplan, *Ungentlemanly Art*.

8. Some significant analyses include Dorothy George, *English Political Caricature*, Lancelot Hogben, *Cave Painting to Comic Strip*; M. Thomas Inge, *Comics as Culture*; David Kunzle, *Early Comic Strip*; Judith O'Sullivan, *Great American Comic Strip*; Charles Press, *Political Cartoon*; Thomas Wright, *History of Caricature and Grotesque*.

Notes

9. John Geipel, *Cartoon*, 31.

10. Henry Stubbe, *A Further Justification*, 2.

11. William Charles is included in *Mantle Fielding's Dictionary of American Painters, Sculptors, and Engravers*, 62, and cited by Arthur Bartlett Maurice and Frederic Taber Cooper, *History of the Nineteenth Century in Caricature*, 143, 159. See Elise K. Kenney and John Merriman, *The Pear*. The pear image was visually appropriate (the hefty king's large jowls), matched the initials for Louis-Philippe (la poire), and inspired dozens of images and slogans. See "'La Poire de France': Caricatures of Louis Philippe," *Chronicle of Higher Education* 37 (6 Nov. 1991): B60.

12. Kunzle, *Early Comic Strip*, 109–110, cites allegations that Louis XIV countered satire with war. Geipel, *Cartoon*, 74, and Shikes, *Indignant Eye*, 148–50, present the case of Philipon; William Murrell, *A History of American Graphic Humor*, 2:173–74, discusses Governor Pennypacker. The Pennsylvania "Gag Law" was in effect from 1903–1907, although it was reputedly never enforced. The significance of *The Masses* trial is discussed in Richard Fitzgerald, *Art and Politics* and Zurier, *Art for the Masses*, 61–64. "Indicts the Masses and 7 of its Staff," *New York Times*, 20 Nov. 1917, p. 4, col. 5; "Masses Jury Disagrees," *New York Times*, 6 Oct. 1918, p. 9, col. 6.

13. Charles Baudelaire, "De L'essence du rire" in *Oeuvres Complètes*; also Werner Hofmann, "Comic Art and Modern Caricature in the Western World," *Encyclopedia of World Art*, 3:762.

14. R. E. Williams, "Humorous Cartoon," *Encyclopedia Americana*, 1988 ed., 5:734.

15. Murrell, *Graphic Humor*, 1:3–6.

16. Press, *Political Cartoon*, 13, summarized cartoonist Alan Dunn's category scheme, which consisted of comic art, the social cartoon, and the political cartoon. Dunn's political cartoon was characterized as "comment championing a specific political faction or point of view."

17. One notable early exception to the historic male bastion is found in Mary Darly, a recognized London caricaturist who published an instruction manual on caricature in 1762; see Draper Hill, ed., *The Satirical Etchings of James Gillray*, xv.

18. Britta Dwyer, "Nineteenth Century Regional Women Artists: The Pittsburgh School of Design for Women, 1865–1905" (Ph.D. diss., University of Pittsburgh, 1989); Phyllis Peet, "The Emergence of American Women Printmakers in the Late Nineteenth Century" (Ph.D. diss., University of California, Los Angeles, 1987). Microfilm.

19. Frances (Fanny) F. Palmer (1812–1876), was an English-born artist who designed and executed over 200 lithographs for Currier and Ives. See *Dictionary of Women Artists,* s.v. "Palmer, Frances;" Charlotte Streifer Rubinstein, *American Women Artists,* 68–70.

20. Robbins and Yronwode, *Women and the Comics,* 7.

21. Heinz Werner, *Comparative Psychology of Mental Development,* 67–82.

22. The classic reference is *History of Woman Suffrage,* Elizabeth Cady Stanton, Susan B. Anthony, and Matilda Joslyn Gage, eds., vols. 1–3; Susan B. Anthony and Ida Husted Harper, eds., vol. 4; Ida Husted Harper, ed., vols. 5–6; see also Inez Haynes Irwin, *Story of the Woman's Party.* Modern interpretations include Eleanor Flexner, *Century of Struggle,* Aileen Kraditor, *Ideas of the Woman Suffrage Movement, 1890–1920;* Beverly Beeton, *Women Vote in the West;* Stephen Buechler, *Transformation of the Woman Suffrage Movement;* Ellen Carol DuBois, *Feminism and Suffrage;* Christine A. Lunardini, *From Equal Suffrage to Equal Rights.*

23. Note the near to total exclusion of women's work in the following: Foreign Policy Association, *A Cartoon History of United States Foreign Policy; American Presidency in Political Cartoons;* and *Image of America in Caricature and Cartoon.*

Chapter 2

1. Rather than use the term *broadside* for any printed sheet including those with illustrations, its use is recommended for textual forms, with *broadsheet* reserved for pictorial ones. See Kunzle, *Early Comic Strip,* 4.

2. See Kunzle, *Early Comic Strip;* Martinus Joseph Schretlen, *Dutch and Flemish Woodcuts of the Fifteenth Century;* Richard T. Godfrey, *Printmaking in Britain.*

3. Kunzle, *Early Comic Strip*, 3; See also Foreign Policy Association, *A Cartoon History*; and *Image of America in Caricature and Cartoon*.

4. Shikes, *Indignant Eye*, 3.

5. The book was illustrated by several engravers, including Albrecht Dürer, to whom the best examples have been attributed.

6. Cesare Ripa, *Iconologia*, Edward A. Maser, "Introduction" in Ripa, *Baroque and Rococo Pictorial Imagery*, vii–xi.

7. Analysis of this cartoon is taken from Frank Weitenkampf, *Political Caricature in the United States*, 18.

8. Freud, *Jokes*, 16–89.

9. William F. Fry, Jr., *Sweet Madness*; 143, maintains that the black frame around the drawing communicates the message "this is not real."

10. Gombrich, "Cartoonist's Armoury," (see chap 1, n. 7), 142.

11. Maurice and Cooper, *Nineteenth Century in Caricature*, 2.

12. Geipel, *Cartoon*, 14.

13. Gombrich, "Cartoonist's Armoury."

14. E. McClung Fleming, "Symbols of the United States" in Conference on American Culture, *Frontiers of American Culture*, 2.

15. Fleming, "Symbols of the United States," 9–10.

16. Martin Grotjahn, *Voice of the Symbol*, 92. See also Annette Kolodny, *The Lay of the Land*.

17. Marina Warner, *Monuments and Maidens*, 46, 48.

18. Murrell, *Graphic Humor*, 1:12; Michael Wynn Jones, *Cartoon History of the American Revolution*, 159; Sinclair Hamilton, *Early American Book Illustration and Wood Engraving*, 17–18. George, *English Political Caricature*, 1:44, traces the Hat of Liberty or Phrygian cap to sixteenth-century Dutch medals. In 1603 Liberty with scepter and hat was depicted in Cesare Ripa's *Iconologia*, 293. Liberty continued to be an important figure in eighteenth century British prints. See Wendy Shadwell, "Britannia in Distress," *American Book Collector*, 7 (Jan. 1986): 6.

19. Dale Roylance, *American Graphic Arts*, 51; *Image of America*, 49.

20. Warner, *Monuments and Maidens*, 277.

21. Roylance, *Graphic Arts*, 69.

22. America, like Europe, Africa, and Asia, was represented as a person in Ripa's *Iconologia*. In the illustrated 1603 edition she appears fair-skinned and handsome, wearing a feather headdress and a short, loose garment that exposes one breast. Her build is muscular and she is armed with a bow and arrow. A British edition from 1779 describes a tawny-complexioned, "nearly naked" female, George Richardson, *Iconology*, 1:33, while Johann Georg Hertel's 1758–60 German edition, *Historiae et Allegoriae* [Histories and Allegories] depicts a male native chieftain, Ripa, *Pictorial Imagery*, 105. In Wynn Jones, *Cartoon History*, the graphics, mostly British, include 14 representations of America as male Indians, 11 as female Indians, 5 as white men, and 6 as white women.

23. Alton Ketchum, *Uncle Sam*, 24. See discussion of desexualized and enthroned female images in Griselda Pollock, *Vision and Difference*, 145.

24. Press, *Political Cartoon*, 218.

25. Winifred Morgan, *An American Icon*; Ketchum, *Uncle Sam*, 24–25.

26. Shaw, *Abraham Lincoln*, 1:65

27. Maurice and Cooper, *Nineteenth Century in Caricature*, 114–17. The name was taken from a satirical drama, *The History of John Bull* written in 1712 by John Arbuthnot. British cartoonists enjoyed symbolizing Lord Bute as a boot, Lord North as the North Wind or Boreas, and an actor, Mr. Wood, as a stand of trees or woods.

28. See Theodore Roszak, "The Hard and the Soft: The Force of Feminism in Modern Times," in Betty Roszak and Theodore Roszak, eds., *Masculine/Feminine*, 87–104, for a discussion of the supremacy of masculinity as culminating in World War I. An insightful contemporary description is found in Margaret Sherwood, "Uncle Sam," *Atlantic Monthly* 121 (Mar. 1918): 330–33.

29. Roylance, *Graphic Arts*, 146.

30. Russel Crouse, *Mr. Currier and Mr. Ives*, 4.

31. Press, *Political Cartoon*, 236.

32. Roylance, *Graphic Arts*, 147, 170.

33. Elizabeth Hawkes, "Magazines and Their Illustrations" in *The American Magazine*, 27–28; Michael Schau, *All-American Girl: The Art of Coles Phillips*.

34. Charles Rosen and Henri Zerner, *Romanticism and Realism,* 37.

35. Werner, *Comparative Psychology,* 67–82; Gombrich, "The Cartoonist's Armoury," 142.

36. See Frank Mott, *A History of American Magazines.*

37. Mott, "Judge," *American Magazines,* 3:553.

38. Mott, "Judge," *American Magazines,* 3:554.

39. Mott, "Life," *American Magazines,* 4:560. Mott, "Literary Phases of Postbellum Magazines." *American Magazines,* 3:268. Rowland Elzea, "That Was 'Life' (And Its Artists)," *The American Magazine,* 10–15, 78.

40. Mott "Judge," *American Magazines,* 3:555; "Life," 4:565.

41. Morton Keller, "Introduction" to Albert B. Paine, *Thomas Nast,* xxxii.

42. Paine, *Thomas Nast,* 179.

43. Consistent with the evolution of figures such as Britannia, Farmer George/John Bull and Brother Jonathan/Uncle Sam, the tiger, originally intended as derogatory, was later appropriated by Tammany supporters as a positive identification.

44. Lisa Tickner, *The Spectacle of Women,* 32.

45. Beard was the brother of Daniel Beard, founder of the United States Boy Scouts. M. Thomas Inge, "Mark Twain and Dan Beard's Collaborative Connecticut Yankee." Unpublished manuscript.

46. "Puzzle" was signed "J. N." [Josh Nolan], an anagram for Sloan's name.

47. Joan M. Ferrante, *Woman as Image in Medieval Literature.*

48. According to Mary Lefkowitz, "The Greeks' most important legacy is not, as we would like to think, democracy; it is their *mythology.*" *Women in Greek Myth,* 9.

49. Tickner, *Spectacle of Women,* 209. A similar argument is found in Marina Warner, "Eternally Female," *New York Times,* 18 May 1986, sec. 6, pp. 34–35, 44, 48.

50. Martha Banta, *Imaging American Women,* 484.

51. See Warner, *Monuments and Maidens,* 28, for a discussion of artistic devices distinguishing allegorical women.

52. The boy's discontinuity in his perception of his mother arises during the formation of gender identity, an identification with his father. The girl,

who identifies with her mother, does not abandon her early (anaclitic) love object.

53. Carl G. Jung, *Four Archetypes*, 15.

54. Erich Neumann, *Origins and History of Consciousness*, 199. See also Neumann, *Great Mother*.

55. "We must conclude that any relationship of matriarchal cast or undertone produces hostility. This is true for any culture that allows women to threaten men's position—from on high, as it were. That has evidently been the situation in the United States, for a variety of reasons. The result has been a rampant misogyny in all of our humor." Jesse Bier, *Rise and Fall of American Humor*, 21.

56. American women called themselves *suffragists*, with few exceptions; the British militants, in contrast, adopted the term *suffragette*.

57. "A good caricature, like every work of art, is more true to life than reality itself." Annibale Carracci quoted in Geipel, *Cartoon;* 56.

58. See Tickner, *Spectacle of Women*, 213–26, for a discussion of the womanly woman and her opposite.

59. Walter Blair in *Native American Humor*, 517, observed that the portrait of Mrs. Partington from 1854 was resurrected to become "Aunt Polly" for the 1876 *Adventures of Tom Sawyer*.

60. Henri Bergson, *Laughter*.

61. See Judith Fryer, *Faces of Eve*, 27–84.

62. H. Spielmann, "On Charles Dana Gibson—Apostle of American Beauty and Humour," *The Magazine of Art*, 1 (new series, 1903): 16.

Chapter 3

1. Flexner, *Century of Struggle*, 63–64.

2. *History of Woman Suffrage*, 1:67. The vocabulary shifts over the course of the campaign, beginning with *woman's rights* (which in the late nineteenth century raised the *woman question*), and with advocates of woman suffrage becoming *suffragists*. See Nancy Cott, *Grounding of Modern Feminism* for a history of the term *feminist*.

3. *History of Woman Suffrage*, 1:67–69.

4. Ellen DuBois, *Feminism and Suffrage*, 40–41.

5. *Proceedings of the Woman's Rights Convention, Aug. 2, 1848*, 3. *History of Woman Suffrage*, 1:76.

6. Eleanor Flexner, *Century of Struggle*, 11.

7. Caroline Sherman Bansemer, "A Colonial Dame," *Harper's Monthly* 97 (1898): 229. See also Karen Berger Morello, *The Invisible Bar*, 1–7; and Ida Husted Harper, "A Brief History," in Frances Maule Bjorkman, ed., *Woman Suffrage*, 3.

8. *Guardian*, 8 Sept. 1713.

9. Abigail Adams to John Adams, 31 Mar. 1776, in Charles Francis Adams, ed., *Familiar Letters of John Adams and his Wife Abigail Adams during the Revolution*, 149–50.

10. Constantia [Judith Sargent Murray], "On the Equality of the Sexes," Parts 1 and 2. *Massachusetts Magazine*, Apr. 1890, 223; Mar. 1890, 133. Courtesy Alice Marshall Collection.

11. Carolyn W. Korsmeyer, "Mary Wollstonecraft," in Carol C. Gould and Marx W. Wartofsky, eds., *Women and Philosophy*, 100.

12. "Convention at Worcester," *The Liberator* 8 (2 Mar. 1838): 35.

13. Margaret Fuller, *Woman in the Nineteenth Century*, 24, 37.

14. Jessie Bernard, *Female World*, 80.

15. Barbara Welter, "The Cult of True Womanhood," *American Quarterly* 18 (1966): 152.

16. Barbara Solomon, *In the Company of Educated Women*, 14–26.

17. Solomon, *Educated Women*, 44, 46–47.

18. Alice Kessler-Harris, *Out to Work*, 22.

19. Kessler-Harris, *Out to Work*, 47.

20. Note that the little girl differs from the women only in size and skirt-length. Her basic features and mannerisms have predestined her for this society.

21. Flexner, *Century of Struggle*, 83.

22. This illustrates Bergson's view of humor as a powerful social corrective, used to keep unconventional members under social control.

23. Judith Papachristou, *Women Together*, 41.

24. Nancy A. Hewitt, *Women's Activism and Social Change*, 40.

25. Hewitt, *Women's Activism*, 40.

26. Elizabeth Cady Stanton, *Eighty Years and More*, 83.

27. Karen Blair, *The Clubwoman as Feminist*, 20.

28. Blair, *Clubwoman as Feminist*, 113.

29. Judith Schwarz, *Radical Feminists of Heterodoxy*.

30. "All inhabitants of this Colony of full age, who are worth £50 . . . and have resided within the county in which they claim a vote, for twelve months immediately preceding the election." Felice D. Gordon, *After Winning*, 208–209.

31. Alice Marshall Collection.

32. Kirk H. Porter, *A History of Suffrage in the United States*, 140.

33. Horace Bushnell, *Women's Suffrage*, 32.

34. Porter, *History of Suffrage*, 140. Aileen Kraditor, *Ideas of the Woman Suffrage Movement*, presented a similar analysis.

35. Porter, *History of Suffrage*, 238, in 1918 identified "the thought of woman 'leaving her proper sphere'" as the greatest impediment to the movement. "It is this sentiment [glorification of the womanly], prejudice if you wish to call it so, that has been the most effectual block to woman suffrage. It has not been crooked politics, the liquor interests, the corrupt element, nor yet ignorance and undemocratic selfishness that has kept women from the ballot."

36. Horace Bushnell, *Women's Suffrage*, 31.

37. Bushnell, *Women's Suffrage*, 63.

38. In the early years of the woman's rights campaign the church was identified as "the only consistent opposition." Porter, *A History of Suffrage*, 141.

39. Lyman Abbott, "Why the Vote Would Be Injurious To Women," *Ladies' Home Journal* 27 (Feb. 1910): 21–22.

40. Anne M. Benjamin, *A History of the Anti-Suffrage Movement in the United States*; Flexner, *Century of Struggle*, 306, suggests its existence was accelerated by the holding of a nonbinding referendum on women's municipal suffrage.

41. Rosalind Rosenberg, *Beyond Separate Spheres*, 54.

42. Carrie Chapman Catt and Nettie Rogers Shuler, *Woman Suffrage and Politics*.

43. *Proceedings of the Eleventh National Woman's Rights Convention*, New York, 1866, 3.

44. Dedicated to helping tired and wounded soldiers, approximately 7,000 local chapters were formed. See Flexner, *Century of Struggle*, 106–107.

45. DuBois, *Feminism and Suffrage*, 79–104.

46. DuBois, *Feminism and Suffrage*, 81.

47. Flexner, *Century of Struggle*, 154–55. The Fourteenth Amendment, which enfranchised blacks, sanctioned Congressional representation penalties should the right to vote be denied adult males. The Fifteenth Amendment prohibited suffrage restrictions based on "race, color, or previous condition of servitude." Suffragists objected to the use of the term *male citizen* and the refusal to prohibit sexual discrimination along with discrimination based on race and color.

48. The American Woman Suffrage Association claimed that women's vote would have minimal social impact and, unlike the National, endorsed the proposed Constitutional Amendment on minority rights that omitted women. Attendance at American's conventions was restricted to official delegates only.

49. DuBois, *Feminism and Suffrage*, 196.

50. Flexner, *Century of Struggle*, 226. Another view is that the two represented similar ideologies. See Buechler, *The Transformation of the Woman Suffrage Movement*, 12–13.

51. Flexner, *Century of Struggle*, 266. It was she who allegedly rejected Rogers's cartoon (figure 1.1).

52. Caroline Katzenstein, *Lifting the Curtain*, 116–17, 174.

53. Katzenstein, *Lifting the Curtain*, 138, 179. See Inez Haynes Irwin, *Story of the Woman's Party* and Lunardini, *Equal Suffrage to Equal Rights*.

54. Beverly Beeton, *Women Vote in the West*, 1–4.

55. Beeton, *Women Vote in the West*, 141–42. Beeton noted that there were few women in the Rocky Mountain region, except in Utah, and that

neither they nor their opponents were mobilized. Giving women the ballot was partly a publicity tactic and more easily accomplished in a territory where a referendum was not required and voters were ineligible to elect the President.

56. Harper, "Brief History," (see Chap. 3, n. 7), 19.

57. Beeton, *Women Vote in the West,* 78.

58. Harper, "Brief History," 25.

59. *Maryland Suffrage News* 9 (18 Sept. 1920).

60. Flexner, *Century of Struggle,* 154. See also Amy Erdman Farrell, "'You Can't Have a Revolution Without a Press': Feminist Periodicals in the Twentieth Century." Paper presented at meeting of American Studies Association, Toronto, Nov. 1989.

61. British suffrage papers used cartoons earlier than the Americans. The *Woman's Journal* became the official paper of the National American Woman Suffrage Association in 1909 to 1912. Kraditor, *Ideas of the Woman Suffrage Movement,* 154.

62. *Common Cause,* the paper of the British National Union of Women's Suffrage Societies, in Tickner, *Spectacle of Women,* 21.

63. Designs were sometimes borrowed freely or reworked.

64. *Woman Voter* 5 (June 1914):10. William Frauenglass, "A Study of Attitudes Toward Woman Suffrage Found in Popular Humor Magazines, 1911–1920" (Ph.D. diss. New York University, 1967), 125, using a sampling technique, reported 73 percent of the jokes and cartoons on suffrage in *Life* were negative.

65. "Judge's Artistic Alphabet," *Judge* 72 (9 June 1917).

66. Moore was sent to England to observe British suffrage activities, an experience that may have increased her sympathy for the movement, although her beliefs on suffrage in these images are ambiguous. "Leaves for England Today to Study Suffrage Question," *Detroit News,* 26 Feb. 1913, p.1, col. 6.

67. Tickner, *Spectacle of Women,* 80–91.

68. Katzenstein, *Lifting the Curtain,* 186.

69. Jacqueline Van Voris, *Carrie Chapman Catt,* 142.

70. Doris Stevens, *Jailed for Freedom*; Lunardini, *Equal Suffrage to Equal Rights*, 138.

71. Catt and Shuler, *Woman Suffrage and Politics*, 496.

72. Anna Kelton Wiley Papers, Schlesinger Library, Radcliffe College.

Chapter 4

1. This was a series on the modern woman. The fact that Rogers was chosen attests to feminist connections that continued beyond suffrage and her professional activities in the New York City area. See Rogers, "Lightning Speed," 395.

2. Facts concerning the Rogers's genealogy are courtesy Elliott Hersey of New Hampshire; *History of Penobscot County Maine*, 478.

3. Pauline Ames Plimpton, *The Ancestry of Blanche Butler Ames and Adelbert Ames*.

4. Blanche Butler Ames, ed., *Chronicles from the Nineteenth Century*, 1:46.

5. *Who's Who in America*, 9th ed., s.v. "Proper, Datus DeWitt."

6. The genealogy is courtesy Lewis G. Proper of Rochester, New York. See also Walter A. Knittle, *Early Eighteenth Century Palatine Emigration*.

7. Courtesy Col. Louis W. Proper of Fairborn, Ohio.

8. [William G. Cutler, ed.,] *History of the State of Kansas*, 1557.

9. Kay Boyle, *Words That Must Somehow Be Said*, 93.

10. Alice B. Griffith to author, 9 Nov. 1989. *Ninth Census of the United States*, 1870; *Topeka Daily Commonwealth*, 26 Feb. 1871, p. 4, col. 2.

11. Boyle, *Words*, 22–23, 93. A document in the biographical file of the Kansas Historical Society reveals that in 1892 D. J. Evans, former superintendent of schools, was employed by the U.S. Navy Department in Washington, D.C.

12. At least two women artists were daughters of Confederate soldiers: Marietta Andrews and Anne Goldthwaite. See Appendix B.

13. Allender's marriage presumably ended in divorce or annulment after her husband abandoned her. O'Neill was divorced at least once, Alexander King, "Profiles: Kewpie Doll," *New Yorker* 10 (24 Nov. 1934), 22–23; *Notable American Women, 1607–1950*, 2:650.

14. William D. Barry, "Women Pioneers in Maine Art," in Alicia Faxon and Sylvia Moore, eds., *Pilgrims and Pioneers*, 47.

15. Mary E. Barker Rogers, "Down East" (Patten, ME: unpublished manuscript, n.d.), 135. Courtesy of Susanne MacLean Boone.

16. [Lou Rogers], "Lightning Speed Through Life," *Nation* 124 (13 Apr. 1927), 396.

17. Farnsworth Art Museum, Ida Proper Collection.

18. "Suffragist Painter and Sculptor Strike Out for Themselves as Exhibitors of Their Work," *New York Evening Sun*, 26 Dec. 1912. "News and Notes of the Art World," *New York Times*, 22 Dec. 1912, Sec. 5, p. 15, col. 2; Another review described her style as "an excellent success," "delightful," where "the whimsical is not obtrusive . . . , but there is enough of it to keep banality at a comfortable distance." "Art at Home and Abroad," *New York Times*, 29 Mar. 1914, p. 11.

19. Rogers, "Lightning Speed," 397.

20. "Heterodoxy to Marie" Inez Haynes Irwin Papers, Schlesinger Library, Radcliffe College, 17–59.

21. "The Campaign in New Jersey," *Woman Voter* 6 (Dec. 1915): 10.

22. "Suffrage Cartoons for Street Crowds," *New York Times*, 19 July 1915, p. 7, col. 5.

23. Pauline Ames Plimpton to author, 21 May 1986.

24. William H. Taft, "Votes for Women," *Saturday Evening Post*, 188 (11 Sept. 1915): 5.

25. Boyle, *Words*, 21.

26. Nina Allender to Margaret Foley, ca. July 1912, Margaret Foley Papers, Schlesinger Library, Radcliffe College.

27. Nina Allender to Margaret Foley, ca. Dec. 1912, Schlesinger Library, Radcliffe College.

28. "Cartooning for Suffrage," *Suffragist* 6 (2 Mar. 1918): 8.

29. Diana Korzenik, "The Art Education of Working Women 1873–1903," in Faxon and Moore, eds. *Pilgrims and Pioneers*, 33.

30. Rogers, "Lightning Speed," 396.

31. Lawrence Campbell to author, 30 June 1986.

32. Lawrence Campbell to author, 2 Oct. 1986. See also Marchal Landgren, *Years of Art*.

33. *Notable American Women, 1607–1950*, s.v. "Preston, May Wilson," 3:99; Rubinstein, *American Women Artists*, 166.

34. *McGraw-Hill Dictionary of Art*, s.v. "Obrist, Hermann," 4:236. She also studied with Walter Thor and Wilhelm von Debochitz.

35. Other Paris teachers included Raphael Collin, Claudio Castelucho, and René Prinet, *Woman's Who's Who of America*, s.v. "Proper, Ida Sedgwick." Ida Proper Collection, William A. Farnsworth Library and Art Museum.

36. *Dictionary of Women Artists*; Ness and Orwig, *Iowa Artists*; *Woman's Who's Who*.

37. The name Nina Evans was listed in 1889. Katherine Kovacs to author, 18 Feb. 1987. "At the Art School." Newspaper clipping in Corcoran Archives, 1889–1890. Women students earned the prize for the first four years. (see Appendix B).

38. Cheryl Liebold telephone conversation with author, 2 Oct. 1990. The Pennsylvania Academy of the Fine Arts launched the careers of Mary Cassatt, Alice Barber Stephens, and Cecilia Beaux. *The Pennsylvania Academy and its Women, 1850–1920*.

39. *In This Academy*, 209–211. Boyle, *Words*, 20–21.

40. *Notable American Women, 1607–1950*, s.v. "O'Neill, Rose Cecil," 2:650–651; Shelley Armitage conversation with author, 4 Nov. 1989. The Artists' Suffrage League and Suffrage Atelier in England had published many posters by this time, see Tickner, *Spectacle of Women*.

41. Lucy Shelton Caswell, "Edwina Dumm: Pioneer Woman Editorial Cartoonist, 1915–1917," *Journalism History* 15 (Spring 1988): 2–7.

42. Erik Erikson, *Childhood and Society*, 266–68.

43. Inez Haynes Irwin, *Story of the Woman's Party*, 20.

44. "Cartooning for Suffrage," *Suffragist* 6 (2 Mar. 1918):10.

45. Jennette A. S. Jeffrey to Blanche Ames, 22 Apr. 1915, Blanche Ames Collection, Schlesinger Library, Radcliffe College.

46. Individual scrapbooks were given to the Sophia Smith Collection at Smith College and Schlesinger Library, Radcliffe.

47. "Mrs. Oakes Ames of North Easton Hostess," *Brockton Times*, 14 Jan. 1915. Blanche Ames Collection, Schlesinger Library, Radcliffe College.

48. The exhibition included paintings by her former Seattle teacher, Jessie Fisken.

49. *Woman's Who's Who*, s.v., "Ida Sedgwick Proper." *Annual Report of the New York State Woman Suffrage Association*, 65. Vera Boarman Whitehouse Collection, Schlesinger Library, Radcliffe College.

50. "A Dozen of the Most Distinguished Illustrators in the World and Every One of Them American," *Vanity Fair* 4 (Aug. 1915): 28–29.

51. *Notable American Women, 1607–1950*, s.v. "Preston, May Wilson," 3:99. Rubinstein, *American Women Artists*, 166.

52. An enigmatic note in the Farnsworth collection explained that the war had done something to her spirit, causing her to store her canvases in an attic and rarely attempt to paint.

53. Ida Proper to Mrs. Fuller, c. 1932. Courtesy Maine Author Collection, Maine State Library.

54. See Trina Robbins and Catherine Yronwode, *Women and the Comics*, 33–36.

55. Examples of Ames' paintings are preserved at the site, while some of her cartoon originals are found at her alma mater, Smith College. Nina Allender's suffrage art is maintained by the National Woman's Party in its Washington, D.C. offices. A small collection of Proper's paintings, though not including her suffrage art, is found at the Farnsworth Library and Art Museum in Rockland, Maine.

Chapter 5

1. See Kraditor, *Ideas of the Woman Suffrage Movement*, 43–52, for an analysis of the historical shifts in justification and Porter, *History of Suffrage*. The origin of these principles is discussed in Olive Banks, *Faces of Feminism*,

where she traces the dual influence of evangelicalism and the Enlightenment in nineteenth-century feminism.

2. See Dennis E. Curtis and Judith Resnik, "Images of Justice." *Yale Law Review*, 96 (1987): 1727–72.

3. "Another Inaugural Ceremony." *Judge*, 64 (1 Mar. 1913).

4. For the development of Uncle Sam see Morgan, *An American Icon* and Ketchum, *Uncle Sam*.

5. Charles Barnard, "The Bartholdi Statue," *St. Nicholas* 11 (1884), 725–32.

6. Warner, *Monuments and Maidens*, 250–51.

7. Warner, *Monuments and Maidens*, 250, 281; Ripa, *Iconologia*, 1603 ed., 63–64.

8. For the portrayal of bare feet in art see H. W. Janson, *History of Art*, 54, 133.

9. Although cartoons drawn by women are emphasized in this discussion, cartoons by men are included as a supplement or contrast to women's images. Men's cartoons were often found in the suffrage press, attesting largely to conviction, but perhaps further encouraged by their wives.

10. Published in the *Maryland Suffrage News*, this cartoon may have been drawn by May Florence Gelletly, a cartoonist active in the Baltimore area. See *Dictionary of Women Artists*, s.v. "Gelletly, May Florence."

11. Kraditor, *Ideas of the Woman Suffrage Movement*, 45–46.

12. "141 Men and Girls Die in Waist Factory Fire," *New York Times*, 26 Mar. 1911, 1. Kraditor, *Ideas of the Woman Suffrage Movement*, 155; Patricia Hills, "John Sloan's Images of Working-Class Women," *Prospects* 5 (1980): 167, reported that over 150 died.

13. Thomas Nast, (cartoon), *Harper's Weekly* 25 (30 Apr. 1881).

14. Alice Sheppard, "Tactics of Persuasion: Pro-Suffrage Cartoons by American Women." Paper presented at meeting of National Women's Studies Association, Seattle, 1985.

15. Elizabeth Barrett Browning, "Now press the clarion to thy woman's lip." Tickner, *Spectacle of Women*, pl. viii, cites this as the inspiration for a suffrage Bugler Girl. In Ripa's *Iconology* ed. Richardson, 2:16, classic

symbolism is explained: "the trumpet signifies that the voice of Fame resounds like this instrument, and encourages men to imitate the virtuous."

16. Tickner, *Spectacle of Women*, 151.

17. Cott, *Grounding of Modern Feminism*, 20.

18. Housekeeping, a symbol of woman's sphere that suffragists sought to challenge, was nonetheless upheld as a symbol of feminine virtue. See Mabel Potter Daggett, "Women: The Larger Housekeeping," *The World's Work* 24 (Oct. 1912): 664–70.

19. The view of government as enlarged housekeeping was used in the nineteenth century by the Woman's Christian Temperance Union (WCTU). See Kraditor, *Ideas of the Woman Suffrage Movement*, 68.

20. The idea was repeated in photographic form, where children sought the ballot.

21. "Woman Suffrage Number," *Puck*, 77 (20 Feb. 1915): 8.

22. The National American Woman Suffrage Association supported the war effort. See Van Voris, *Carrie Chapman Catt*, 130–41.

Chapter 6

1. See Tickner, *Spectacle of Women*, 153.

2. Kenneth E. Boulding, *The Image*, 5–6.

3. Daniel Boorstin, *The Image*, 185.

4. Tickner, *Spectacle of Women*, 163–64.

5. Flexner, *Century of Struggle*, 311, reported an association between anti-suffrage and business, especially the railroad.

6. She shares a physique and social activity with Hokinson's club women of two decades later.

7. This may be the work of Hendrik Van Loon, who supported the National Woman's Party. The name, however, was printed as "Frederick" in the *Suffragist*.

8. "Women Start League Against Suffragists." *New York Times*, 14 May 1908, p. 8, col. 7. Lyman Abbott, "Why the Vote Would Be Injurious to Women," 21–22.

9. See Kate Douglas Wiggin, *Rebecca of Sunnybrook Farm.*

10. In her original drawing, Ames offered the caption "The Dog Gives Them Away." See *Woman's Journal* 46 (2 Oct. 1915):314, for a discussion of Reardon's role.

11. Brewers attempted to conceal their financial efforts against suffrage, but a 1918 Senate Judiciary Committee report on pro-German and Bolshevik propaganda disclosed their involvement. See Flexner, *Century of Struggle,* 307.

12. U.S. Bureau of the Census, *Statistics of Women at Work,* 32.

13. "City Tie-Up Strike Gets New Backing," *New York Times,* 19 Aug. 1915, p. 9, col. 6; "Show We Depend on Working Women," *New York Times,* 22 Aug. 1915, p. 4, col. 8.

14. "Woman's Place in the World," *Woman Voter* 6 (Oct. 1915): 16–17.

15. Daniel Parker Livermore, *Woman Suffrage Defended,* 121–38.

16. Alice Stone Blackwell, "Objections Answered" in Bjorkman, ed., *Woman Suffrage,* 171, 173.

17. The reversal in male and female size was a device utilized by Marietta Holley, whose turn-of-the-century humor books promoted woman's rights. See Jane Curry, ed., *Samantha Rastles the Woman Question.*

18. "Modern Representative Government" was printed in Brooklyn for the Woman Suffrage Party and used as a suffrage flier. Sophia Smith Collection.

19. Blackwell, "Objections Answered," 186, 189, 207.

20. Blackwell, "Objections Answered," 178, 191.

21. Blackwell, "Objections Answered," 192.

22. Blackwell, "Objections Answered," 195, 202, 207.

23. Lou Rogers, "American Chivalry in Perfect Flower," (cartoon), *Judge* 68 (15 May 1915).

Chapter 7

1. Some suffrage artists created drawings that were realistic and relied on conventions of illustration rather than cartooning. Their work represented events and situations with little use of symbolism. Others incorporated

allegorical figures (angels, Liberty, Justice, Democracy), seeking to inspire faith in women's mission rather than to interpret political conditions. For posters featuring these graphic forms, see Paula Hays Harper, "Votes for Women? A Graphic Episode in the Battle of the Sexes," in Henry A. Millon and Linda Nochlin, eds. *Art and Architecture in the Service of Politics*, 150–61.

2. Freud assumed this to reflect primary process thought characteristic of the unconscious mind. See Sigmund Freud, *The Standard Edition of the Complete Psychological Works of Sigmund Freud*, especially 22: 74–75.

3. Gombrich, "The Cartoonist's Armoury," (see chap. 1., n. 7), 136–38.

4. Irwin, *Story of the Woman's Party*, 133–43.

5. See Tickner, *Spectacle of Women*, 209, for a discussion of Joan of Arc as "archetypal Militant." Marina Warner, *Monuments and Maidens*, 147, 164–65. A sculpture of Joan of Arc was photographed for the cover of the *Suffragist* 4 (4 Apr. 1916).

6. Lou Rogers, "If Lincoln were Alive" (cartoon), *Judge* 66 (20 June 1914).

7. Howard D. Hadley, "The Woman's Party and the Presidential Campaign," *National Magazine* 44 (July 1916): 562.

8. Irwin, *Story of the Woman's Party*, 164.

9. Irwin, *Story of the Woman's Party*, 56.

10. Gombrich, "Cartoonist's Armoury," (see chap. 1, n. 7), 138–39.

11. See Tickner, *Spectacle of Women*, 16–18, for a discussion of the British poster by this title.

12. J. E. Murphy, "Famous Characters of the Cartoonists," *Cartoons* 3 (Feb. 1913): 84.

13. Following establishment of the Woman's Party, Irwin, *Story of the Woman's Party*, 163, wrote: "Newspaper cartoonists began to introduce the new Party into their pictures. Alice Paul in the figure of a little deer, big-eyed and wistful, stood timidly among a group which included the elephant, the donkey and the bull moose."

14. "Lou Rogers—Cartoonist," *Woman's Journal* 44 (2 Aug. 1913): 243.

15. Rogers seemed to discover that a woman with a cat (indirect influence) was a more flexible symbol than the turtle of anti-suffrage.

16. See Thomas Nast's front page cartoon, "The Democratic Camel" (cartoon), *Harper's Weekly* 22 (8 June 1878). One suffrage cartoonist, Edwina Dumm, used the camel for Prohibition. See Edwina Dumm, "Ring Around a Rosy," (figure 1.17) *Columbus Monitor*, (7 Dec. 1916).

Chapter 8

1. T. E. Perkins, "Rethinking Stereotypes," In British Sociological Association, eds, *Ideology and Cultural Production*, 148.

2. Ernest Earnest, *American Eve in Fact and Fiction*, 1.

3. Earnest, *American Eve*, 62.

4. Earnest, *American Eve*, 208.

5. Fryer, *Faces of Eve*, 24–25.

6. Banta, *Imaging American Women*, 46.

7. Stephen Gould, *Mismeasure of Man*; Roberta Frankfort, *Collegiate Women*.

8. A number of early women leaders were indeed married, including Lucretia Mott, Amelia Bloomer, Lucy Stone, and Elizabeth Cady Stanton. Mrs. Stanton raised seven children, see Elisabeth Griffith, *In Her Own Right: The Life of Elizabeth Cady Stanton*.

9. Oliver Jensen, *Revolt of American Women*, 47.

10. William Frauenglass demonstrated that the number of jokes concerning suffrage had declined strikingly by 1918, shortly before passage of the Nineteenth Amendment. See William Frauenglass, "Attitudes Toward Woman Suffrage" (chap. 3. n. 64) 129.

11. Robinson, of liberal views himself, was most likely influenced by his wife, Sally Whitney, who studied with Rodin in turn-of-the-century Paris, see Albert Christ-Janer, *Boardman Robinson*, 9–10. As Mrs. Boardman Robinson she was later associated with New York City's feminist Heterodoxy Club. See Judith Schwarz, *Radical Feminists of Heterodoxy*, 124.

12. British suffrage artists relied on a Mrs. John Bull figure in much the same way. See Tickner, *Spectacle of Women*, 17, 31, 39.

13. Tickner, *Spectacle of Women*, 216, 167.

14. La Touche Hancock, "American Caricature and Comic Art," Part 2. *Bookman* 16 (1902): 268. One wonders whether the editors of *Cartoons Magazine* were committed to women's advance or exploiting women cartoonists as novelties.

15. Because Americans did not posit a category of "sweated labor" as did the British, it is appropriate to group women's employment, a fact which may have encouraged aspiring women professionals of Greenwich Village to identify with factory workers on the Lower East Side.

16. U.S. Bureau of the Census, *Statistics of Women at Work,* 32.

17. This portrayal gave rise to the image of the "unteachable" donkey. "Cartooning for Suffrage." (See chap. 4, n. 44).

Chapter 9

1. See Bettina Friedl, *On to Victory,* for a collection of suffrage plays.

2. "'The Suffragist' as a Publicity Medium," *Suffragist* 6 (23 Feb. 1918): 9.

3. Marshall B. Davidson, *Drawing of America,* 214.

4. For example, the cartoon women categorized as *glamorous, matronly,* and *lifelike* by Katherine Meyer, John Seidler, Timothy Curry, and Adrian Aveni, "Women in July Fourth Cartoons: A 100–Year Look." *Journal of Communication* 30 (1980): 21–30.

5. Patricia Hills reported that Sloan's wife, Dolly, was the model for the suffragist in "She's Got the Point." See Patricia Hills, "John Sloan's Images of Working-Class Women," *Prospects* 5 (1980): 168.

6. Reprinted in the *Woman Voter* 4 (Sept. 1913): 7.

7. Hills, "John Sloan's Images," 176, 168. She described Sloan's women as "embodiments of innocence removed from the 'class struggle,'" 189.

8. Tickner, *Spectacle of Women,* 220.

9. Tickner, *Spectacle of Women,* 220.

10. George W. Kelling, "An Empirical Investigation of Freud's Theory of Jokes," *Psychoanalytic Review* 58 (1971): 477.

11. Warner, *Monuments and Maidens,* 174.

12. Nineteenth-century women were classified into two types: chaste and

unchaste, Floyd Dell, *Love in the Machine Age*, 169. Chaperoning of young women was designed to protect their purity and to prevent contamination of virtuous women by the immoral types. Ray Strachey asserted that the system really functioned to protect men's "honour," in Gillett, *Worlds of Art*, 156. Suffragists, of course, upheld women's virtue as an argument for the ballot; antis pointed out that prostitutes would vote.

13. Porter, *History of Suffrage*, 239.

14. E. P. Richardson, *Painting in America*, 390–91.

15. *New York World*, 10 June 1906, quoted in Bennard B. Perlman, *The Immortal Eight*, 196.

16. Zurier, *Art for the Masses*, 135, 138.

17. Zurier, *Art for the Masses*, 127.

18. See Tickner, *Spectacle of Women*, for the history and role of the Artists' Suffrage League and the Suffrage Atelier in England.

19. For a different viewpoint see Paula Hays Harper, "Votes for Women?" (See chap. 7, n. 1). Her analysis overlooks the fact that the posters by Ames and O'Neill she examined were published as small printed cartoons.

20. Gillett, *Worlds of Art*, 140.

21. Mary E. Barker Rogers, "Down East" (see chap. 4, n. 15), 131. Courtesy Susanne MacLean Boone.

22. Rosenberg, *Beyond Separate Spheres*, 54.

23. Erikson, *Childhood and Society*, 266–68.

24. See Cott, *Grounding of Modern Feminism*, 13–15. The term *suffragette* was used little by activists in the United States. See William L. O'Neill, *Feminism in America*, xxiii–xxiv.

25. Tickner, *Spectacle of Women*, 275. Barbara Taylor, *Eve and the New Jerusalem*, x; Mari Jo Buhle, *Women and American Socialism*, 290; Cott, *Grounding of Modern Feminism*, 14.

26. In Buhle, *Women and American Socialism*, 290, after Edna Kenton, "Edna Kenton Says Feminists Will Give—." *Delineator* 85 (July 1914): 17.

27. Kenton, "The Militant Women—and Women." *Century* 87 (Nov. 1913): 15.

28. Beatrice Forbes-Robertson Hale, *What Women Want*, 184.

29. Marie Jenney Howe, "Feminism," *New Review* 2 (Aug. 1914): 441.

30. June Sochen, *The New Woman,* 5.

31. Schwarz, *Radical Feminists of Heterodoxy,* 28.

32. Buhle, *Women and American Socialism,* 292.

33. Cott, *Grounding of Modern Feminism,* 4–5.

34. Cott, *Grounding of Modern Feminism,* 5.

35. Buhle, *Women and American Socialism,* 290.

36. Crystal Eastman, "Now We Can Begin," in *On Women and Revolution,* 52–57.

Archives

Alice Marshall Collection, Camp Hill, Pa.

Corcoran Gallery, Washington, D.C.

Denver Historical Society, Denver, Colo.

Kansas Historical Society, Topeka, Kans.

Library for Journalism and Communication Arts, Columbus, Ohio, Edwina Dumm Collection.

Library of Congress, Washington, D.C., National Woman's Party Collection.

Maine State Library, Augusta, Maine, Maine Author Collection.

Pennsylvania Academy of the Fine Arts, Philadelphia, Archives.

Princeton University Library, Princeton, N.J., Miriam Holden Collection.

Schlesinger Library, Radcliffe College, Cambridge, Mass., Blanche Ames Collection, Margaret Foley Collection, Inez Haynes Irwin Collection, Alice Park Collection, Vira Boarman Whitehouse Collection, Anna Kelton Wiley Collection, Woman's Rights Collection.

Sophia Smith Collection, Smith College, Northampton, Mass., Blanche Ames Collection, Woman's Rights Collection.

Periodicals

Birth Control Review (New York: 1917–40)

Cartoons (Chicago: 1912–20)

Judge (New York: 1881–1939)

Life (New York: 1883–1936)

Maryland Suffrage News (Baltimore: 1912–20)

The Masses (New York: 1911–17)

Puck (New York: 1877–1918)

Suffragist (Washington, D.C.: 1913–21)

Woman Citizen (New York: 1917–27)

Woman's Journal (Boston: 1870–1917)

Woman Voter (New York: 1910–17)

Select Bibliography

Books

Adams, Charles Francis, ed. *Familiar Letters of John Adams and his Wife Abigail Adams during the Revolution.* New York: Hurd and Houghton, 1876.

Allgemeines Lexikon der Bildenden Künstler von der Antike bis zur Gegenwart. Edited by Ulrich Thieme and Felix Becker. 37 vols. 1915. Reprint 1965.

The American Magazine, 1890–1940. Exhibition Catalogue. Edited by Dorey Schmidt. Wilmington, Del.: Delaware Art Museum, 1979.

The American Presidency in Political Cartoons 1776–1976. Edited by Thomas C. Blaisdell, Jr., Peter Selz, and Seminar. Rev. Ed. Salt Lake City: Peregrine Smith, 1976.

Ames, Blanche Butler, ed. *Chronicles from the Nineteenth Century: Family Letters of Blanche Butler and Adelbert Ames,* 2 vols. Clinton, Mass.: Colonial Press, 1957.

Andrews, Marietta Minnigerode. *My Studio Window.* New York: E. P. Dutton, 1928.

Artists of the American West: A Biographical Dictionary. Edited by Doris Ostrander Dawdy. 3 vols. Chicago: Sage, 1974–1985.

Banks, Olive. *Faces of Feminism: A Study of Feminism as a Social Movement.* New York: Basil Blackwell, 1986.

Banta, Martha. *Imaging American Women: Idea and Ideals in Cultural History.* New York: Columbia University Press, 1987.

Baudelaire, Charles Pierre. *Oeuvres Complètes.* 1868. Rev. ed. Paris: Gallimard, 1961.

Beeton, Beverly. *Women Vote in the West: The Woman Suffrage Movement, 1869–1896.* New York: Garland Publishing, 1986.

Benjamin, Anne M. *A History of the Anti-Suffrage Movement in the United States From 1895 to 1920: Women Against Equality.* Lewiston, N.Y.: Edwin Mellen Press, 1991.

Bergson, Henri. *Laughter: An Essay on the Meaning of the Comic.* Translated by Cloudesley Brereton and Fred Rothwell. New York: Macmillan, 1911.

Bernard, Jessie. *The Female World*. New York: Free Press, 1981.

Bier, Jesse. *The Rise and Fall of American Humor*. New York: Holt, Rinehart, and Winston, 1968.

Bjorkman, Frances Maule, ed. *Woman Suffrage: History, Arguments, and Results*. New York: National American Woman Suffrage Association, 1913.

Blair, Karen J. *The Clubwoman as Feminist: True Womanhood Redefined, 1868–1914*. New York: Holmes and Meier, 1980.

Blair, Walter. *Native American Humor*. 1937. Reprint. San Francisco: Chandler, 1960.

Boorstin, Daniel. *The Image: A Guide to Pseudo-Events in America*. 1961. Reprint. New York: Atheneum, 1975.

Boulding, Kenneth E. *The Image: Knowledge in Life and Society*. Ann Arbor: University of Michigan Press, 1956.

Boyle, Kay. *Words that Must Somehow Be Said*. Edited by Elizabeth S. Bell. San Francisco: North Point Press, 1985.

British Sociological Association. *Ideology and Cultural Production*. Edited by Michele Barrett, Philip Corrigan, Annette Kuhn, and Janet Wolf. New York: St. Martin's, 1979.

Brooks, Van Wyck. *John Sloan: A Painter's Life*. New York: E. P. Dutton, 1955.

Bruère, Martha Bensley, and Mary Ritter Beard, eds. *Laughing Their Way: Women's Humor in America*. New York: Macmillan, 1934.

Buechler, Steven M. *The Transformation of the Woman Suffrage Movement: The Case of Illinois, 1850–1920*. New Brunswick, N.J.: Rutgers University Press, 1986.

Buhle, Mari Jo. *Women and American Socialism, 1870–1920*. Urbana: University of Illinois, 1981.

Bushnell, Horace. *Women's Suffrage: The Reform Against Nature*. New York: C. Scribner, 1869.

Callen, Anthea. *Women Artists of the Arts and Crafts Movement, 1870–1914*. New York: Pantheon, 1979.

Campbell, Mary, and Gordon Campbell. *The Pen, Not the Sword*. Nashville: Aurora, 1970.

Canemaker, John. *Winsor McCay, His Life and Art*. New York: Abbeville, 1987.

Catt, Carrie Chapman, and Nettie Rogers Shuler. *Woman Suffrage and Politics: The Inner Story of the Suffrage Movement*. New York: C. Scribner's Sons, 1923.

Charlesworth, Hector. *The Canadian Scene; Sketches: Political and Historical*. Toronto: Macmillan, 1927.

Christ-Janer, Albert. *Boardman Robinson*. Chicago: University of Chicago Press, 1946.

Christy, Howard Chandler. *Liberty Belles*. Indianapolis: Bobbs-Merrill, 1912.

City Life Illustrated, 1890–1940. Exhibition Catalogue. Wilmington, Del.: Delaware Art Museum, 1980.

Conference on American Culture. *Frontiers of American Culture*. Edited by Ray B. Browne, Richard H. Crowder, Virgil L. Lokke, and William T. Stafford. West Lafayette, Ind.: Purdue University Studies, 1968.

Coolidge, Mary Roberts. *Why Women Are So*. New York: Henry Holt, 1912.

Cott, Nancy F. *The Bonds of Womanhood: "Woman's Sphere" in New England, 1780–1835*. New Haven: Yale University Press, 1977.

————. *The Grounding of Modern Feminism*. New Haven: Yale University Press, 1987.

Crane, Bonnie L. *Blanche Ames: Artist and Activist*. Exhibition Catalogue. Brockton, Mass.: Brockton Art Museum, 1982.

Crane, Walter. *Cartoons for the Cause: Designs and Verses for the Socialist and Labour Movement, 1886–1896*. 1896. Reprint. London: Journeyman Press, 1976.

Crouse, Russel. *Mr. Currier and Mr. Ives: A Note on their Lives and Times*. Garden City, N.Y.: Garden City Publishing, 1930.

Curry, Jane, ed. *Samantha Rastles the Woman Question*. Urbana: University of Illinois Press, 1983.

[Cutler, William G., ed.] *History of the State of Kansas.* Chicago: A. T. Andreas, 1883.

Davidson, Marshall B. *The Drawing of America: Eyewitnesses to History.* New York: Abrams, 1983.

Dell, Floyd. *Love in the Machine Age: A Psychological Study of the Transition from Patriarchal Society.* New York: Farrar and Rinehart, 1930.

Dictionary of Canadian Biography. Edited by W. Stewart Wallace. Toronto: Macmillan, 1945.

Dictionary of Women Artists: An International Dictionary of Women Artists Born Before 1900. Edited by Chris Petteys. Boston: G. K. Hall, 1985.

Dictionnaire critique et documentaire des peintres, sculpteurs, dessinateurs et graveurs de tous les temps et de tous les pays. Edited by Emmanuel Bénézit. 10 vols. Nouv. ed. Paris: Grund, 1976.

DuBois, Ellen Carol. *Feminism and Suffrage: The Emergence of an Independent Women's Movement in America, 1848–1869.* Ithaca, N.Y.: Cornell University Press, 1978.

Earnest, Ernest. *The American Eve in Fact and Fiction, 1775–1914.* Urbana: University of Illinois Press, 1974.

Eastman, Crystal. *Crystal Eastman On Women and Revolution.* Edited by Blanche Weisen Cook. New York: Oxford University Press, 1978.

Eastman, Max. *Enjoyment of Living.* New York: Harper and Bros., 1948.

Encyclopedia of World Art. New York: McGraw-Hill, 1959–1987.

Erikson, Erik H. *Childhood and Society.* 2d ed. rev. New York: W. W. Norton, 1963.

Faxon, Alicia, and Sylvia Moore, eds. *Pilgrims and Pioneers: New England Women in the Arts.* New York: Midmarch Arts Press, 1987.

Ferrante, Joan M. *Woman as Image in Medieval Literature, from the Twelfth Century to Dante.* New York: Columbia University Press, 1975.

Fink, Lois Marie. *American Art at the Nineteenth-Century Paris Salons.* New York: Cambridge University Press, 1990.

Bibliography

Fischer, Katrina Sigsbee. *Anton Otto Fischer, Marine Artist: His Life and Work.* Brighton, England: Teredo Books, 1977.

Fitzgerald, Richard A. *Art and Politics: Cartoonists of the Masses and Liberator.* Westport, Conn.: Greenwood Press, 1973.

Flexner, Eleanor. *Century of Struggle: The Woman's Rights Movement in the United States.* 1959. Rev. ed. Cambridge, Mass.: Harvard University Press, Belknap Press, 1975.

Foreign Policy Association. *A Cartoon History of United States Foreign Policy: 1776–1976.* New York: William Morrow, 1975.

Frankfort, Roberta. *Collegiate Women: Domesticity and Career in Turn-of-the-Century America.* New York: New York University Press, 1977.

Franzen, Monika, and Nancy Ethiel, comps. *Make Way! 200 Years of American Women in Cartoons.* Chicago: Chicago Review Press, 1988.

Freud, Sigmund. *Jokes and their Relation to the Unconscious.* Translated by James Strachey. New York: W. W. Norton, 1960.

————. *The Standard Edition of the Complete Psychological Works of Sigmund Freud.* 24 vols. Translated by James Strachey. London: Hogarth Press, 1953–1974.

Friedl, Bettina, ed. *On to Victory: Propaganda Plays of the Woman Suffrage Movement.* Boston: Northeastern University Press, 1987.

Fry, William F., Jr. *Sweet Madness: A Study of Humor.* Palo Alto, Calif.: Pacific Books, 1963.

Fryer, Judith. *The Faces of Eve: Women in the Nineteenth Century American Novel.* New York: Oxford University Press, 1976.

Garrison, Dee. *Mary Heaton Vorse: The Life of an American Insurgent.* Philadelphia: Temple University Press, 1989.

Geipel, John. *The Cartoon: A Short History of Graphic Comedy and Satire.* Cranbury, N.J.: Barnes, 1972.

George, M. Dorothy. *English Political Caricature: A Study of Opinion and Propaganda.* 2 vols. Oxford: Clarendon Press, 1959.

Getlein, Frank, and Dorothy Getlein. *The Bite of the Print: Satire and Irony in Woodcuts, Engravings, Etchings, Lithographs and Serigraphs*. New York: C. N. Potter, 1963.

Gibson, Charles Dana. *The Weaker Sex*. New York: Scribner, 1903.

Gillett, Paula. *Worlds of Art: Painters in Victorian Society*. New Brunswick, N.J.: Rutgers University Press, 1990.

Godfrey, Richard T. *Printmaking in Britain*. New York: New York University Press, 1978.

Gombrich, E. H. *Meditations on a Hobby Horse, and Other Essays on the Theory of Art*. London: Phaidon, 1963.

Gordon, Felice D. *After Winning: The Legacy of the New Jersey Suffragists, 1920–1947*. New Brunswick, N.J.: Rutgers University Press, 1986.

Gould, Carol C., and Marx W. Wartofsky, eds. *Women and Philosophy: Toward a Theory of Liberation*. New York: Putnam, Capricorn, 1976.

Gould, Stephen. *The Mismeasure of Man*. New York: W. W. Norton, 1981.

Griffith, Elisabeth. *In Her Own Right: The Life of Elizabeth Cady Stanton*. New York: Oxford University Press, 1984.

Grotjahn, Martin. *Beyond Laughter: Humor and the Subconscious*. New York: McGraw-Hill, 1957.

———. *The Voice of the Symbol*. New York: Dell, 1971.

Hale, Beatrice Forbes-Robertson. *What Women Want: An Interpretation of the Feminist Movement*. New York: Frederick A. Stokes, 1914.

Hamilton, Sinclair. *Early American Book Illustrators and Wood Engravers, 1670–1870*. Princeton, N.J.: Princeton University Library, 1958.

Hanaford, Phebe A. *Daughters of America: Or, Women of the Century*. Augusta, Maine: True, 1882.

Hess, Stephen, and Milton Kaplan. *The Ungentlemanly Art: A History of American Political Cartoons*. Rev. ed. New York: Macmillan, 1975.

Hewitt, Nancy A. *Women's Activism and Social Change*. Ithaca, N.Y.: Cornell University Press, 1984.

Hill, Draper, ed. *The Satirical Etchings of James Gillray*. New York: Dover, 1976.

Bibliography

Him. *How It Feels to the the Husband of a Suffragette.* 1914. Reprint. New York: George H. Doran, 1915.

History of Penobscot County, Maine. Cleveland: Williams, Chase, 1882.

History of Woman Suffrage. Vols. 1–3 edited by Elizabeth Cady Stanton, Susan B. Anthony, and Matilda Joselyn Gage, Rochester, N.Y.: Anthony, 1881–1886. Vol. 4 edited by Susan B. Anthony and Ida Husted Harper. Rochester, N.Y.: Anthony, 1902. Vols. 5–6 edited by Ida Husted Harper. New York: National American Woman Suffrage Association, 1922.

Hogben, Lancelot Thomas. *From Cave Painting to Comic Strip: A Kaleidoscope of Human Communication.* New York: Chanticleer Press, 1949.

Hoff, Syd. *Editorial and Political Cartooning: From Earliest Times to the Present.* New York: Stravon Educational Press, 1976.

Illustrators of Children's Books, 1744–1976. Edited by Bertha E. Miller et al. 4 vols. Boston: Horn, 1948–1978.

The Image of America in Caricature and Cartoon. Fort Worth: Amon Carter Museum, 1975.

In This Academy: The Pennsylvania Academy of the Fine Arts, 1805–1976. Exhibition Catalogue. Washington, D.C.: Museum Press, 1976.

Inge, M. Thomas. *Comics as Culture.* Jackson, Miss.: University Press of Mississippi, 1990.

Irwin, Inez Haynes. *The Story of the Woman's Party.* New York: Harcourt, Brace, 1921.

Janson, H. W. *History of Art.* 2d ed. New York: Abrams, 1977.

Jensen, Oliver. *The Revolt of American Women.* 1952. Reprint. New York: Harcourt Brace Jovanovich, 1971.

Jung, Carl G. *Four Archetypes: Mother, Rebirth, Spirit, Trickster.* Translated by R. F. C. Hull. Princeton, N.J.: Princeton University Press, 1969.

Katzenstein, Caroline. *Lifting the Curtain: The State and National Woman Suffrage Campaigns in Pennsylvania as I Saw Them.* Philadelphia: Dorrance, 1955.

Keller, Morton. *The Art and Politics of Thomas Nast.* New York: Oxford University Press, 1968.

Kenney, Elise K., and John M. Merriman. *The Pear: French Graphic Arts in the Golden Age of Caricature.* Exhibition Catalogue. South Hadley, Mass.: Mount Holyoke College Art Museum, 1991.

Kessler-Harris, Alice. *Out to Work: A History of Wage-Earning Women in the United States.* New York: Oxford University Press, 1982.

Ketchum, Alton. *Uncle Sam: The Man and the Legend.* New York: Hill and Wang, 1959.

Knittle, Walter A. *Early Eighteenth Century Palatine Emigration.* Philadelphia: Dorrance, 1937.

Kolodny, Annette. *The Lay of the Land: Metaphor as Experience and History in American Life and Letters.* Chapel Hill: University of North Carolina Press, 1975.

Korzenik, Diana. *Drawn to Art: A Nineteenth-Century American Dream.* Hanover, N.H.: University Press of New England, 1985.

Kraditor, Aileen S. *The Ideas of the Woman Suffrage Movement, 1890–1920.* 1965. Rev. ed. New York: W. W. Norton, 1981.

Kunzle, David. *The Early Comic Strip: Narrative Strips and Picture Stories in the European Broadsheet from c. 1450 to 1825.* Berkeley: University of California Press, 1973.

Landgren, Marchal. *Years of Art: The Story of the Art Students League of New York.* New York: McBride, 1940.

Lefkowitz, Mary R. *Women in Greek Myth.* Baltimore: Johns Hopkins University Press, 1986.

Livermore, Daniel Parker. *Woman Suffrage Defended by Irrefutable Arguments, and All Objections to Women's Enfranchisement Carefully Examined and Completely Answered.* Boston: Lee and Shepard, 1885.

Logan, Mary S. *The Part Taken by Women in American History.* Wilmington, Del.: Perry-Nalle, 1912. Reprint. New York: Arno Press, 1972.

Lunardini, Christine A. *From Equal Suffrage to Equal Rights.* New York: New York University Press, 1986.

Mantle Fielding's Dictionary of American Painters, Sculptors, and Engravers. 2d ed. rev. Edited by Glenn B. Opitz. Poughkeepsie, N.Y.: Apollo, 1986.

Marks, Patricia. *Bicycles, Bangs, and Bloomers: The New Woman in the Popular Press.* Lexington, Ky.: University Press of Kentucky, 1990.

Maurice, Arthur Bartlett, and Frederic Taber Cooper. *The History of the Nineteenth Century in Caricature.* 1904. Reprint. New York: Cooper Square, 1970.

Millon, Henry A. and Linda Nochlin, eds. *Art and Architecture in the Service of Politics.* Cambridge, Mass.: MIT Press, 1978.

Milner, John. *The Studios of Paris: The Capitol of Art in the Late Nineteenth Century.* New Haven: Yale University Press, 1988.

Morello, Karen Berger. *The Invisible Bar: The Woman Lawyer in American 1638 to the Present.* New York: Random House, 1986.

Morgan, Winifred. *An American Icon: Brother Jonathan and American Identity.* Newark: University of Delaware Press, 1988.

Mott, Frank Luther. *A History of American Magazines.* 5 vols. Cambridge, Mass.: Harvard University Press, Belknap Press, 1957, 1968.

Murrell, William. *A History of American Graphic Humor.* 2 vols., New York: Macmillan, 1938.

National Woman's Party Papers: The Suffrage Years 1913–1920. Guide to the Microfilm Edition, ed. Donald L. Haggerty. Sanford, N.C.: Microfilming Corporation of America, 1981. Microfilm.

Ness, Zenobia, and Louise Orwig. *Iowa Artists of the First Hundred Years.* Des Moines: Wallace-Homestead Co., 1939.

Neumann, Erich. *The Great Mother: An Analysis of the Archetype.* Translated by Ralph Manheim. 2nd ed. Princeton: Princeton University Press, Bollingen, 1963.

———. *The Origins and History of Consciousness.* Translated by R. F. H. Hull. New York: Pantheon, Bollingen, 1954.

Notable American Women, 1607–1950. Edited by Edward T. James, Janet Wilson James, and Paul S. Boyer. 3 vols. Cambridge, Mass.: Harvard University Press, Belknap Press, 1971.

O'Neill, William L. *Feminism in America: A History.* 2nd ed. rev. New Brunswick, N.J.: Transaction Books, 1989.

O'Sullivan, Judith. *The Great American Comic Strip: One Hundred Years of Cartoon Art.* Boston: Little, Brown, Bulfinch Press, 1990.

Paine, Albert B. *Thomas Nast: His Period and His Pictures.* 1904. Reprint. New York: Chelsea, 1980.

Papachristou, Judith. *Women Together: A History in Documents of the Women's Movement in the United States.* New York: Knopf, 1976.

The Pennsylvania Academy and its Women, 1850–1920. Exhibition Catalogue. Philadelphia: Pennsylvania Academy of the Fine Arts, 1974.

Perlman, Bennard B. *The Immortal Eight: American Painting from Eakins to the Armory Show (1870–1913).* 1962. Reprint. Cincinnati: North Light Publishers, 1979.

Plimpton, Pauline Ames, ed. *The Ancestry of Blanche Butler Ames and Adelbert Ames.* Privately published, 1977.

Pollock, Griselda. *Vision and Difference: Femininity, Feminism, and Histories of Art.* New York: Routledge, 1988.

Porter, Kirk H. *A History of Suffrage in the United States.* Chicago: University of Chicago Press, 1918.

Powell, Kirsten, and Elizabeth C. Childs, eds. *Femmes d'esprit: Women in Daumier's Caricature.* Exhibition Catalogue. Middlebury, Vt.: Johnson Memorial Gallery, Middlebury College.

Press, Charles. *The Political Cartoon.* Rutherford, N.J.: Fairleigh Dickinson University Press, 1981.

Proper, Ida Sedgwick. *Monhegan: The Cradle of New England.* Portland, Maine: Southworth, 1930.

———. *Our Elusive Willy: A Slice of Concealed Elizabethan History.* Manchester, Maine: Dirigo, 1953.

Bibliography

Richardson, E. P. *Painting in America: The Story of 450 Years.* New York: Thomas Y. Crowell, 1956.

Ripa, Cesare. *Baroque and Rococo Pictorial Imagery: The 1758–60 Hertel Edition of Ripa's "Iconologia."* Reprint. Edited and translated by Edward A. Maser. New York: Dover, 1971.

———. *Iconologia overo descrittione di diverse imagini cavate dall' antichità, & di propria inventione.* 1603. Reprint. New York: Georg Olms, 1970.

———. *Iconology: or A Collection of Emblematical Figures.* Edited by George Richardson. 2 vols. London: G. Scott, 1779. Facsimile.

Robbins, Trina, and Catherine Yronwode. *Women and the Comics.* Gurneville, Calif.: Eclipse Books, 1985.

Rogers, Lou. *The Rise of the Red Alders.* New York: Harper and Bros., 1928.

———. *Ska-Denge (Beaver for Revenge).* New York: Harper and Bros., 1929.

Rosen, Charles, and Henri Zerner. *Romanticism and Realism: The Mythology of Nineteenth-Century Art.* New York: W. W. Norton, 1984.

Rosenberg, Rosalind. *Beyond Separate Spheres: The Intellectual Roots of Modern Feminism.* New Haven: Yale University Press, 1982.

Ross, Ishbel. *Ladies of the Press.* New York: Harper and Bros., 1936.

Roszak, Betty, and Theodore Roszak, eds. *Masculine/Feminine: Readings in Sexual Mythology and the Liberation of Women.* New York: Harper & Row, 1969.

Roylance, Dale. *American Graphic Arts.* Princeton: Princeton University Library, 1990.

Rubinstein, Charlotte Streifer. *American Women Artists: From the Indian to the Present.* Boston: G. K. Hall, 1982.

Schau, Michael. *All-American Girl: The Art of Coles Phillips.* New York: Watson-Guptill, 1975.

Schretlen, Martinus Joseph Antonius Maria. *Dutch and Flemish Woodcuts of the Fifteenth Century.* 1925. Reprint. New York: Hacker Art Books, 1969.

Schwarz, Judith. *Radical Feminists of Heterodoxy.* Rev. ed. Norwich, Vt.: New Victoria Publishers, 1986.

Shaw, Albert. *Abraham Lincoln: A Cartoon History*. 2 vols. New York: Review of Reviews, 1929.

Shikes, Ralph E. *The Indignant Eye: The Artist as Social Critic in Prints and Drawings from the Fifteenth Century to Picasso*. Boston: Beacon Press, 1969.

Showalter, Elaine, ed. *These Modern Women: Autobiographical Essays from the Twenties*. 1978. Rev. ed. New York: Feminist Press, 1989.

Sochen, June. *The New Woman: Feminism in Greenwich Village, 1910–1920*. New York: Quadrangle, 1972.

Solomon, Barbara Miller. *In the Company of Educated Women: A History of Women and Higher Education in America*. New Haven: Yale University Press, 1985.

Solomon, Martha M., ed. *A Voice of Their Own: The Woman Suffrage Press, 1840–1910*. Tuscaloosa: University of Alabama Press, 1991.

Stanton, Elizabeth Cady. *Eighty Years and More: Reminiscences 1815–1897*. 1898. Reprint. New York: Schocken, 1971.

Stevens, Doris. *Jailed for Freedom*. New York: Boni and Liveright, 1920.

Stubbe, Henry. *A Further Justification of the Present War Against the United Netherland*. London: H. Hills and J. Starkey, 1673.

Tarbell, Ida M. *The Business of Being a Woman*. New York: Macmillan, 1912.

Taylor, Barbara. *Eve and the New Jerusalem: Socialism and Feminism in the Nineteenth Century*. New York: Pantheon, 1983.

Tickner, Lisa. *The Spectacle of Women: Imagery of the Suffrage Campaign, 1907–14*. Chicago: University of Chicago Press, 1988.

U.S. Bureau of the Census. *Statistics of Women at Work, Based on Unpublished Information Derived from the Schedules of the Twelfth Census*. Washington, D.C.: Government Printing Office, 1907.

Van Voris, Jacqueline. *Carrie Chapman Catt: A Public Life*. New York: The Feminist Press, 1987.

Walker, Nancy. *A Very Serious Thing: Women's Humor and American Culture*. Minneapolis: University of Minnesota Press, 1988.

Warner, Marina. *Monuments and Maidens: The Allegory of the Female Form.* New York: Atheneum, 1985.

Weitenkampf, Frank. *Political Caricature in the United States in Separately Published Cartoons: An Annotated List.* 1953. Reprint. New York: Arno Press, 1971.

Werner, Heinz. *Comparative Psychology of Mental Development.* New York: International Universities Press, 1948.

Who Was Who in American Art. Edited by Peter Hastings Falk. Madison, Conn.: Sound View Press, 1985.

Who's Who in American Art. New York: R. R. Bowker, 1936.

Wiggin, Kate Douglas. *Rebecca of Sunnybrook Farm.* Boston: Houghton Mifflin, 1903.

Woman Suffrage Facts Cartooned. Oleana, Pa.: Holzapfel Publishing Co., n.d.

Woman's Who's Who of America: A Biographical Dictionary of Contemporary Women of the United States and Canada. New York: American Commonwealth, 1914.

Women Artists in the United States. Edited by Paula Chiarmonte. Boston: G. K. Hall, 1990.

Women's History Sources: A Guide to Archives and Manuscript Collection in the United States. Edited by Andrea Hinding, Ames Sheldon Bower, and Clarke A. Chambers. 2 vols. New York: R. R. Bowker, 1979.

The World Encyclopedia of Cartoons. Edited by MauriceHorn and Richard Marschall. New York: Chelsea House, 1980.

Wright, Thomas. *A History of Caricature and Grotesque in Literature and Art.* 1865. Reprint. New York: Frederick Ungar, 1968.

Wynn Jones, Michael. *The Cartoon History of the American Revolution.* New York: Putnam, 1975.

Young, Art. *Art Young: His Life and Times.* New York: Sheridan House, 1939.

Zurier, Rebecca. *Art for the Masses: A Radical Magazine and its Graphics, 1911–1917.* Philadelphia: Temple University Press, 1988.

Page numbers in italics refer to illustrations. Adjoining pages regularly include related text.

Index

House of Representatives (U.S.). *See* Congress
Housekeeping skills, 6, 133, *133*, 179
Housewives, 181, *182–84*
How it Feels to be the Husband of a Suffragette, 118
Howe, Julia Ward, 80
Howe, Marie Jenney, 75, 107, 211
Hughes, Charles Evans, 166–67
Humor magazines, 50–53, 179
Hunger strikes, 91
Husbands, 179, 187
Hutchinson, Anne, 67, *67*
Hyde, William Henry, 52

Icons, 30–34, 37–38, 178
Idaho, 81–82
Ideal woman, 61, 179, 210
Idealism, 6, 11, 191
Identification of women artists with cartoon counterparts, 199
Ideology, 76, 208–15
Illinois, 175
Illustrators, 205, 207
Images, power of, 5–6
Immigrants, 12, 199, 200
Indian princess, 40, *42*
Indians, North American, 40, *41*
Indirect influence, 147, 152
Industrial protection laws, 7–8
Inevitability of suffrage, 130–32
Inner development, 214
Intellectualism, 60, 104, 180, 181, 205
International movement, 23
Interpersonal strengths, 181
Irwin, Inez Haynes, 116, 177
Isabella of Spain, *162*, 163
Isis, 59
Italian artists, 59

Jackson, Andrew, 40
Jane Bull, 87
Joan of Arc, 57, 162, *163*, 168
Job safety, 127, *129*

John Bull, 40, 43–45, *43, 44*, 87
Jokes, 38, 160
Jones, Mrs. Gilbert, 146
Jones, Grace, 169, *170*, 224
Journals and periodicals, 84–89
Judge, 26, 46, 51–52, 54, 106–7, 113, 208
Jung, Carl, 58–59, 62
Jury duty, 193, *194*
Justice, 122–23
Justice personified, 29, 32, 38, 83, 122–23, *123*, 153, 160

Kansas, 79, 82
Keller, Morton, 52
Kennedy, John F., 118
Kenton, Edna, 211
Keppler, Joseph, 30, *30*, 47
Ker, Balfour, 111
Ker, Mary Sigsbee. *See* Sigsbee, Mary Ellen
Kessler-Harris, Alice, 71
Kewpies, 29, 113, 136, *136*
Kirby, Rollin, *164*, 170, 171, 224
Korányi, Anna Soós, 23
Korzenik, Diana, 110
Kraditor, Aileen, 122, 127

Labeling, 37, 39, 160
Ladders, 108, *173*
Ladies' Home Journal, 77, 118, *119*, 146
Ladylike, 189
Lafayette, 126, *126*
Laundry, 193
Lazarus, Emma, 123
League for the Civic Education of Women, 146
League of Women Voters, 8, 93
Leisure, 71
Liberals, 76, 78
Liberator, 74
Liberty, 122
Liberty Bell, 40, 167, 168, 214
Liberty Belles, 168
Liberty personified, 32, 38, 40, *42*, 123–26,

160, 168. *See also* Statue of Liberty
Library of Congress, 59
Life (magazine), 3, 51–52, *52*, 88, 89, 93, 113, *145*, 146
Life preservers, 108, *154*, *190*, 191
Light, 171, 173, 175
Lincoln, Abraham, 53, 123, 163, 165, 166
Liquor interests, 76–77, 144, 146–48, *147*, 186. *See also* Brewers
Literacy, 53
Literacy tests, 13
Lithographic crayon, 206
Lithography, 28, 47, 49
Livermore, Daniel, 152
Livermore, Mary, 84
Locke, John, 68
Lockwood, Belva, 61, *61*
Louis-Philippe, King of France, 27

McCay, Winsor, 124, *125*, 224
McCutcheon, John, 174
McKinley, William, 51
Magazines, Humor, 50–53, 179
Magazine circulation figures, 52
Maids, 189
Male cartoonists, 186, 197, 200
Male images in pro-suffrage cartoons, 7, 205
Male supremacy, 77
Maps of movement's progress, 81, 83, 84
Marianne, 58
Marriage, 105, 106, 109
Martin, Edward, 51
Marx, Karl, 130
Marxism, 130
Maryland, 67
Maryland Suffrage News, 86, 87
"Masculine" women, 25, *25*, 49, 72, 182
Masculinity, 89, 90
Massachusetts Association Opposed to the Further Extension of Suffrage to Women, 78, 143
Massachusetts Normal Art School, 105, 110–11